PABLO ESCOBAR'S STORY

PART 1 THE RISE

SHAUN ATTWOOD

For Stephen Abbott the Ben Nevis power walker

ACKNOWLEDGEMENTS

A big thank you to Mark Swift (Editor at Reedsy),
Jane Dixon-Smith (cover design and typesetting)

SPELLING DIFFERENCES:
UK V USA

This book was written in British English, hence USA readers may notice some spelling differences with American English: e.g. color = colour, meter = metre and = jewelry = jewellery

SHAUN'S BOOKS

English Shaun Trilogy
Party Time
Hard Time
Prison Time

War on Drugs Series
Pablo Escobar: Beyond Narcos
American Made: Who Killed Barry Seal?
Pablo Escobar or George HW Bush
The Cali Cartel: Beyond Narcos
We Are Being Lied To: The War on Drugs (Expected 2019)
The War Against Weed (Expected 2019)

Un-Making a Murderer:
The Framing of Steven Avery and Brendan Dassey
The Mafia Philosopher: Two Tonys
Life Lessons

Pablo Escobar's Story (Expected 2019)
T-Bone (Expected 2022)

SOCIAL-MEDIA LINKS

Email: attwood.shaun@hotmail.co.uk
YouTube: Shaun Attwood
Blog: Jon's Jail Journal
Website: shaunattwood.com
Instagram: @shaunattwood
Twitter: @shaunattwood
LinkedIn: Shaun Attwood
Goodreads: Shaun Attwood
Facebook: Shaun Attwood, Jon's Jail Journal,
T-Bone Appreciation Society

Shaun welcomes feedback on any of his books.
Thank you for the Amazon and Goodreads reviews!

CONTENTS

INTRO

Many authors have tried to dissect Pablo's character, with each only providing a few pieces of the puzzle. The first Escobar book I wrote was part of a series exposing the War on Drugs. Since its publication, I've received requests to write his biography in more detail and without the War on Drugs politics. This new series of books containing approximately 1,000 pages is my response.

After doing a talk about Pablo in London, I was approached by a Colombian. She said that there was far more information available about him in the Spanish-speaking world. On a mission, I ended up getting hundreds of thousands of words translated, which transformed my understanding of his story. Previously, I had viewed him through the filters of the English-speaking world – and many of those authors had an agenda such as portraying certain people or government agencies in particular ways.

This book also includes everything I have learned about El Patrón while researching information for my books on the Cali Cartel and Barry Seal. Since the explosion of interest in Pablo, far more up-to-date information has become available thanks to those closest to him who later became authors, including his ex-lover and TV celebrity, Virginia Vallejo (*Loving Pablo, Hating Escobar*); his son, Juan Pablo (*Pablo Escobar: My Father*); and his former hit man, Popeye (*The True Life of Pablo Escobar* and *Surviving Pablo Escobar*) – who was released and now has a popular YouTube channel. Two of the men chiefly responsible for his demise, Don Berna (*Killing the Boss*) and Carlos Castaño (*My Confession*), have also published books about their roles, which contradict the official story of the police killing Pablo. *In Secret (En Secreto)* by the journalist Germán Castro Caycedo and *The Words of Pablo (La Parábola de Pablo)* by Alonso Salazar also contain lots of information.

These combined accounts helped to revise my earlier versions of the big stories such as the absence of Los Pepes at Pablo's death, and the role of the state in the murder of the presidential candidate Galán, which had largely been overlooked. In 2017, Pablo's nemesis, General Maza, was sentenced to thirty years for conspiring to murder Galán, which had been squarely blamed on Pablo by most authors. This book also contains stories untold in the English-speaking world, such as the death of Pablo's brother, Fernando. It is my hope that I have provided the most detailed and up-to-date account.

CHAPTER 1

ESCAPING THE VIOLENCE

Pablo Escobar was a mama's boy who cherished his family and sang in the shower, yet he bombed a passenger plane and approved methods of torture such as genital electrocution and the forced inhalation of petrol fumes, which made people's eyeballs pop out. For millions worldwide, these contrasts and his rags to riches story have provided endless fascination. To understand how his character was shaped, let's start with his childhood.

Family, poverty, violence and religion all influenced young Pablo. His parents met in El Tablazo, a tiny village in the province of Antioquia, in the cold plateau of the municipality of Rionegro. Roughly an hour's drive south-east of Medellín, El Tablazo is surrounded by fields growing berries, tomatoes and colourful flowers – a landscape that Pablo's father loved and never wanted to leave. Abel Escobar lived with his parents on a farm in northern El Tablazo, about four miles from where Hermilda taught kids at primary school. Nicknamed Abelito, he was an industrious silent man of the fields.

Self-taught in education, Hermilda had been assigned to the school by the Secretary of Education of Antioquia. Committed to the community, she made an immediate impression on the locals, who noticed her fierce spirit and leadership qualities – traits that Pablo would inherit. They marvelled at her ability to make clothes for her children and her chalk drawings of famous paintings such as Da Vinci's *The Last Supper*. Enchanted by the elegant and energetic woman with blonde hair and blue eyes who carried herself in a sophisticated way, mild-mannered Abel proposed.

After Hermilda accepted, they were married on March 4, 1946. She quit teaching and relocated to Abel's farm.

The next year, Roberto was born, followed by Pablo – named after Pablo Emilio, his grandfather – at noon on December 1, 1949. Hermilda liked the name Pablo, equivalent to Paul, because of the story of Paul the Apostle, who had persecuted disciples in Jerusalem before converting to Christianity. The siblings would eventually expand to seven, but Pablo remained Hermilda's favourite. She spoiled him and laughed endlessly at his antics. Whenever he detected that she was ignoring him, he threw tantrums until he was back in her arms. When he was 4, she chastised him for such behaviour, stating that he was a big man on the verge of growing a moustache whom she was embarrassed to carry around. She added that if he didn't start to walk on his own legs, they would shrink and he would be unable to get around for the rest of his life.

When it came to raising children, the parents' personalities clashed. Hermilda overrode Abel's conservative and austere approach by encouraging them to become confident about money and success. She could never have imagined how far her son would take her entrepreneurial spirit. At a white church on a path to El Tablazo, she entrusted Pablo to the Virgin of Fátima, a.k.a. the Blessed Virgin Mary. She prayed that the virgin would make him intelligent and charitable. She believed that a person's highest quality was generosity. Abel tasked the children with farm work. At 3 AM, when it was foggy and cold, Roberto fetched the cows from the pastures and assisted in milking them. He also collected firewood. Although Pablo was quiet and reserved in his early teens, characteristics inherited from his father, he shed those traits after puberty to exude his mother's confidence.

Five more siblings were born: three girls, Alba Marina, Luz María and Gloria, and two boys, Argemiro and Fernando, the youngest. With so many mouths to feed, Abel moved his family to the estate of his neighbour, a political leader who insisted on Hermilda not working, so that she could concentrate on raising her family. Relations with their landlord were so cordial that he became Pablo's godfather on December 4, 1949, at a baptism in an ancient white church now known as the Catedral San Nicolás el Magno in Rionegro.

Lacking money, Hermilda went against the customs of the day and the will of her husband by requesting to resume teaching in Antioquia. As she was married, she was assigned to a school far away as a form of punishment. The family moved to Titiribí, south-west of Medellín, a small town nestled into the mountains with white stucco buildings, an historic church, plenty of palm trees and a backdrop of vibrant green slopes. They lived in a tiny wooden one-bedroom house next to the school. The parents slept on a mattress and the children on another. While Hermilda worked, Abel was unable to gain employment as a farmer or doing odd jobs, so food was scarce. On the weekends, she volunteered to teach poor children to read and write.

Since Pablo's birth, a civil war called The Violence had been raging in Colombia. From the mid-1940s to the late 1950s, the war had claimed approximately 200,000 lives. Some of it involved Conservatives and Liberals butchering each other in the country-side. Both sides also battled the Colombian Communist Party's paramilitary forces. Pablo's region, Antioquia, was hard-hit.

A trigger for the war was the April 9, 1948 assassination of the popular politician Jorge Eliécer Gaitán, a Liberal Party presidential candidate. After his death, rioting lasted for ten hours, killing approximately 5,000 people. Plotting to redistribute the power in their favour, elites manipulated the poor and the peasants into annihilating each other under the banners of liberalism and conservatism. Rural town police and leaders encouraged Conservative peasants to seize the agricultural lands of Liberal peasants, which provoked widespread peasant-to-peasant violence. In regions such as Antioquia, the violence was used as a ruse to steal land from peasant farmers. Large landowners paid gunmen to wreak havoc in the countryside. Coffee crops on the way to the market were stolen. The displaced and destitute swelled the populations of the towns and contributed to Colombia becoming a country of big cities.

True to its name, the civil war involved barbarous methods of torture and slaughter, including crucifixion, hanging, scalping, quartering and beheading. Infants were sometimes killed slowly, and at other times bayoneted. Schoolgirls were gang-raped in front of their parents. Foetuses were sliced from wombs and replaced by live roosters. Political enemies were put aboard airplanes and dropped from great heights – a tactic the authorities used years later against the Medellín Cartel.

Picar para tamal – to cut like a tamale – involved slowly chopping up a living person. With bocachiquiar, hundreds of small slices were made until the person bled to death. It imitated how fishermen removed the scales from a type of fish called bocachico. The Flower Vase Cut began with the severing of the head, arms and legs. The limbs were stuffed down the neck, turning the headless torso into a vase of body parts. A victim stabbed in the neck, who had his tongue pulled out through the gap and hung down his chest, was wearing a Colombian Necktie.

Living in Titiribí and with The Violence escalating around them, Pablo's family had tried to avoid the excesses of politics, but local Conservatives known as the Rabble of Goths took offence to Hermilda teaching their children and alleged that something wicked lay at the root of her liberal spirit. They were warned to leave, but having no safe place to go, Hermilda and Abel locked their doors at night and prayed.

One night, frantic screams frightened the family. Some of Pablo's neighbours were dragged from their homes and killed. Trembling, Pablo heard machetes hacking the front door and threats of murder. He clung to his mother, who was crying and praying to the Holy Child of Atocha, a Roman Catholic deity popular in Latin America, depicted by a child under 12 years old dressed in a feathered hat, a blue robe and reddish-brown cape with a scallop shell attached, carrying a bread basket, a staff and a drinking gourd. She had learned the prayer from her grandmother, whose trust in the Holy Child was absolute:

"Glorious Child of Atocha, supernal Divine Majesty, I greet you and adore you and beg you to give me your mercy in memory of the ineffable joy your Blessed Mother felt when she received you in her arms and when the angelic choirs sang joyfully for all places the sweet harmonies of the Gloria in Excelsis Deo, in praise to the Almighty for your coming into the world for the good of the human lineage."

"We will all be killed," Abel said, "but at least we can try and save the kids." They instructed the kids to lie silently on a mattress and covered them with blankets.

Roberto gave Pablo a baby's bottle. "Don't cry. We're going to be all right."

The front door was so strong that the mob eventually quit trying to break in. Hermilda credited the Holy Child for bolstering the door's strength. The mob doused the door with petrol and attempted to light it. Hermilda pledged to build a church if the Holy Child saved them – which she did years later on land purchased by Pablo for his Medellín Without Slums project.

They heard a disturbance outside, people running away and silence, followed by voices and *bang-bang-bang* on the door. "Come out. You're safe." The new arrivals identified themselves as soldiers opposed to the mob, but Hermilda was too terrified to open the door.

Eventually, the family emerged to see some of their peasant neighbours dangling from the school beams, hung upside down by their feet with their heads missing. Blood was pouring from their necks onto the corridor floor, which stuck to the feet of Pablo and his family.

With burning buildings illuminating the street, the survivors were told to immediately abandon the area. Roberto carried his brother, who clung to him tightly. Pablo would never forget the people on fire in the gutters, the limp bodies hanging from lampposts and the stench of charred meat coming from corpses soaked in petrol. With Pablo crying for a baby's bottle, Roberto said, "Can I go back for it?"

"You cannot go back," Abel said. For two hours, they fled on foot under army protection.

Believing they had been saved by the Holy Child, the atmosphere was heavily religious wherever they settled. They had a figurehead of the Holy Child with realistic blood. After Hermilda told Christ's story, young Pablo was so sad that when lunch was served, he put a piece of meat in his corn cake and took it to the figurehead. "Poor man, who made you bleed? Do you want a little meat?" This act convinced his mother that he was kind and religious. For the rest of his life, Pablo would always try to sleep with a nearby image of the Holy Child.

CHAPTER 2

GRANDPARENTS

Hermilda enchanted Pablo with stories about his grandfather, Roberto Gaviria, the mayor of Cañasgordas, Antioquia, who smuggled whiskey from Urabá, where the northern part borders the Caribbean Sea. With foresight and a creative flair, Don Roberto the bootlegger had outsmarted everyone, including the authorities. One of his methods was to hide whiskey in a coffin and to create a fake funeral procession with relatives dressed in black and ready to start sobbing as they approached checkpoints. The coffin was buried in the cemetery, extracted at night and taken to a shop. The whiskey was transferred to eggs with holes drilled in them to drain out their contents.

After getting warned that someone had informed on him, Don Roberto continued with the coffin, but without the whiskey. During the burial ceremony, the police arrived to arrest him. He protested his innocence, but the police insisted on opening the coffin, only to find it full of stones. Believing that Don Roberto was a crazy old man, they dismissed the smuggling allegation. Pablo wanted to copy his grandfather's success.

Don Roberto moved from Cañasgordas to Frontino, where he supported his family through goldmining. After the stock market crash of 1929 and the economic downturn, he lost his fortune and had to leave. On the road, his wife, Grandmother Ines and the children worked as minstrels and performed at inns, where they sang, played music and told jokes and stories in exchange for food and lodgings. Eventually, they arrived in Medellín and settled in La Toma.

Drawing on the work of the writer Tomás Carrasquilla, Grandmother Ines developed a variety and comedy show called "Fruits of my Land." Following several seasons of success, she toured Argentina in the 1940s. Pablo and the other grandchildren were told exaggerated stories about Grandmother Ines performing privately for a powerful fan, Evita Perón, the First Lady of Argentina from 1946 to 1952. Impressed by the comedy performance and flamenco dancing, Evita awarded Grandmother Ines a 10-year position of heading an asylum for widows. As a devout Catholic, Grandmother Ines admired Evita's populism.

It is unknown when Grandmother Ines returned to Colombia, but her sons started to base themselves in Medellín in the late 1940s. Hernando Gaviria became a popular streetcar driver, a trade unionist and the founder of a newspaper, which encouraged protests and strikes. Skilled with the guitar and violin, Gustavo became a serenade player, charming lovers during his evening performances. Hermilda was assigned to teach in El Tablazo, where she met and married Abel.

CHAPTER 3

GROWING UP IN MEDELLÍN

Antioquia's Education Ministry moved Hermilda to the Guayabito School by Rionegro. The family lived in a large room in an old school building, which had two classrooms and a bathroom. As the boys grew older, they walked roughly two hours to school. With a sewing kit, Hermilda repaired their uniforms. In worn-out shoes, Pablo trekked to school with Roberto. Rather than wear shoes with holes in them, he decided to go barefooted. His teacher sent him home. Humiliated, Pablo told his mother that he needed new shoes to stay in school. As she had spent her pay on food, she deliberated her options and shoplifted a pair. At home, she noticed that each shoe was a different size. Disheartened, she confessed to a priest, who advised her to return the shoes and get them on credit. She bought the shoes and arrived home, exhausted and anxious. With such a large family to feed, she complained about their lack of money.

"Don't worry, Mom," Pablo said. "Wait until I grow up. I'll give you everything."

The shoe problem was avoided after Hermilda bought a bicycle on credit. The journey time to school was halved. With Pablo on the cargo rack, Roberto sped away, sometimes racing a friend, other times just trying to beat his personal best. It was the beginning of his love of bicycles. As Pablo grew, Roberto complained about transporting his brother's weight up hills, so Hermilda bought a bike for Pablo, and the brothers raced.

Out of all six siblings, Pablo bonded the most with Roberto, who was intelligent and had a passion for mathematics and electronics, skills that would be employed by the Medellín Cartel. He enjoyed watching Roberto construct things such as radios, but rather than join in, he sat around as if lost in thought.

During the holidays, their cousins visited. Pablo enjoyed the company of his favourite cousin, Gustavo Gaviria – who was small and thin with penetrating dark eyes and a square face. In the countryside, they collected guavas and aimed slingshots at birds. On an old bridge over a river, Roberto would get at one end and Gustavo the other. When Pablo was in the middle, they would shake the bridge. He would scream and run to his mother, who punished Roberto by lashing him with a belt.

The brothers sometimes played pranks on Abel. On a Holy Friday, it was traditional to search for mysterious lights that would lead to gold treasure. In the evening, Abel and a neighbour went on a treasure hunt until they saw a spooky light that sent some of the locals running scared. Hiding his fear to appear brave, Abel approached the light – a cookie jar containing a candle, hanging from a tree by a rope that someone had used to make the mysterious light go up and down. He returned home angry and yelled, "Who would want to mess with me like that?"

Having noticed that her sons had come home in an excited state just before Abel had arrived, she named the culprits and belted Roberto so hard that he wrapped himself in a blanket to bandage the bleeding. Her favourite son received no punishment on the grounds that he was too young.

Believing that a city would be safer and offer better educational opportunities for her children, Hermilda moved her family into her mother's house in Medellín, where kids played on the streets without any problems. Just like with any city, murders happened, but not so often yet. Although they loved the steady climate averaging around 22.2°C or 72°F in the City of Eternal Spring, all of the fast cars and endless people intimidated the brothers, who were accustomed to the countryside.

Medellín is in the mountain-ringed and narrow Aburrá Valley in the Andean foothills of north-western Colombia, more than

250 miles of mountainous terrain from Bogotá. Sephardic Jews on the run from the Spanish Inquisition founded Medellín in 1616, satisfied with the sanctuary its isolation provided. Early commerce was created by ranchers and coffee planters who worked on the slopes and offered their goods in the city. The arrival of cheap hydroelectric power in the twentieth century brought manufacturing to Medellín, where textile, brewing and chemical industries flourished. The residents had a reputation for being tough, tenacious, hard-working and full of local pride. With countryside workers flocking there, Medellín's population exploded from 275,000 to 1.3 million between 1952 and 1977. By 1990 it was 2.5 million, and Pablo's wars had turned the city into the murder capital of the world.

Living in a big house in the Francisco Antonio Zea neighbourhood, Grandmother Ines was an astute businesswoman whose family owned a dye company called Dicolor factory, which supplied coloured aniline to bakeries and aqueduct companies. They had their own formulas for the production of wax and bitumen, and they bottled sauces and spices and sold them to supermarkets. Under her loving but stern hand, Pablo and Roberto had to go to church and pray every morning. Working at Mora Hermanos, an appliance store, Roberto demonstrated an early ability in electronics. He assembled the family's first TV, prior to which they had watched shows in their neighbours' homes. Their favourites were *Gilligan's Island* and *Bonanza*.

Pablo was a timid teenager with a pompadour hairstyle who wore shorts. At 13 years old, he took turns with Roberto to spy on his grandmother's maid in the shower. He was stood on a chair when Grandmother Ines approached. Roberto fled. Catching Pablo, his grandmother shifted the chair. He fell and broke a finger.

On bicycles, delivering dentures to dentists earned the brothers money, half of which they gave to Grandmother Ines. When they had saved enough, they decided to lose their virginities by dressing up and going to a brothel. Two stunning ladies escorted them to a room, and instructed them to wait. They reappeared with towels, soap and hot water. Naive to the etiquette of brothels, the boys assumed that something bad was about to happen and fled. Their friends mocked them and explained that the women had intended to wash them before giving them a massage and having sex. It took the brothers another two months to save up enough to return to the brothel.

A plague wiped out the family's small amount of cattle in El Tablazo, which forced Abel to leave the countryside. The family moved to a suburb south of Medellín called Envigado, a quiet town which would feature throughout Pablo's life. It was in the mountains to the south-east of the Aburrá Valley. The State Social Housing Institute assigned them a house in a neighbourhood where a typical home had a mud roof and a courtyard.

By the middle of the 1960s, they had settled down in a one-storey, three-bedroom house in La Paz, Envigado, which was a relatively new neighbourhood built on a farm with only a few homes and unpaved streets. Wearing a hat and a poncho provided by Hermilda, Abel worked as a night watchman. Despite their low incomes, the residents of La Paz always had food. There was a neighbourhood sector for journalists, one for families of various origin and one for university professors, which was a hotbed for the left-wing ideology Pablo absorbed. The most dangerous resident of La Paz was a cannabis smoker affectionately known as Arturo Malo, because he was harmless.

The main celebration of the year was the Feast of the Virgin. Pablo and his siblings, escorted by Hermilda, would watch the musical procession with drummers and wind instruments, accompanied by gunpowder explosions and a crazy cow – a bovine skull with flames and horns that frightened and excited the children.

Pablo and his brothers were happy teenagers. They walked and played in the countryside, with its many farms, ponds and streams. They spent hours in their favourite part of the forest, which they named The Little Jungle, where on moonlit nights, they played war games, hide and seek and cops and robbers. They startled young lovers and encountered hippies, who introduced them to cannabis.

Pablo and his friends often walked to Cerro La Paz, at the top of the neighbourhood. It provided a view of the Aburrá Valley, with Medellín in the middle, the city expanding along the slopes of the mountains and riverbanks as its population ballooned. From Cerro La Paz, they took old roads to other towns. To reach the municipality of El Retiro, they headed east up a mountain range and through a farm called the Cathedral, where years later Pablo would build his own prison, protected by thick forest and frequent fog. He would buy numerous properties in the area, which, with his familiarity of the landscape, would provide hideouts.

Veering south, they would arrive at Sabaneta and Caldas, which provided a view of the city of Itagüí – where Pablo's brother Roberto would eventually be incarcerated – and the town of La Estrella, which hosted the Festival de Ancón, a.k.a. the Colombian Woodstock. With the news portraying hippies as invading demons, Hermilda warned her children about the dangers of the festival. With their friends also similarly warned, the teenagers couldn't resist joining the hippies high on cannabis, LSD and rock 'n' roll. The Conservative leaders of Medellín unleashed the authorities on the hippies in an attempt to banish them from La Estrella.

After Hermilda gave him permission to let his hair grow long, Pablo started to carry a comb in his pocket. His obsession with gazing at his reflection in windows did not go unnoticed by his friends, who mocked him for constantly adjusting his hair. Over time, he learned to conceal his vanity.

When rivals from other neighbourhoods entered La Paz, conflicts erupted. If the rivals were chasing girls, rocks were often thrown, sometimes leaving the combatants bleeding from their heads. Intense rivalry was also felt during soccer games. Pablo played hard to win, but if his team was going to lose, he was known for storming off the pitch.

Abel turned a bedroom into a shop with shelves. It went out of business within months for lack of customers. Pablo painted the room his favourite colour, light blue, and stocked the shelves with books on politics, including works by Mao and Lenin. He added issues of the *Reader's Digest*, which he'd asked his friends to steal from their parents. He offered a *Reader's Digest* rental service to his neighbours. To challenge his fears, he entered a cemetery at midnight and stole a skull, which he cleaned, painted and used as a paperweight.

The call of El Tablazo's beautiful fields was too much for Abel, so he abandoned the city to rebuild his farm. From then on, Pablo's only contact with his father was on occasional visits. His absence took its toll, and probably motivated Pablo to be more devoted to his own children. Even when he was the most wanted man in Colombia, he wrote stories for Juan Pablo, whom he affectionately called Grigory, and for his little ballerina Manuela, he made cassette recordings of poems and nursery rhymes. He always reminded them how special they were and how much he loved them.

What he lacked due to his father's absence, Hermilda attempted to compensate for by providing unconditional love and support, rendering him more of a Gaviria than an Escobar. In later years, he made little effort to see his father, whereas he went out of his way to see his mother, even putting his life on the line. Hermilda described his condition as "mama-itis." She said he couldn't go twenty days without seeing her, even when he was on the run. A car would arrive and she would have to wear a mask on route to his hideout. When she challenged him about the mask, he would say that it was necessary because under torture and in great pain she might have revealed his location.

In later years, as money poured in from his illegal activity, Abel remained oblivious. When he first heard the rumours, he refused to believe them. As the evidence mounted, he demanded that his son come clean. A master of persuasion, Pablo insisted that he was a successful real-estate investor and that the rumours were motivated by envy over his quick fortune. He even quoted the champion road racing cyclist, Martín Emilio Rodríguez Gutiérrez, a.k.a. Cochise: "The people in Colombia die more of envy than of cancer."

In his early teens at Baccalaureate High School of the University of Antioquia, Pablo was elected president of the Council for Student Wellness, which demanded transportation and food for indigent students. He learned about revolutionary activity, the theory of liberation, Camilo Torres Restrepo the guerrilla priest and Fidel Castro's Cuba. He found out about the US meddling in Central and South America for its own advantage, which often increased the suffering of the poor. He hated that the poor were the biggest victims of violence and injustice. He led demonstrations against class division.

During this time, he absorbed anti-imperialist phrases, which became mantras for the rest of his life. He heard rumours that the CIA had facilitated the assassination of Jorge Eliécer Gaitán, the deceased presidential candidate who had defended workers' rights and promised an equitable land reform. Gaitán's death had ignited The Violence that had threatened Pablo's family. He learned about America's animosity towards Fidel Castro and Cuba, the failed Bay of Pigs invasion, and the assassination of Patrice Lumumba, the first democratically elected prime minister of Congo, who had helped his country gain independence from Belgium.

He started to despise the way that society was structured: a tiny per cent owned the majority of the land and wealth, while more than half of Colombians lived in poverty. He claimed that he would kill himself if he had not made a million pesos by the age of 30. He viewed smuggling as the road to riches. In between studying, he smuggled Marlboro cigarettes and cannabis.

According to his brother, Roberto, in his book, *Escobar*, Pablo developed an interest in history, world politics and poetry. At the public library, he read law books. He practised public speaking on student audiences at lunchtime or on the soccer field. Roberto remembers him speaking passionately about becoming the president of Colombia and taking ten per cent of the earnings of the richest people to help the poor to build schools and roads. To create jobs, he wanted to encourage Asian manufacturers to build plants in Colombia.

In school, Pablo grew restless. Distrustful of authority figures, he felt more at ease with the street gangs. For money, he experimented with small scams. Believing that school was a waste of time, he dropped out for two years. On the dangerous streets, he refined his techniques and learned from his mistakes. Hermilda convinced him to resume his education, so he could get the three grades necessary to graduate. As he adored his mother, he enrolled in Enrique Vélez School.

Pablo spent more time with his cousin Gustavo. One of their earliest transgressions was forging educational diplomas. Using clay, they took imprints of the keys to the faculty lounge. When the teachers were absent, they entered the lounge and stole blank diplomas and copied the official seal. After studying the teachers' handwriting, they filled out grades on the diplomas, which they signed. Using the same keys, they stole the answers to exam questions, which they sold.

"How are you guys doing in algebra?" Pablo would ask his schoolmates.

"Not well at all."

"It's so difficult."

"From now on, you'll all be doing fine." He waved a copy of the final exam. The students' test results improved so much that the teachers grew suspicious and changed the tests.

Eventually, the headmaster summoned his mother. "Pablo is going to be suspended for a few days."

"Now what's he done?" Hermilda said.

"Pablo imagines that he's the students' leader. The boys all obey him. Standing on a desk, he told his classmates that the exams were so hard they would all fail, and he told his teacher not to give them the exams."

Whenever he felt injustice, Pablo would rise and speak, but

for the most part he sat around in school in silent contemplation, inserting bits of paper into his mouth. His schoolmates remember him as mostly quiet. He ended up in arguments with his teachers, whom he viewed as absurd and foolish. School was a waste of time when he could be earning money smuggling. Eventually, he was expelled in 1969.

After his mother scolded him, he said, "Mother, I keep on telling you: I want to be big and I will be. I'm poor, but I'll never die poor. I promise."

While Pablo disliked education, Roberto excelled. Studying electrical engineering at the Science and Electronics Academy in Medellín, he learned how to repair and build any electronic device, skills that would be employed to install electronics in submarines that transported cocaine and to build complex security systems. Although one of the younger students, he became the head of the technical department. To study accounting, Roberto enrolled in University Remington. Hoping that the financial knowledge would help him run a business, he had not anticipated that his skills would be needed by Pablo, who lacked knowledge of money-laundering.

When not working, Roberto was cycling, cheered on by his assistant, Pablo, who washed his bike, prepared his uniform and captured and killed a pigeon for good luck. Competing in Colombia, Panama and Ecuador, he became a professional, and was ranked number two in Colombia in 1966. After attending a course in Germany, he was appointed onto a technical team, which selected Colombian cyclists to compete internationally. He became a coach for the Cycling League of Caldas. In Manizales, he set up the Osito Bicycle Factory, named after his nickname Osito or Little Bear. His income enabled him to buy a car and to save Hermilda's house from foreclosure. Thinking his life was set, he had no idea that Pablo and Gustavo would build a criminal enterprise that would consume them all.

Before the crimes escalated, Pablo co-founded a local chapter of the Boy Scouts, organised home dances, mowed grass and camped on the weekends. At the Colombia de Envigado cinema, he enjoyed action movies such as James Bond, and Mexican and cowboy films. Shorter than his contemporaries, he banned them from calling him shorty or midget. Early signs of his entrepreneurship manifested when he started a bicycle repair shop and bicycle rental business. With money he made legitimately, he purchased a motorbike, which he later used to commit crimes.

On the streets of Medellín, some of Pablo's leadership and criminal traits started to emerge. Although the youngest in his group, he'd take the lead. When the police confiscated their soccer ball, he encouraged the group to throw rocks at the patrol car, which cracked a window. The police rounded up several of the group and threatened to keep them in jail. Only Pablo spoke up to the commander. He told them they hadn't done anything bad. They were tired of the ball being taken and they'd pay to retrieve the ball. Some of the kids in the group ended up in business with Pablo later on. His activism led him to throw stones at police cars. The student protests of the 60s were global, and Pablo participated at the University of Antioquia. He yelled, "Fucking pigs," while hurling rocks, and bragged that he was going to start his own revolution.

CHAPTER 4

EARLY CRIME

Raiding orchards for oranges was profitable. Pablo and Gustavo bumped into displays of oranges, watched the fruit roll downhill and collected it later. They knocked on houses and sold them, and offered them at markets.

At first, their work with gravestones was legitimate. Pablo's uncle who had established himself as a serenade singer, also manufactured aluminium headstones, which Pablo and Gustavo sold in towns. From gravediggers, they obtained the names of the deceased and tracked down the nearest relatives, to whom they offered options such as religious drawings, the most stylish fonts and flower vases. Over time, they targeted the San Pedro Cemetery, the final destination for Medellín's wealthy. From luxury vaults, they stole marble gravestones and sold them to recyclers, but business was slow due to the absence of narco-violence.

Pablo learned how to hotwire a car from a friend. When the Bishop of Medellín arrived in their neighbourhood, the boys stole his Cadillac and cruised around. When they got back, police were swarming the area, so they left the car in a remote location.

Pablo used his motorbike and talkative nature to impress girls. He drove around in a white wool poncho, his shirt untucked, the sleeves rolled up and the top half of the buttons open – a button preference that persisted throughout his life. Distrustful of barbers, he cut his own hair with scissors and kept a tortoise-shell comb in his shirt pocket. Years later when rich, he ordered 500 such combs from the US. He was known to rise late and spend hours in the bathroom, showering, brushing his teeth and preening. After he became a fugitive, he joked to his son about not having the luxury of visiting the dentist, hence the need for such lengthy brushing sessions.

By 16, he was confident on the streets. With his comb in his shirt pocket, he often admired his reflection in windows. In later years, he imitated the mannerisms of Al Capone and *The Godfather* played by Marlon Brando. Smoking cannabis intensified his deep thinking. He grew quieter. When asked a question, he paused silently and gazed down before replying. Some wondered whether he was imitating *The Godfather*, but it was a natural characteristic exacerbated when stoned. A trait noticed and disliked in both Pablo and Gustavo was their inability to look people directly in the eyes while talking to them.

Young people partied in La Paz in garages and hung out in ice-cream shops. Pablo despised the ostentatious outsiders who danced with the local girls, especially if they were from the rival El Dorado neighbourhood. He threw rocks at their expensive cars and fights erupted between the locals and outsiders. When an outsider in a convertible gatecrashed a female's 15th birthday party, Pablo called him a rich son-of-a-bitch and a letch. The outsider punched Pablo in the nose, knocking him down.

On another occasion, a girl refused to dance with a drunk who made a scene. Pablo aimed a revolver and shot him in the foot. The drunk reported it to the police, who issued a warrant for Pablo's arrest. After the drunk dropped the charges, Pablo was released from jail. A criminal record for shooting somebody in the foot may have stood in the way of his plans for millionairehood and the presidency. At the DAS office in Medellín, equivalent to the FBI headquarters, he requested his police file, and was relieved to find that it was clean.

To obtain money for his accelerating lifestyle, he committed more brazen crimes. The cousins robbed a truck full of soap, and bought a more expensive Italian motorbike to take girls on dates. They held up cinema box offices at gunpoint. With a rifle, Pablo walked into banks and calmly told the staff to empty their safes.

With a smile, he chatted to the tellers, while awaiting the cash.

Unable to perceive that Pablo had shed his sense of fear, some mistakenly ascribed his bravado to drugs. The results he achieved from his cleverness and farsightedness – including eluding the police – boosted his faith in himself. He rationalised his banditry as a form of resistance to a rigged society. A formidable combination of intelligence and street smarts enabled him to rise above his contemporaries, some of whom sought his advice and joined his gang. Those who were nervous or frustrated felt safe in his company. He earned their respect by remaining calm and cheerful in dangerous situations.

The cousins stole cars in various ways. Pablo told a journalist, "I had just left my high school and bought a Lambretta [motorbike] with Mario Henao, my brother-in-law, and Gustavo Gaviria, my cousin, and we started working with it, Gustavo and me. At that time the Renaults were a sensation.

"Then we got people in a couple of car stores and, when they were going to deliver a car, they gave us duplicates of the keys. We waited for the car to leave the agency and we continued to where the driver got off, locked it and entered somewhere. There we arrived and the one who was sitting on the back of the motorbike would open the car and leave with it.

"I remember a guy who once took out a cherry-coloured Renault 4 and left happily, whistling, singing, tapping the rudder until he arrived in front of the bride's house. There he parked it and came down to call her to show it to her. But when he came out holding her by the hand, the car was already around the corner."

On other occasions, drivers were forced from their cars, which were dismantled at chop shops. Cars were difficult to resell if they had been reported as stolen, so they bribed workers at the dealerships to issue car certificates and keys. They obtained plates from cars written off by insurance companies.

Bribery solved police problems. After a year of stealing cars, Pablo's relationship with the police was so strong that the police chiefs followed his orders. Complaints about him reselling stolen cars were ignored. Money from selling car parts was used to bribe officials to issue car certificates, so that the stolen cars could be resold without having to be chopped. The officials receiving the complaints about what he was doing were the same ones issuing him the titles.

He started a protection racket: people paid to prevent their cars from being stolen. Always generous with his friends, he gave them stolen cars with clean papers. Those receiving new cars were told to pick them up from a factory. If the workers detected the forged paperwork, his friends told them, "These titles were made by Pablo," which prompted them to surrender the keys. By now he was dictating orders from home, managing the logistics and collecting the cash. His bank deposits shot up from $50 in February 1973 to almost $5,000 by November.

CHAPTER 5

MEETING VICTORIA

In La Paz, the Henaos owned a general store and were one of the wealthiest families. The father used a Chevrolet truck to deliver jelly beans, made from guava pulp and panela, enjoyed throughout Colombia. Sponsored by his family, the son Mario Henao had studied psychology in college. Out of eight Henao children, Pablo and Gustavo hung out with Mario. The threesome modelled themselves on James Dean's *Rebel Without a Cause*. Their constant pranks disturbed the neighbourhood.

Joined by their younger brothers, including Pablo's brother Fernando, the threesome attended weekly dances, where the music ranged from rumba to new wave. At a dance in 1974, Pablo noticed one of the Henao sisters, Victoria, who was only 13, but taller than him, eleven years older. Regarded as a local beauty, Victoria had shoulder-length brown hair and an expression of strength and determination accentuated by swimming over half a mile a week. Curious about her, he located her best friend, whom he asked for dating advice.

When Mario learned that his friend was not looking to date one of his older sisters, he confronted Pablo. "How can a guy as old as you, 24, mess with a girl so young? Show her respect and move on."

Despite Mario's warning, Pablo was falling in love. The Henaos also represented the wealth he craved. Although street smart, he had to overcome shyness to declare his love to Victoria, which she accepted and maintained until he died.

With the help of friends, they met on Saturday evenings for a couple of hours, keeping the relationship secret from her parents. She appreciated his naughty smile, chivalrous gestures and his passion for helping the poor. To disguise his criminal activity, he claimed to travel during the week on legitimate business.

When Victoria's mother found out, she was unhappy with the age difference and the lower-class status of Pablo's family. She viewed him as an unstable hooligan with a reputation among the ladies. But her attempts at stopping the relationship only strengthened the lovers' resolve. Victoria was only allowed to attend local parties accompanied by her brothers, so Pablo sent her gifts delivered by her best friend, including romantic musical records, a designer watch and a turquoise ring embedded with pearls. Believing that Pablo was a driver, Nora mocked his job status and his taste in clothes, including his poncho. After he brought Victoria home one afternoon, Nora ordered him to respect her daughter and stay outside.

With obstacles intensifying their feelings, their dates increased. He taught her to drive his mustard-coloured Renault 4, which included risky manoeuvres near cliffs that thrilled them both. When parked, Pablo would announce that he was going to build a school or a university for the poor. Afterwards, they ate at restaurants with views of Medellín.

CHAPTER 6

WORKING FOR THE GODFATHER

Victoria's perfect gentleman was always on the verge of police trouble. In late 1974, he was stopped in a stolen Renault 4 and incarcerated at La Ladera prison. His cellmate was Don Alberto Prieto, a.k.a. the Godfather, a powerful contraband kingpin who specialised in transporting cigarettes, electronics, jewellery and clothing in shipping containers from America, England and Japan. The goods entered a north-western section of Colombia via Panama. Pablo listened to the Godfather explain how his business functioned, including which judges and legislators in Bogotá he bribed:

"In the town of Turbo in the jungle of the Caribbean Sea, where flies travel in clouds, the goods are lowered from medium-sized vessels. Cowboys disguise them in trucks carrying bananas. They reach Medellín by crossing the Western Cordillera and the Cauca River, and ascending the Central Mountain Range to the Aburrá Valley. Over twenty-four hours, they pass through the posts of the National Navy, the Army, the police and the Departmental Guard of Customs. Everyone watches them travel along what they call the Highway to the Sea, but nobody stops them because of the Fly: the man travelling ahead of the convoy to pay the bribes."

As cellmates, they became friends. Pablo admired the man who helped the indigent with food and medicine, and even paid for lawyers and bail bonds for the poorest. He financed social projects through a nun, who with the blessing of Christ stored some of the Godfather's contraband at the convent. Pablo was impressed by the Godfather's political visitors, including Alberto Santofimio, a.k.a.

Santo, a heavyweight in the Liberal Party, who would later become the head of the Medellín Cartel's political division.

Due to a cardiac emergency, the Godfather was moved to the Santa María clinic and released months later due to a lack of evidence. After two months, Pablo's case was dismissed because the paperwork had vanished thanks to the Godfather. The Attorney General's Office added a note to his file about irregularities in the case, including the deaths of witnesses.

Having graduated from prison, Pablo went on a crime spree with Gustavo. They used different colour motorbikes to confuse the authorities. Using a red motorbike and a white one, they robbed the Manrique theatre. They held up banks and stole trucks full of goods. Hired as gunmen, Pablo drove while Gustavo shot, contributing to the rise in what the media reported as "murderers on a motorcycle."

Pablo met the Godfather at a soccer game. "The way to make money," the Godfather said, "is to protect the merchandise for the guy with the money, and that's me. I'm offering you a job. I want you to protect my trucks and to reduce worker theft."

"I will work for you," Pablo said, "if you'll hire my cousin Gustavo, too." Due to his confidence and determination, the Godfather agreed to hire them as bodyguards. He also appreciated that Pablo did not get drunk or smoke.

Pablo applied his organisational skills to contraband, a thriving business in Colombia, which was steeped in corruption. Medellín was known as a hub for smugglers. Those who got caught typically bribed their way free. If they were unable to pay a bribe, the police would usually confiscate their contraband rather than incarcerate them. It was the cost of doing business and customary.

With numerous police on the payroll of crime bosses, it was hard to differentiate between the police and the criminals. The police not only gave their criminal associates freedom from jail, but they also committed crimes for the gangs, including kidnappings and contract killings. Shootouts sometimes occurred between different police on the payrolls of rival gangs.

The court system was the same. Judges who earned $200 a month could charge up to $30,000 to dismiss a case. Judges who refused were threatened or beaten. Court staff could be bribed to lose files, which was cheaper than paying a judge. If that didn't work, the judge was killed. The court system was considered the softest target in law enforcement, and Pablo would master the art of manipulating it.

Pablo bought the Godfather's poorly paid workers seafood and wine. He offered them half of his salary to work with him. If they stopped stealing, he'd come back and take care of them in two weeks. The workers agreed and returned their stolen goods.

Pablo gave his mother enough money for her to ignore the rumours of his crimes. He invested in an old Zastava car and attached a banner on the back window – ANTIOQUIA FEDERAL – which represented a widely held belief in his area that hard-working Antioquians, a.k.a. paisas, were almost a separate species from regular Colombians, and that the bureaucracy enforced by the central government in Bogotá was impeding their achievements. Another phrase popular in Medellín backed up this assertion: "We the people prostitute ourselves for everything."

In a country of tradition and formality, the early Antioquians stood out as frontier families who conquered the wild, mountainous hinterland and lived off subsistence agriculture. In the late 1800s, the proceeds from exporting coffee helped to finance their colonisation. Usually, coffee barons controlled the estates across Colombia, but in Antioquia, many family farms gave birth to the stereotype of the hard-working paisa individualist. The small farms operated in a democratic fashion outside of the traditional framework. The boom in coffee and mining created Antioquia's first merchants and financiers. During the early 1900s, Medellín filled with cotton factories, which created fortunes for families such as Ospina, Restrepo and Echavarría, whom Pablo would target for kidnapping. In the 1950s, the textile industry slumped and was replaced by other industries, which increased the working class. The emergence of the cocaine business in the 1970s provided an opportunity for the unemployed.

After proving himself as a hard worker, the Godfather gave Pablo the position of the Fly. Specialising in cigarettes, he drove across Colombia in a jeep ahead of anywhere from half a dozen up to forty trucks with contraband. Along the way, he paid the necessary bribes. During this time, he started to stay up extremely late, a habit he maintained throughout his life. He liked to say, "The brain works better at night."

He was absent when the police pulled over the Godfather's trucks and threatened to seize the cigarettes. With Gustavo, he sped to the scene and negotiated the release of the cargo in record time. Delighted with his performance, the Godfather offered him ten per cent of the business. Pablo demanded fifty. The Godfather called Pablo crazy. Pablo said it was fair because the Godfather had sometimes lost more than half of the goods. Even after his fifty per cent, the Godfather would still make more money because there would be no theft. The Godfather agreed to forty per cent and put Pablo in charge of a convoy of thirty-five trucks. The increased responsibility meant more time away from Victoria, which upset her.

Through the contraband business, he became adept at nationwide smuggling and avoiding government taxes and fees. Supervising two convoys a month earned him up to $200,000. He stashed his profits in hiding places in the walls of his home. He installed special electronic doors that only he could open. He recruited Roberto as an accountant, in charge of handling the payroll, making investments and depositing money into bank accounts with fake names. Money was invested in real estate, construction businesses and farms. As his brother was handling so much money, he gave him a gun.

Giving half of his salary to the Godfather's workers earned their respect and the name El Patrón or the Boss. He bought his mother a house, a taxicab for Gustavo and an Italian bicycle for his brother. He donated truckloads of food to the homeless. He took about twenty members of his family to Disney World in Florida, where he accompanied his son on the rides.

One of the Godfather's bodyguards who raised fighting cocks took Pablo to meet a woman at the Holy Trinity, a dangerous neighbourhood with criminals and prostitutes, where people fought face-to-face duels to the death over love and honour. The neighbourhood had its own slang, with killing known as pimping out and corpses called dolls. Pickpockets called ticklers travelled internationally and returned with fortunes. By an airport, the Holy Trinity was ideally situated for trafficking. With no customs or immigration checkpoints to stop them, smugglers boarded planes headed for America with suitcases packed with weed.

In a small coliseum, Griselda Blanco was presiding over cockfighting. In a cloth hat and a zebra-striped dress, the Queen of Cocaine was sat in a throne-like chair, surrounded by relatives. The circular stands were occupied by workers and locals, cheering at roosters, with whiskey and gambling in full flow. During a break, the bodyguard and Pablo approached Griselda. "Here's a man who is useful." After chatting, she invited Pablo to visit her in a few days.

The daughter of a prostitute, Griselda had entered cocaine early. As the demand increased, the Holy Trinity traffickers had created a saying: "Cannabis is like silver while cocaine is more than gold." Small planes brought coca paste from the south, landed at Medellín airport and dropped the paste onto the northern part of the runway, from where the Holy Trinity smugglers would take it to labs. After processing, it continued by land on its journey to Urabá and eventually to Panama. By the middle of the 1970s, the sons of the Holy Trinity prostitutes were investing their cocaine fortunes in homes in the wealthy El Poblado neighbourhood, which for a time became known as the Hills of the Holy Trinity.

Griselda was an exotic Caribbean beauty when she had married Pestañas, who had pioneered the use of light aircraft for transporting cocaine and had established fake companies in Panama and Ecuador. Pablo admired him as a fine captain who dressed in green suits and white ties, who despite his wealth had maintained a thuggish charisma hewn from an impoverished background. El Patrón kept a photo of the handsome Pestañas published in *The Colombian*, sporting sideburns and a goatee. He had many lovers, luxury cars and travelled worldwide. His restless nature kept him on the move. Not long after their marriage, his own crime partners assassinated him at a petrol station because they were jealous of his success and power. Before he could draw his gun, he was shot at point-blank range.

Griselda then married Darío Sepúlveda. Inspired by *The Godfather*, they named their first son Michael Corleone. Sepúlveda's control of the cocaine business through violence and war was short-lived, and when he died, Griselda became the boss. She turned her children and their associates into soldiers. Through them and her alliances with the police and the Army, she wiped out her enemies, including the father of one of her children. So many of her lovers died that she became known as the Black Widow. Not wanting to end up like Pestañas, she killed her own crime partners first, threw them lavish funerals and publicly mourned the loudest. The boss of Army intelligence in Medellín warned journalists to avoid Griselda because she was so evil and cunning.

Pablo claimed to be the son of these wars. He and Gustavo were apprentice bandits during a time when the bosses were fighting over business, honour and women, or just because they wanted to. Their unstoppable mayhem spilled over into New York and Miami.

Pablo's other source of income was kidnapping, which led to an early murder. The kidnapping of Sanin was unusual because the hostage was attempting to shake down his own brother. Pablo and Victoria's older brother, Mario, agreed to hold Sanin at a farm near Envigado. After the ransom was paid, they were going to split the money three ways. While Mario remained at the farm, Pablo went for the cash. Neighbours noticed suspicious activity and contacted the police, who arrived at the farm. To avoid getting in trouble, Sanin told the police that he had been kidnapped by Mario, who ended up in prison for nine months.

At night on a motorbike, Pablo followed Sanin around Medellín, biding his time. After Sanin entered a garage, Pablo slowed down and sprayed Sanin with bullets.

Another early murder occurred during a robbery. On a motorbike, Pablo and an accomplice shot at a policeman who was transporting money for a department store. The policeman returned fire, wounding Pablo's accomplice. After they had shot the policeman dead, they escaped with the cash. Oddly enough, a 12-year-old boy had witnessed the crime. Years later, the boy would become one of Pablo's most loyal hit men, known as Popeye.

Diego Echavarría Misas was a powerful industrialist who lived in a remake of a medieval castle. Widely respected in the higher social circles, he yearned to be revered as a philanthropist. But no matter how many schools and hospitals he opened, the poor were not fooled by his attempts to mask his malevolence.

The workers in his textile mills toiled endlessly in cruel conditions for a pittance. He fired hundreds of them in an abusive way and without a severance pay. Like many wealthy landowners, he expanded his territory by forcefully evicting peasant communities. Attempting to defend their homes, some peasants were imprisoned or murdered. The rest were forced to settle in the slums.

El Patrón had heard enough about Echavarría. One day, his kidnapping became news. His family paid the ransom, but his fate remained a mystery. After six weeks, his body was found in a hole near Pablo's birthplace. He had been tortured, beaten and strangled. The poor celebrated his death. Although many people believed that Pablo had brought them justice, with no evidence linking him to the crime, he was not charged. On the streets, people stopped to shake his hand or bowed to him in reverence.

He learned that murder provided cheap and effective PR. He ordered the murders of people who tried to prevent his accumulation of power, including those who denounced him, refused to abide by his rule or declined his bribes. Focussing people on their mortality or that of their families brought their behaviour into line. He killed without remorse, just to increase his reputation and earnings, and to help his business grow in a world of opportunists and cutthroats.

In 1975, Pablo accompanied the Godfather to a meeting of all of the bosses held in Bogotá. After arriving in a private plane, they stayed in a mansion protected by gangs of heavily armed bodyguards. The bosses agreed to finance a paramilitary army to counteract kidnappings. With business out of the way, there was a raucous party. Pablo envied the orgies they rewarded themselves with.

Observing the Godfather interacting with the other bosses such as Griselda, the King of Marlboro and the Bravos, Pablo absorbed how they made business decisions and decided who to kill. He learned about bribing the most powerful people, including politicians, judges and police chiefs.

CHAPTER 7

MARLBORO WAR

Many of the Spanish texts describe how Pablo was shaped by the disagreements among the contraband bosses, which culminated in the Marlboro War. In the mid-1980s, he told a journalist, "In this country, one is made in war. I [first] got involved in a war, in a very violent war that was the Marlboro War. I swear that not even the countrymen – unless they were bandits at that time – knew that such a war existed … It was before the cocaine began and that [war] was where the first capos came from and where the first hit men came from. The sicarios were born there. The Marlboro War was the prelude to all the wars that came after.

"It seems to me that if we are going to remember and make history, you have to split things into three parts. Let's say until 1973 it was contraband and smugglers. From 1973 to 1979 were the first two generations of hard smuggling of cocaine, and from 1980 until now is the last straw, which is what the gringos named it, supposedly the [generation] of cartels.

"In that first period lived the most courageous man of Antioquia called Ramoncachaco, who was Don Alfredo's workman, the first man in this country to be called Padrino, whom they made issues with, but since they were never able to prove [accusations] against him, they made up an excuse to put him in jail. At that time, for his safety, he was using a television screen, which is now called a closed circuit, but at that time people saw it as something extraterrestrial, and they used the existence of that screen to put him behind bars, accusing him of smuggling.

"Of course, Don Alfredo was always a contrabandist of

cigarettes, whiskey, watches and second-rate pianos. He bought all that up there in the US, brought it by ship, smuggled it through Turbo or Tolú. Once he got thirty-eight trucks loaded. I remember a famous scandal that took place which became a part of history, in which people from the smuggling business began to get into the drug trade. At that time I was a worker of Don Alberto's, another smuggler, who I consider to be my teacher, because he was a warrior and because he was intelligent and skilled.

"It happens that there was so much contraband at that time that the pressure came on the authorities to the point where a scandal broke out and, as a result, the first commander in the history of Antioquia police fell, supposedly for helping the smuggler's convoy: It was Colonel Ibáñez.

"The story is that Don Alberto loaded thirty-two trucks – six fewer than Don Alfredo who had the national record with thirty-eight – and we smuggled them through Turbo and then we sent them to Medellín along an old, broken trail that connected to the sea. Just imagine how the situation in the country was at that time [lacking infrastructure].

"On that tour, all the police along the way received money. It is that, man, that time the Community Action meetings and even the police inspectors of the roads came out to ask for money because the [operation] became general gossip from when we unloaded the merchandise and then the boxes went from the ship to some barrels and from the barrels to the beach and from the beach to the trucks. So we started, and when the convoy crossed through Santa Fe de Antioquia, we found a lieutenant and his patrol of six police officers – many for that time – with the order to arrest and confiscate the merchandise. The lieutenant was not taking money or wanting to trade anything, but the ones below, those who let us out of Turbo and the ones we gave money to down the road [did cooperate]. So when they stopped us, we went down to the ground to talk. Now I remember the words Don Alberto said to the officers:

"'Look, Lieutenant, for you to get rid of these thirty-two

trucks you need, first of all, thirty-two cops that know how to drive a truck, thirty-two assistants and sixty-four freighters, and, in addition, a thousand riflemen because you're going to have to kill me right here. Better said, you either receive this money here or you are putting your life at stake.'

"And the thirty-two trucks entered Medellín, but since the gossip had also reached here, the gossip flew to Bogotá and there they thought that Colonel Ibáñez had received money and they removed him without investigating anything. That time they sent Don Alberto and all those involved in the smuggling to jail again. I remember how, laughing, he told me about the investigation:

"'Do you know what they asked me?' he said. 'They asked me which military people I knew. Then I answered about the judge that I knew, about General José María Córdoba, General Santander ... He asked me if I knew Colonel Ibáñez. He asked whether he was my friend. I told him no, that I had never seen him.' And it's just that he never saw the colonel, and the colonel was a straight and narrow person, but so the police could show they were taking action, those of Bogotá took revenge on him. Do you understand?

"Returning to the topic, let's go back to Ramoncachaco who had already gone from the contraband business with Don Alfredo's group to the cocaine group, and now he was independent and began to show that for the first time, he was being talked about. He already had, for example, the fashionable car that was the Nissan Patrol four-wheel with nickel-plated wheels, a silver-plated grill, and pimped out more or less like those of the emerald traders of Boyacá. The car was from 1971 and he changed it out later on for another, a 1972. For the years I remember at that time, this man continued to do so well that he soon bought a plane. That was an example of how, after some time passed, many decided it was better to switch to the cocaine business.

"Ramoncachaco went personally for the cocaine to Ecuador and he even told me that the first time he went there with a plane – I think his plane was the first aircraft that left this country for drugs – everything seemed so easy. He came back and came back and became richer and richer.

"Later, there were three small planes that became famous: that of Jaime Cardona, who even died in a plane crash with part of his family, Don Alberto's plane and Ramoncachaco's plane. They were one-engine planes.

"So, I was telling you that this man went to Quito for the first time, with a flight plan that he acquired legally. He bought his merchandise, packed it in his suitcases and, when he got back to Medellín, he went through customs and saw that no one knew what it even was. Nobody knew [what he was doing]. Listen to me: he told me no one was even looking at him. They supposedly searched around the clothes and checked them and the product was in there, and nobody knew what it was … Those of that time worked with cocaine straight up and began to mobilise complete fortunes.

"All in all, Marlboro's smuggling continued into its heyday, so that here was a mix of what could be called the Mafia of the time, which were the strongest smugglers, and those that were just beginning in the drug trafficking, whom had also been in the cigarette business.

"In this business were names like Jaime Cardona, Ramon-cachaco, Mario Cacharrero and another one called El Pariente, who is alive and at some point owned about ten cars. Pariente was a tall fat massive man. He began to carry, I do not know in what form, his merchandise, and he bought those LTD long cars. He was the bomb: he would drive around in the centre of Medellín with those huge cars and the people would gawk at them. He was famous for his cars.

"That is the first phenomenon that I saw of drug trafficking from my position as a young man because let's say that I was still studying. I had barely finished high school. Look: I've been thinking about these things and I'm seeing more and more clearly that those were for me the examples that determined the future of my life and the future of many, many young people who were beginning to live with illusions – without much desire to work in a factory or in a warehouse. This is just what we saw – and that's why I'm telling you – that the opulence added to the adventure and added to the power that money gives. You ain't gonna tell me that money does not empower and does not give fame – and neither will you be able to deny that there is not a single human in this world who does not like silver, fame and power. And more so at that age.

"Well, the capos of drug trafficking that I admired at that time were then Jaime Cardona, Mario Cacharrero, Ramoncachaco and of course El Pariente with his cars, and a guy named Evelio Antonio Giraldo who was the first death within the Mafia in Medellín. He was killed in 1972. He was killed there, near *The Colombian*, in a gas station over Juan del Corral. He was shot several times when he was next to his car, a 1968 Dodge Demon. There they used dum-dum bullets – they made those bullets popular – with a Magnum that is a massive revolver. Really big. It was used a lot. And it's still being used.

"I saw the corpse of that guy and the holes he had were impressive because that projectile is made of lead, a lead core as described by those who know, reinforced with a copper shield to the base, so that when it touches skin, the lead is flattened and the copper is still there, firm, and then the bullet becomes, imagine, a mushroom. And as the bullet does not enter straight but enters spinning, it starts twisting at a high speed because the gun barrel has what they call an anima or a groove, an alembic carved inside so that when the lead gets fired it turns it into like a spinning top. Then think about the embrasures that it gets to drill in the victim's body. That was the first death of the cocaine business ... It is a story that nobody in this country knows. Of course, at that time there had already been dead people but not from the cocaine business, but from the Marlboro War.

"The business brought lots of money. It started here, developed here and went to the United States. It happened because Don Alfredo was bringing in so many trucks. Don Alberto was entering as many as Jaime Cardona and many others. The cigarettes came out to the market and as the saturation in every corner was increasing every day, the competition increased, the price went down and everyone lost money.

"Then the first bullets came. As a result, things heated up. With Ramoncachaco already in the cocaine business, he was killed because he had been involved in the cigarette business before. He was, shall we say, the second dead man of this war.

"[Things became] so belligerent and so hard that whenever they saw somebody involved in this business they would kill him in the street as soon as they saw him. And they all knew each other. And, besides, the city was not that big. Then you measure the mortality here and in the US, because in the States those who dispatched the shipments to the three capos and then those who left from Colombia fleeing from death began to die.

"I got to live that war closely. I felt it over my head and counted the dead from here in Medellín – more than sixty – and I left, man, bless God, I came out alive. I was from a generation that was made in the war. Of course, here it seems that we all did, we do and we will be made out of it, but I say that I got to be closer to many of the guys of my time. Look at one thing: I got to see, for example, how the first man was killed from a motorcycle. And I got to see, once in a while, people returning from the afterlife – like with Don Alberto.

"It happened that one day, Don Alberto started drinking with two guards and when they finished, they started his car. But one of them had inhaled a line of cocaine and, with some people, cocaine produces delirium – ideas of persecution and aggression and so many mental issues. One of the bodyguards – an ex-policeman, by the way – who was in the back seat became paranoid, took out a revolver and he shot the man. [Alberto] recalled that the car stopped and he managed to open the door, but he fell there without being able to move. Dead to the others, but he said he listened to everything, saw everything, understood what was happening. That he saw as the ex-policeman went away about six or seven metres to get a taxi and he had him in his sight and he could not do anything. Then he said he remembered something that I always repeated to him:

"'Boss, one has to always be armed. One with a gun next to him becomes like a different person. If something happens to you, at least shoot in the air, get attention. The weapon must always be close to you when you drive or when you sit down at the table. Better said, always. It is just that everybody in this country of wars has to carry a weapon because otherwise he is fucked.' I used to tell him that and I saw that on that day he had not listened to me.

"Going back to the story, you see, Ramoncachaco was killed in the Alivar gas station that is exactly six blocks away from the Olava Herrera airport. They shot him with a Magnum revolver, with flat bullets cut off at the tip, at 3:57 in the morning. Who-ever is familiar with these bullets will understand me well when I describe what that war was like. And they shot him at the time he was pouring gasoline into the Nissan Patrol, as a cassette player was playing music and he was dancing salsa on the ground while filling the tank with gasoline. And when he fell, because the first bullet sent him backwards, so powerful was the impact of that cut-out bullet that he was left without a gesture of pain or fear or tragedy. Ramoncachaco was left smiling. He remained, as they said then, with the salsa that was being played at that moment smeared on his face.

"They called him Ramoncachaco because he dressed nicely – but he had a bum vibe – because he was a bum, a fine bum, well-dressed, with suits with billiard tablecloth fabric or olive suits or dark green suits and light green or white ties and white stockings and a white or yellow handkerchief that looks well with green and patent leather shoes, wine-coloured. Imagine it. The man was a thug: a thug because he had nonetheless come from below.

"So I'm telling you, just on the surface, who they were: let's say the mirrors of my youth. I do not say my idols, but the examples that I had at a time when one already decided definitively the path that they will follow in life. And of all of them, I repeat that the one that served me the most was that of my teacher who is still alive: Don Alberto [the Godfather]."

When a policeman on Pablo's payroll was moved to another district, he snitched out the Godfather's operation. The police waited to ambush a convoy of trucks. They would all get rich confiscating so many goods. El Patrón had stopped for lunch and told the convoy to continue without him. Thirty-seven trucks were seized. A driver called Pablo, who said to tell the other drivers not to speak to the police. With the police after him, he took a bus back to Medellín. Lawyers got the drivers released but were unable to retrieve the merchandise.

The accusations against the Godfather multiplied. He was reported to the president for running an illegal business and bribing over 200 members of law enforcement. It was alleged he had conspired to kill multiple witnesses. With no evidence against him of any major crimes, he was charged with having a television circuit without the appropriate legal documents. Evidence of drug trafficking, including a weighing scale, were found on a raid at his home. After serving a year in prison in Cartagena, he retired from the business, which he believed was being overrun by bloodthirsty individuals from desperate backgrounds. After advising the other bosses to retire, too, he told them, "Pablo and those warriors will keep the business going. They are unstoppable."

CHAPTER 8

COCAINE

A supply of competitive and organised gangsters, and its ideal geographic location, paved the way for Medellín's dominance in cocaine. Before Pablo's rise, its savvy smugglers used air connections, communications and the banking system to their advantage. Experts in money-laundering, evading currency controls, trading in black markets and kidnapping proliferated. Gangs taught kids to pickpocket and flew them to New York to fleece Christmas shoppers. Trainee murderers learned how to perform surveillance and abductions.

Before Colombian dominance, Cuban traffickers in Miami managed the wholesale cocaine market, supplied by refineries in Peru and Bolivia. They recruited Colombians to smuggle the drugs. As demand for cocaine increased, the Colombian gangs saw the profit potential. They set up refineries to produce record amounts of drugs, and distributed them through a network they had already established to sell cannabis.

The earliest traffickers from Medellín traversed dangerous dirt roads, flew over perilous mountain slopes and landed on short strips in Peru and Bolivia to get to villages in the Andes. They paid the locals to grow coca bushes, and to remove the leaves every three months. The leaves were soaked in kerosene, and grey residue was filtered out, leaving the paste. Then it was dissolved in sulphuric acid and potassium permanganate and filtered. Ammonium hydroxide was added and it was filtered again, finally producing cocaine base. The traffickers flew paste and base back to Colombia.

In jungle and forest labs, cooks mixed the base with ether and acetone. The chemical reaction produced cocaine hydrochloride, a fine white salt. Packed into plastic, the cocaine was placed aboard light aircraft, and flown to transshipment points on Colombia's north coast.

Only 1,100 miles from Barranquilla, a bustling Colombian seaport flanked by the Magdalena River, Miami provided an ideal entry port for the cocaine invasion. The underlings of the Colombian gangsters blended well into the cosmopolitan city, but they did not go unnoticed for long. Whereas the old-school Italian Mafia preferred to dispose of its enemies quietly, the Colombians publicly massacred each other and Cuban rivals. Armed gangsters in cars chased each other, culminating in machine-gun battles. Even Dadeland Mall was sprayed with bullets by a Colombian assassin. TV news broadcast the aftermath of the battles, with journalists at the scene of what appeared to be war zones. As the bodies piled up, the morgues were forced to rent extra space.

Working for the Godfather had introduced Pablo to operations in local villages processing coca paste from Peru, Bolivia and Ecuador. With the coca plant growing widely in the jungles and mountains of South America, cheap paste was abundant. Cocaine was so scarce that none of the kitchens were getting busted. Colombians were selling it to middlemen, who transported it to America, where it was sold to wealthy customers. The US authorities were focussed on cannabis and heroin coming from Mexico, not cocaine.

Intrigued, Pablo set about learning everything he could about cocaine from an associate of the Godfather who produced it. He also studied the history of cocaine, including Freud's experiments, as detailed in Appendix A of this book. He calculated that he could make more from a single load of cocaine than he could from a convoy of trucks smuggling contraband.

Pablo and Gustavo went to Ecuador and Peru. Suppliers of cocaine paste were offering it for $60 a kilo when a kilo of cocaine was selling for up to $60,000 in America. By cutting the cocaine with two thirds of another substance, a kilo could fetch almost $200,000. In Renault 4s, they smuggled the paste from the Andean mountains across three countries. They had separate cars for each country, with the relevant country's licence plate. The paste was hidden in spare tyres, a fender or a compartment they had installed above the petrol tank, which the checkpoint police never searched.

The first batch of paste ended up in a house with covered windows, where it was transformed into cocaine. The cooks lived on the second floor. Most of the first floor had been renovated into a kitchen. The cocaine was cooked in old refrigerators that Pablo had converted into ovens. Hoping for feedback on his first batch, he gave away ten samples. The majority said they preferred it to weed and requested more. Some said it gave them energy. Others said it calmed them down. Pablo didn't like it. He preferred smoking pot. With Mario out of prison, Pablo put him in charge of the facility. As a cook, Mario learned to increase the quality and quantity of cocaine. Pablo's sister, Alba Marina, hid chemicals such as ether and acetone at the school where she worked.

Trucks replaced the Renault 4s. They could carry up to twenty kilos of raw material disguised by a cargo of potatoes. More workers were hired. Pablo's customers were exporters, including the Ochoa brothers, who smuggled it out of Medellín.

Problems manifested in Ecuador. Some of his men were stopped by the police, murdered and disposed of with signs around their necks which read, "So you know who you are dealing with." After learning that his Ecuadorian contacts had betrayed him, he transferred the work to intermediaries and recruited more Colombians for the southern route. In Peru, he established new channels for shipments of coca paste.

As his network expanded, El Patrón formed alliances with dictators, militias, governors, Mafia leaders and even Nazi fugitives in Bolivia, whose leader was Klaus Barbie, a.k.a. the Butcher of Lyon, who during World War II had ordered the deaths of up to 14,000 people. Pablo marvelled at the Nazi stronghold in the middle of the jungle, where troops marched in uniforms and worshipped Adolf Hitler.

CHAPTER 9

MARRIAGE

By the age of 25, Pablo had surpassed his goal of making one million pesos and his friends joked that he no longer had to honour his pledge of killing himself for not achieving it. But Nora remained unimpressed. An ideal suitor for her daughter should have a regular job or at least study. Also, she had heard rumours about his crimes. She told her daughter to end the relationship.

In September 1975, Victoria celebrated her quinceañera – an important ceremony for a girl's 15th birthday to mark her passage to womanhood, to give thanks to God for his blessings and to present a young woman to the community. After Pablo didn't show up – he was in Ecuador – she yelled at him.

In March 1976, the couple met at an ice cream shop. "I'm going on a long trip," he said. "I won't be back for months."

"My mother told me not to come here to say goodbye," she said, her big brown eyes shining sadly. "She told me to let you go."

His usually calm face tensed. "She didn't want you to say goodbye! We can't go on like this! Let's run away and get married in Pasto."

Her face lit up. "OK. Yes. Let's."

"We can spend tonight at Gustavo's."

After she didn't return home, Nora sent Mario to find her.

"Your brother's searching for us," Pablo said. "We need to leave for Pasto right away. To get there, we need to change planes at Cali."

In La Paz, Mario and his siblings went door-to-door hunting for Victoria. He believed that she had been dragged away. After someone revealed the couple's travel plans, he headed to the airport, read the passenger registries and learned that they had boarded a flight for Cali.

Nora got on the phone to her mother in Palmira. "Can you go to Cali and stop them from leaving?" she asked Lola.

After locating and surprising the runaways, Lola said to Pablo, "For you to take this little girl, you have to get married."

In a truck, two of Pablo's friends headed for Cali. When they arrived at the airport, they found the couple with Lola. Smooth-talking Pablo had convinced Victoria's grandmother of his honourable intentions. Bowled over by his charm, Lola asked the couple to accompany her to Palmira, where she would have the bishop oversee the ceremony.

Victoria married in the clothes she had eloped in: green army pants and an orange and beige jumper. Pablo's two friends gave him a card to celebrate the regrettable mistake he had made. After a week at Lola's, they lived in a house in La Paz for a few months. Victoria cooked Pablo one of his favourite meals: dice fried cooking bananas scrambled with scallions and eggs, with grilled meat, rice and beetroot salad. His preferred breakfast was a corn patty with scrambled eggs, chopped onions and tomatoes, with coffee.

Marriage did not stop Pablo's affairs. His indiscretions with a school principal and a widow came to Victoria's attention, but did not break their bond. Swearing undying love, he told her to ignore rumours from jealous people who wanted to destroy their relationship. As his affairs continued with beauty queens, she suffered in silence. Whenever tension increased, he gave her roses.

CHAPTER 10

COCAINE ARREST

One of Pablo's drivers, Vulture, racked up profits from coca-paste trips, and bought an expensive car, motorbike and clothes. His relative in the DAS, the Colombian equivalent to the FBI, asked about the source of his cash. Vulture said he was transporting potatoes, but the relative remained suspicious.

In early June 1976, a headline in *The Time* disrupted Pablo's honeymoon period: "Cocaine was seized in Itagüí, worth twenty-three million pesos." He gazed at the photos and read the article. Near the Ecuadorian border in Ipiales, DAS agents had watched his men stash contraband in the rims of a Ford truck, which they had tracked to Medellín. Days later in Itagüí, the DAS had stopped the truck and found ten kilos in the spare tyre. Under orders to accept bribery, so that they could arrest the head of the gang, the agents had taken money and told the driver to tell Pablo that they would "let the goods get to Medellín in exchange for a cash payment."

The next morning, Pablo, Gustavo and Mario arrived at an ice cream shop with $5,000. After warmly greeting the agents, Pablo invited them to sit at an outdoor table. "Everything in life has a solution," he said, while employing a tactic he used to sharpen his senses: rolling a cylinder of paper with his right ring and middle fingers. With the agents faking interest, he added, "I'll give you $5,000 in advance of a bigger figure and everything will be in order."

As soon as he offered the cash, an agent announced, "You are wanted for attempted bribery." Three DAS vehicles screeched up and everybody was arrested, including the two drivers, for drug trafficking and attempted bribery.

After a night in holding cells in Medellín, they were transported north to the Bellavista prison, an overcrowded hellhole with desperate men lying on the floor next to each other on makeshift mattresses or sitting on walls or milling around the decrepit building. Forced to survive on a diet of rotten-meat soup, the majority were malnourished. It was renowned for subhuman conditions and violence.

Convinced that he wouldn't be incarcerated for long, Pablo grinned confidently for his most infamous mugshot, holding the sign 128482 of the Prison of the Judicial District of Medellín. In no other photo would he ever display such an impressive smile and the teeth he spent so much time brushing to keep pristine. The next day, his mugshot was on the front page of the newspaper.

Preparing to give a speech, his brother was with the coaching staff of the national bicycling team when he saw the mugshot. As soon as possible, he called his mother.

"I've been crying for hours," Hermilda said. "Did you know about this?"

"No, I swear. I knew he was doing contraband, but not this. I'll do whatever I can to help him."

Pablo's glee faded when a rumour started that his group included undercover police trying to infiltrate the prison gangs. Tipped off that they were going to be attacked, they braced to defend themselves. Things calmed down when an inmate called Blackie, who had earned the respect of the other prisoners, vouched for them and told the others to leave them alone. Blackie had heard of Pablo, who later rewarded him with a job.

Having received death threats, the judge assigned to Pablo's case, Manda Espinosa, announced, "If I have to die to get someone as important as him into jail, then I shall die."

In a Dodge truck, Roberto and a friend went to visit Pablo, taking turns to drive for eight hours. Roberto was shocked by how bleak it was inside the prison.

"Don't worry about my situation," Pablo said. "I'll take care of it."

"OK," Roberto said. "When I get back to Medellín, I'll tidy up your records to show that the money has all come from real-estate deals."

While Pablo was incarcerated, Victoria started to show signs of pregnancy. In the queue for prison Visitation, with Pablo's sister, Alba Marina, and Gustavo's wife, Victoria vomited. The news of the pregnancy lifted Pablo's spirits, which the prison had worn down. While he schemed to be transferred to a different prison, Victoria moved into her mother's house.

Through bribery, Pablo, Gustavo and Mario were transferred to the Yarumito prison, Itagüí, which had outdoor recreation, including soccer. Every day, Hermilda and Victoria visited with fresh food. He bribed a judge, but after two months, it was decided that he would be tried in a military court, which was more difficult to corrupt. His lawyer warned that he could get a long sentence.

At Visitation, Victoria sensed that Pablo planned to escape. "You're not going to do anything that crazy," she said.

Although he said no, the next night, he told a guard that he needed to stretch his legs to reduce his stress. After being allowed onto the soccer field, he asked the players to keep kicking the ball as far as possible. He followed it, jumped over the wall and hid at a friend's house in La Paz.

The warden called Hermilda: "Your son has escaped. I need you to convince him to come back otherwise I'm going to end up in jail. If he comes back immediately, I promise there will be no repercussions."

When Pablo called his mother, she relayed the message from the warden, and urged him to return. "Think about Victoria! She's three months pregnant. Why make her suffer like this by going on the run?" Pablo and his mother showed up at the prison with X-rays of a sick person. Claiming he'd been ill, he showed them to his military escorts, who were satisfied about his absence.

Due to all of the evidence, the case was strong against Pablo and his co-defendants. With nothing to lose, he gambled on getting a new judge by filing a motion to move the trial to Ipiales, the city near Ecuador where the truck had been intercepted by the DAS. Without the decision being approved by the Supreme Court of Justice, the motion was granted. The three men were handcuffed and escorted out. Seeing his mother arrive for a visit, he smiled until a guard hit her with a rifle butt to get her out of the way. Unable to intervene, he gave the guard a death stare.

In Ipiales, he spread his money around the prison. The guards treated them and their visitors well. They allowed him to go to a hotel to spend time with Victoria. But the new judge refused to accept bribery. For his own lawyer, Pablo hired the judge's brother, so that a new judge would be required. The next judge accepted cash from Pablo's lawyer. Pablo paid the driver of the truck to take the fall. Sentenced to less than five years, he ended up in a prison with good facilities. He gave the driver's family a house, a car and money.

In August 1976, the charges against Mario and Gustavo were dropped. An inmate with a pet rabbit was released. The rabbit went to another inmate, who was released. After a third time, it became known as the lucky rabbit. Finally, Pablo ended up with the rabbit, and he was released in November, after five months of incarceration.

He took a long bus journey north to Medellín. Walking to Hermilda's house with his belongings in a backpack, he bumped into a relative, whom he hugged and asked for a coin. At a payphone, he recited some code and hung up. At Hermilda's, he nestled into a sofa. Although he was exhausted from the day's travel, his expression remained resolute. A couple of hours later, an associate brought $200,000 and a Toyota SUV.

Over dinner, Roberto tried to dissuade his brother from investing in coca paste. He was making so much money in contraband, why would he want to risk everything on cocaine? Pablo said not to worry, he was going to make some fast money from cocaine, and return to contraband because the police only confiscated contraband without incarcerating you.

"Getting in trouble for cocaine hurts me, too," Roberto said. "I'm a successful businessman. My stores are selling lots of bikes. The government pays me a salary for coaching. I don't think the government will allow me to coach the national team if my brother is a drug dealer."

Before his first day of release was over, El Patrón had organised a coca-paste mission. The next day, he learned that his smuggler had been pulled over at a checkpoint. The police had examined the A/C system and found the cash. Pablo and Gustavo sped to the province of Risaralda, where they bribed the police to release the vehicle and the money. Not wanting any further mishaps, the cousins headed to Ecuador, where contacts Pablo had made in prison helped him to source coca paste and advised him about the best smuggling routes.

Judge Espinosa frowned on his release. Having refused his exoneration, she added some notes to the file that death threats had been received by her, the case detectives and even the head of the DAS. Rather than have her killed, Pablo condemned her to always have to walk to work. Whenever she bought a car, it was stolen and thrown off a cliff or burnt.

Over a month later, Pablo and Gustavo were pulled over by the two DAS agents who had previously arrested them. The agents took them to a remote area by a garbage dump, tied their hands together and forced them onto their knees. Assuming that he was about to be executed, Pablo remained calm and tried to convince the agents to take money instead of killing them. He later credited his proximity to death with giving him a certain eloquence for the fifteen minutes it took to negotiate his freedom. After roughing them up, the agents demanded a million pesos in exchange for their lives. Gustavo went to get the money.

Once freed, Pablo told Gustavo that he was going to kill the agents because being forced onto his knees at gunpoint was unforgivable. Gustavo was initially reluctant, but Pablo said if they were not murdered, they would suffer blackmail from the agents for the rest of their lives. Emboldened by their success, the two agents were about to kidnap one of his workers. They considered Pablo an easy drug-trafficker target.

On March 30, 1977, Pablo's men kidnapped the agents and took them to a house. El Patrón made them get onto their knees. As they begged for their lives, he put a gun to their heads and fired multiple times. The news reported the discovery of their bodies.

CHAPTER 11

EXPORTATION

With 15-year-old Victoria about to give birth, Pablo rented an apartment next to a supermarket in Medellín's Castropol area. After thirteen years of staying in Hermilda's house, he finally moved out. A few weeks later, he bought a Porsche Carrera.

On February 24, 1977, Juan Pablo was born. The proud father ran around singing salsa songs and telling everybody, "He was born male, a gentleman! He's a boy!" They hired a nanny called Sofia. The arrival of a grandson and Pablo's increased wealth softened his mother-in-law's attitude towards him. It was the beginning of what Pablo and his men would call the Golden Age.

When enough money had come in, Pablo moved to the prestigious Provenza neighbourhood in El Poblado, with lots of white stucco houses. His mansion was diagonal to the Campestre Club, frequented by the traditionally rich, who publicly frowned on the traffickers, while secretly coveting their business. When asked who they had sold their properties to, they replied wealthy cattle ranchers. Other Mafia bosses owned property in the neighbourhood, including the Ochoas and the Castaños.

Pablo and Victoria ate at restaurants with views of the city lights and shopped at boutiques. He bought Hermilda a house in the Estadio neighbourhood, and relocated his sisters into apartments near his mother. Yet again, Roberto urged him to stop and focus on real-estate investments, but El Patrón was addicted to the power, money and lifestyle.

Rather than host meetings in locations such as ice-cream parlours, he intended to run his business from his new house, until

Mario cautioned him not to mix business with family. Instead, he opened an office near El Poblado church, but eventually he bought the fourth floor of a new office building by the Oviedo shopping centre. He continued to invest in premium Medellín real estate. In his late 20s, Pablo had realised his dream of becoming a multimillionaire.

Expanding his business, Pablo bribed an Ecuadorian Army colonel to oversee the transportation from the coca-paste sellers to the Colombian border. A dozen workers with blocks of wood hoisted onto their shoulders travelled for twenty hours through the jungle. Due to the smells released from making cocaine, Pablo established kitchens in the jungle.

Pondering the American market, he calculated that he could make higher profits if he stopped selling cocaine to exporters in Medellín. By 1977, cocaine had become increasingly popular overseas. It was considered relatively harmless, and many thought it would be legalised. Even the DEA issued a report that stated, "It is not physically addictive ... and does not usually result in serious consequences, such as crime, hospital emergency room admissions or both."

He compared the illegality of cocaine to America's prohibition of alcohol, from which the Kennedy family had prospered. Through legalisation, he hoped that his business would be legitimised, and his story would become a legend similar to the Kennedys. He even settled on a brand name: ESCOBAR COCAINE. He paid special attention to any news about the Hells Angels motorcycle gang, which he wanted to recruit for distribution after legalisation.

Shipping cocaine seemed easier and far more profitable than smuggling bulky strong-smelling cannabis. Security checks at airports were lax. Passengers were hardly ever searched. Their luggage was never X-rayed.

Testing the export business, Pablo and Gustavo loaded 100 kilos of cocaine into a Piper Seneca plane. The pilot took off for Miami's Opa Locka airport, mostly used by rich Americans. Back in Medellín, he waited to hear if the plane had made it. When the news arrived, the cousins hosted a party in a nightclub. For over a year, small planes carried up to 400 kilos to Opa Locka airport, two to three times a week. For refuelling, they stopped at Barranquilla, at the northern tip of Colombia or in Haiti's capital city, Port-au-Prince. A new verb was created to describe when a shipment had reached America: crowning. After each crowning, parties with gunpowder shook Medellín, with passers-by unaware of the nature of the celebration.

His smugglers took drugs on flights and returned with large amounts of cash. Up to forty kilos could be packed into used airplane tyres, which pilots would discard at Miami. They were taken to a dump, followed by one of his workers who would retrieve them. The cocaine was distributed through a network of Latinos in Miami. Continuously changing his methods, he had Colombian and US citizens board planes with cocaine in their suitcases or in specially made clothes. Holding up to five kilos, the suitcases had double walls. They were paid $1,000 and their flight tickets. Some wore shoes with hollowed-out bottoms, manufactured with the cocaine sewn inside. As well as passengers, Pablo recruited crew members, including stewardesses, pilots and co-pilots, who breezed through airports without getting searched. People in wheelchairs could smuggle up to $1 million worth of cocaine in the frames. Some smugglers dressed as nuns. Others posed as blind, with canes packed with drugs. Some swallowed cocaine in condoms. If the condom opened, they died. Newspapers reported such tragedies.

With the authorities obsessed with eradicating the drug that they had demonised for decades – cannabis – cocaine slipped into the US unnoticed. The federal government had classified cannabis as a Schedule 1 substance, more harmful than cocaine, and equally as harmful as heroin, where it remains to this day.

Over time, instead of sending people with suitcases, Pablo just sent the suitcases. They were checked onto a flight and picked up at the other end. Airport officials were bribed with hundreds of thousands of dollars to look the other way. An official on a meagre salary ended up getting arrested with $27 million in his bank.

Periodically, Pablo flew to Miami to oversee the distribution. Posing as the head of the Fredonian Petroleum Company – an example of his sense of humour because there is no petroleum in Fredonia, Antioquia – he rented out a floor of the Omni Hotel, where his customers partied all night. After they had paid in cash, the customers would get keys to cars in the hotel's garage. They would drive away with the cocaine hidden in the rear, each kilo stamped with the brand name Diamond Emerald. On the phone, he used words such as emeralds and diamonds, hoping to avoid providing any evidence to the DEA.

In 1987, Pablo told a journalist about his history with planes:

"Airplanes amaze me more than cars. When I was a kid, I painted airplanes into my notebooks, on pieces of paper I would find, on the walls with a coal smudge. Wherever I could, I painted planes because at that moment I already knew that someday I would be rich and have my own plane. Around eighteen, I confessed it to a friend and laughed because that day we did not have a penny in our pockets. But then came the cocaine business that was [smuggled] inside whatever was at hand, such as between canes or between rosaries, and [eventually] the planes appeared, carrying up to 60 kilos per trip. But 60 was a lot.

"The planes at the beginning were small planes that were left in bad condition, simply because there was no serious infrastructure in Colombia. Light aircraft that flew from the coast to Florida, for example, without going down an intermediate track, with an inexperienced pilot who had never done such flights. For instance, a sports driver who was the only person available. Then each flight was an odyssey because they sent themselves to the front, to either kill themselves or to become millionaires.

"Just imagine, one of the first routes that I knew went through near Bermuda, but since in Bimini was the first American radar, these men knew at what point to get down to eight, nine metres high on the surface of the sea, aware that there may be waves ten and eleven metres high. And as they usually crossed at night at that point, they went blindly: all they saw was the phosphorescent board of their wristwatch and the red lights of the compass. Nothing else. That's how many were lost. That's how the first one I had was lost."

CHAPTER 12

BROTHER'S DEATH

When it came to approaching girls, Fernando was shy. Initially, he had lacked the nerve to talk to Piedad, so he had sent her letters through friends. After receiving a positive response, he had visited her on Pablo's red motorbike. On the weekends, they had gone on walks with Hermilda and stayed at Abel's farm. The lovers had sometimes quarrelled, but Fernando had quickly restored their harmony by bringing gifts of perfume and music.

Piedad had been warned by her mother: "Those people are into bad things. Your relationship with Fernando is at your own risk."

After completing school, Fernando had gone to work at Roberto's bicycle factory in Manizales. Every week, he had returned to Medellín to see Piedad. After he had proposed, she agreed to get married after her graduation.

An omen occurred in early December 1977 when Piedad's newspaper deliverer died in a pond with his girlfriend. "It's good to die with your boyfriend," Piedad said.

"Don't talk such nonsense," her mother replied.

On December 23, she graduated. With Fernando absent from the ceremony, his sister Gloria brought roses. When placing them on the table, she noticed that two of the roses had withered. "That's bad luck," she said.

"You all talk too much nonsense," Piedad's mother replied.

Christmas 1977 was celebrated like never before by Pablo's family. The house was adorned with an expensive tree, a nativity scene and coloured bulbs. The family prayed and prepared custard and donuts. On Christmas Eve at Hermilda's house, gifts were exchanged, including a house for Pablo's mother in the Stadium sector, and an RV for Fernando, the youngest brother. Even neighbours benefited: Pablo covered the costs of a girl's surgery, education for another and one had his mortgage paid.

On December 24, Fernando picked up Piedad in the new vehicle Pablo had given as a Christmas gift. He drove to Abel's farm in El Tablazo. In the evening, they visited their mothers' houses to exchange Christmas greetings. Then they went out to celebrate her graduation. When Piedad uncharacteristically didn't return home, her mother had a sleepless night. She got in a taxi to search for her daughter.

"I woke up watching a fatal accident take place," the driver said.

"What car was involved?"

"A red Toyota."

"Do you know the name of the deceased?"

"No. They said it was a couple."

"Take me to the morgue," she said, grief-stricken.

After identifying the bodies, she hurried to Hermilda's house, where the mothers embraced, sobbed and prayed.

Hermilda called Pablo: "Fernando and Piedad were killed!"

Shock coursed through Pablo's body. After the words had sunk in, he said, "What happened?"

"Nothing is known." She sobbed.

Devastated, Pablo went to Envigado to launch an investigation. He heard various accounts, all of which ended with three dead at the bottom of a ravine, including a policeman. Listening attentively, he tried to piece everything together. Fernando had stopped on a ravine near a residential area. While they were petting inside, the vehicle had aroused local suspicion because it was brand new and lacking licence plates. Its authorisation paper was absent, perhaps blown off by the wind. Taking the lovers by surprise, a drunken policeman had pistol-whipped Fernando, who had scrambled to get behind the wheel and attempted to flee at a high speed. A police car in pursuit had rammed the Toyota, a risky manoeuvre that sent both vehicles over a cliff.

At the police station, the surviving members of the patrol had told the commander what had happened. Knowing Pablo's reputation, he had responded, "You don't know what you've done. You are all so fucked."

For the autopsies, Pablo paid René Meza a healthy sum. As a Liberal leader of Envigado, Meza was allied with Pablo, who was considering entering politics as a way to earn immunity from prosecution.

In the La Paz neighbourhood, hundreds attended the funeral. Men brought Fernando's coffin to Piedad's house. Her school-mates in uniform – white shirts, stockings and red shoes – carried her coffin. The two processions went to the Church of Santa Gertrudis in the main park. While they were buried in adjoining tombs, everyone was crying.

The small army of older well-dressed bodyguards with Pablo and Gustavo projected their power. After leaving the funeral in two SUVs, they travelled two blocks until the police stopped them and demanded ID papers.

"We don't have them," Pablo said.

"Where's your permits to carry weapons?"

"We don't have any."

"Why don't you have ID papers or weapons permits?"

"Because we're bandits." In the wake of his brother's death, El Patrón's aura was so powerful that the police backed down and allowed the men to continue. The bodyguards cheered.

CHAPTER 13

BUSINESS RISING

American demand for cocaine was so high that Pablo could sell any amount. To keep expanding, he needed more paste. He found suppliers in the Upper Huallaga Valley of northern Peru. Planes replaced men carrying bricks through jungles. He started to build runways in the Antioquia and Magdalena Medio areas. As well as planes taking cocaine to America, ships were used. A ship carrying bananas from the Caribbean to Miami could transport up to 800 kilos in its hold. The cocaine ended up in houses in Florida, stashed underground. Distributors who paid cash upfront bought bulk cocaine, which they collected from the houses and sold to their customers.

The size of the bribery increased. To enable the police on his payroll to get promotions and pay increases, El Patrón allowed them to confiscate massive amounts of cocaine. The media recorded the busts and reported them on the news. The seizures enabled the authorities to get more money from America to fight the War on Drugs. The confiscated cocaine was reported as destroyed, returned to Pablo and exported to the US.

Even though his brother had cautioned him about cocaine, so much money was coming in that Roberto felt that he had little choice but to launder it for Pablo, who lacked accounting skills. Roberto spread it among different banks and continued to invest in legitimate businesses such as real estate. He told his brother that they had enough money to buy their own island and live happily for the rest of their lives, but Pablo mocked the prospect of sitting on a deck chair sipping a cool drink, when he was running an exciting business that would make him a billionaire.

Streamlining his operation brought in millions, and attracted the attention of other traffickers, including two of the Castaños: Fidel and his younger brother, Carlos. El Patrón instinctively trusted Fidel, whose connections in Bolivia produced bulk paste. Fidel was a sportsman who jogged thirty kilometres a day in intense heat. He dressed smart but low-key, didn't smoke and only drank the occasional glass of fine wine. He never bought fancy cars and sometimes travelled on foot or took public transport. His associates were envious of the art and wine collection at his property, Montecasino, which was considered the most elegant house in Medellín.

Pablo sent aircraft to collect 500 kilos of raw material, which vehicles delivered to his kitchens in Antioquia. Delivering messages from his brother and other traffickers, Carlos Castaño was a regular at Pablo's office, which up to 300 people visited daily, including businesspeople, bikers, company directors, journalists, politicians, soldiers and an assortment of foreigners seeking opportunities in trafficking. Its car park had up to 100 vehicles. The wait to see him sometimes lengthened to three days, during which the visitors remained in the clothes they had arrived in, reluctant to go anywhere in case they lost their place in the queue. The police were usually there to pick up bribery cash. For a share of the profits, smaller traffickers wanted him to ship their product to America.

By offering high rates of return, he attracted investors. A stake of $50,000 would be repaid with $75,000 in two weeks. If the drugs were busted, investors received half of their money back. To obtain capital, people sold their cars and houses or cashed in savings. Pablo set up a form of insurance whereby businessmen could invest a few thousand dollars for a share in a shipment. After it was sold in America, the profits would be distributed. He guaranteed their original investment even if the shipment was seized. For providing this insurance premium, he took ten per cent of the American value of the cocaine. He even offered businessmen loans to invest and his most loyal acquaintances were granted allocations of up to ten kilos without having to put up any cash.

Despite his sober nature, he went out most nights. As a VIP, he sat in nightclubs surrounded by adoring women. While the rest were boozing, he drank water and smoked weed. By 2 AM, he would head for his car, which led a convoy of women to a penthouse he owned near the El Diamante baseball stadium.

After 200 million pesos went missing from his office, a guard was suspected of theft. Having rescued the employee from the prison island of Gorgona, Pablo was hurt by the betrayal. The cash was found at the guard's house. Pablo summoned his workers to the pool. The guard was tied to a crane and sank repeatedly. After he drowned, El Patrón told a stunned audience that he would kill anyone who stole so much as a peso. Wrapped in a rug, the victim was thrown onto a dump at Moravia called the Curve of the Devil.

A hit man put petrol on the rug. "Dust you are and dust you will become." He dropped a match.

So far, Pablo's rise had been unstoppable. Immensely wealthy, he had all of the Medellín traffickers at his feet and the respect of traffickers nationwide. He was allied with key sectors of the military, economic and political establishments, and was revered as a leader on social issues.

He moved his family to a mansion in the Santa María de Los Ángeles neighbourhood, not far from the Medellín Country Club, which he tried to join. Attempting to erase his poor background and criminal origins, he longed to be accepted by the higher social class, but perceiving him as a threat, they rejected him. After his application for the country club was declined, he flew into a rage and paid the employees to go on strike for higher pay, which forced the club to close temporarily. He instructed them to take a truck full of dirt across the golf course, tear it up and fill the swimming pool with dirt.

In Medellín, the traditionally rich were known as the white people. They formed a business lodge to prevent the traffickers from taking over the local companies. Attempting to buy shares in a cement factory located in Puerto Triunfo near Hacienda Nápoles, El Patrón sent a representative to negotiate.

"We can't sell shares to that man," he was told.

"So, how much is the whole factory worth?"

"It's not for sale."

"So, how many do we have to kill so they will sell it?"

Years later, Pablo told a journalist about his business challenges: "Look, people say, 'Those mobsters make big bucks so easily.' Is that true? This is hard-earned money. And well worked, because to get ahead in a company like this, you have to have an industrial mentality. This is not about grabbing a kilo of cocaine and telling a sailor: 'Take it away. Sell it.' No. This requires having cold blood to handle a trigger and shooting whoever must be shot, to having intelligence to put your fingers on the keys of a calculator and look to see how much you are going to invest and how much you are going to pay and how much you want to earn. And after that, one must have patience to get into the jungle, flying in planes and being so shrewd as to buy from a policeman to a general if he agrees."

By investing in land and construction, the traffickers controlled areas where they could move freely. Al Capone had employed this strategy in the Cicero suburb of Chicago, which he controlled electorally and with all of the authorities in his pocket.

Pablo converted the small town of La Estrella into a stronghold for his men. At the southern end of the Aburrá Valley, La Estrella had hosted the Colombian Woodstock he had visited as a child. It had many Catholic convents, and a park with the Los Trece Botones tavern, an old house frequented by bandits. As long as they prayed to the Virgin of Chiquinquirá, the patron saint of the municipality, they could shoot each other for the slightest reasons such as a soccer result. As devout parishioners, they sponsored neighbourhood groups for the purpose of worship and hired bands for processions.

For his 4th birthday, Juan Pablo received a yellow Suzuki mini-motorbike, custom-built for his size with stabiliser wheels on both sides. Taking a break from the office, Pablo gave his son a driving lesson by removing the stabiliser wheels and running along holding the motorbike. After Juan Pablo's confidence had improved, Pablo removed his hands to allow his son to ride without any stabilisation. Juan Pablo enjoyed the day so much that he fell in love with motorbikes.

By 1981, Pablo was often travelling to America with his family, Roberto, Gustavo and his bodyguard, Pinina. He owned real estate in Miami, including a mansion on a private beach. On one trip, his limo driver – unaware that he was transporting El Patrón – suggested they do a tour of the FBI's Museum.

"No. That's not a good idea," Roberto said in Spanish.

"Nobody will know who we are," Pablo said. Inside, they saw themselves on a massive wanted poster, so they fled.

In Washington DC, Pablo decided to test the security at the FBI building. While the rest of his family surrendered their passports to get a tour, he gave false ID papers, which the FBI failed to detect. After the tour, they headed to the White House, where Victoria took the iconic photo of him holding his son's hand outside of the gate. As usual, he was dressed nondescript like a harmless family man in dark trousers, a light shirt with its sleeves folded to the elbow, his trademark moustache and his curly hair combed to the right. The occupants of the White House could never have imagined that the man flooding the world with cocaine was outside. In Dallas, he visited the location of JFK's assassination. In Texas, he bought a mechanical bull, which sent people flying in Colombia.

CHAPTER 14

ALLIANCES WITH MAFIA BOSSES

Pablo bought two aircraft for personal use: a Hughes 500 helicopter and an Aero Commander plane. His first helicopter visit was to Fabio Ochoa Sr, the patriarch of a big family of adventurous men and strong women. His sons – Jorge, Juan David and Fabio – would end up classified as a powerful faction of the Medellín Cartel.

Unlike the other bosses, the Ochoas had grown up with money from over 100 years of horse breeding and they owned a restaurant. They created the Paso Fino horse race, famous in Medellín. The animal business dated back to Grandfather Abelardo Ochoa, who became wealthy from selling ribbons to railroads in the early 1900s. He paid for one of his sons to study veterinary medicine in France. While in Europe, Abelardo bought animals, including pigs, donkeys, goats, sheep and cattle, which he believed would improve the Colombian breeds. He omitted horses because he felt that the domestic animals were already well-suited to their environment. In 1927, his animal improvements earned him the Cruz de Boyacá medal.

By the 1970s, Abelardo's son, Fabio Sr, owned the Las Margaritas stables by the Cattle Fair. Approximately 600 animals kept the family busy. The restaurant at Las Margaritas attracted horse lovers and traffickers, who arrived with beautiful women in expensive cars, which contrasted the ethic of the discreet hard-working Antioquian.

The Ochoas lived at La Loma, a hilltop property south of Medellín, where friendly pet ponies ate out of visitors' hands, and also at Hacienda Veracruz, where they bred horses and had their own zoo. They regularly attended horse shows, and Jorge collected vintage Harley-Davidsons. Jorge and Juan David were stocky, but nothing compared to their father.

At home, Fabio Sr occupied a chair customised for a man with an immense girth. Although he never got caught with his hands in the trafficking operation, some authors have claimed that Fabio Sr was the true godfather of the Medellín Cartel. In the 2006 documentary film, *Cocaine Cowboys*, the former Medellín Cartel associate Jon Roberts mentioned Fabio Sr: "As many people want to believe that Pablo Escobar was the king of cocaine, they can believe that, but the man that was really the king was Ochoa." Visiting Fabio Sr at the Ochoa's La Clara estate in south-eastern Antioquia, Pablo respected the old man's advice and folk wisdom.

Jorge Ochoa had entered the cocaine business in Miami, where he worked in a wood factory. When asked for cocaine, he obtained it from Colombians in the Miami community. Over time, he sourced it uncut by having Fabio Jr send it from Medellín.

A natural lover of horses, Fabio Jr enjoyed working in the stables. By befriending the visitors, he built a network of trafficking contacts. After purchasing half a kilo of cocaine, with the help of two associates, he sealed it in the base of a pair of shoes, which was transported to Miami by a friend who worked on a Caribbean cruise. That first shipment was the start of a multibillion-dollar enterprise.

Due to the sudden wealth from unsure origins that was invested in massive estates and luxury items, people started to call the traffickers magicians. Their four-door Toyota trucks were called narco-Toyotas. In bidding wars, they overpaid for whichever art their advisers recommended. Their tasteless architecture multiplied in city centres. To avoid confiscation, property was put in carefully selected names. With the complicity of a corrupt bureaucrat, one trafficker registered property using the fingerprint and name of his pet monkey.

For Pablo to become a billionaire, it would take the ideas of a man of mixed German-Colombian descent who worshipped both John Lennon and Adolf Hitler: Carlos Lehder.

On September 7, 1947, Lehder was born in Armenia, a small town in central Colombia, a mountainous area renowned for its coffee plants. His father, Wilhelm Lehder, a tall blond German, had moved to Colombia before World War II and was considered a dangerous Nazi sympathiser by the police, who suspected him of running a fascist spy ring out of his hotel. As an engineer, he had helped to build the infrastructure that linked rural towns. Aloof and unfriendly, Wilhelm preferred to spend time alone in coffee shops.

Lehder's mother Elizabeth was the opposite of Wilhelm in manner and appearance. The ex-beauty queen came from a poor background. She was gregarious, artistically talented and adhered to a moral code. The youngest of four children, Lehder inherited some of his mother's physical traits, only reaching a height of 5 foot 4 and a weight of approximately seventy kilos. His two brothers grew tall and his sister had Down syndrome. As a young man, he was a charismatic risk taker, especially when it came to charming girls.

Wilhelm wanted Elizabeth to stay at home with the children, but she found that stifling. Eventually, they obtained a legal separation. Initially, Lehder sided with his father and was angry at his mother for wanting to travel the world. After he calmed down, he stayed with her in Central America, but returned to Colombia.

Handsome, intelligent and ambitious, Lehder was constantly in trouble at school and was ultimately expelled for throwing an inkwell at a blackboard after a teacher had attempted to discipline him. Ahead of his time, he self-studied, absorbing as much knowledge as he could from books and the news. Setting his sights on becoming an actor, he wrote to a Hollywood film company.

In his late teens, he moved to Michigan to join his architect brother. Living half like a hippie, he enjoyed the Beatles and polished up his English. Eventually, he got a job as a waiter in

Long Island, and dealt weed on the side. He married a beautiful Cuban college student he had met in Canada and they settled in a condominium in Miami. His initial attempts at crime were unsuccessful. He was arrested for the interstate transportation of stolen cars. In 1973, at 24, he was arrested for smuggling cannabis and sentenced to four years.

In minimum-security federal prison in Danbury, Connecticut, he rubbed shoulders with a more polished type of prisoner: white-collar criminals, Vietnam War protesters ... Unlike the typical Colombian smuggler, Lehder now spoke fluent English, enabling him to absorb knowledge from the eclectic mix of prisoners, which he filed away for future use. His cellmate was George Jung – whose life story was portrayed in the movie *Blow*, starring Johnny Depp. It was a meeting that changed their lives forever, and is detailed in Appendix B in this book: Norman's Cay.

After Lehder told Jung about the profit margin on cocaine, which he could easily source from Pablo and Gustavo, the cellmates set about planning a cocaine empire. They gleaned knowledge from fellow prisoners, such as smuggling routes from pilots and money-laundering schemes from bankers. Lehder's dream was to make millions from cocaine and to use the proceeds for revolutionary goals, including the destabilisation of imperialistic America.

After their release, they put the plan into effect, both becoming multimillionaires. Over time, Lehder ousted Jung from their partnership. To create a transshipment zone for the refuelling of aircraft heading to America, Lehder invested in a Bahamian Island called Norman's Cay. At first, he presented himself as a charming businessman to the locals, whose properties he bought. To deal with those who refused to leave, he imported a small army of German mercenaries with guard dogs, machine guns and helicopters. After getting their lives threatened, the diehards fled.

For five years, pilots brought anywhere from 300 to 5,000 kilos to Norman's Cay. The 5,000 kilos were worth $150 million wholesale and they arrived in a plane with 28-year-old Jorge Ochoa, who with Pablo, Lehder and Gacha would be classified as the leaders of the Medellín Cartel by the US. The cocaine packages were marked with the letters CIA. Larger planes meant bigger cargoes. At Norman's Cay, big loads were divided among smaller planes destined for Florida, creating a Federal Express-type method of delivery. Bales of cocaine were offloaded at remote airstrips or dropped into the water, where high-speed motorboats were waiting.

Lehder charged fees for other traffickers to use his airstrip. They brought cannabis, amphetamines and Quaaludes. Years later in court, he was alleged to have made $300 million from 1979 to 1980. Never had more drugs destined for America come from such a tiny place. With so much of it entering his state, the attorney general for Florida said in 1980, "Through an accident of geography, Florida has become an internal port of entry for illicit drugs entering the US. We now accept the fact that the drug industry is indeed the biggest retail industry in Florida." Lehder's success put him at the top of the DEA's most wanted Colombian smuggler list, supplanting Griselda Blanco.

Pablo was delighted with the amount of cocaine going through Norman's Cay. Every week in the late 1970s, he made millions, distributing cocaine to states as far away as Colorado for $72,000 a kilo, California for $60,000 and Texas $50,000. Depending upon the sizes of the loads, his pilots made up to $1 million per flight. The pilots revered his organisation as the most efficient to work for. The merchandise was always on time.

Sometimes, pilots didn't make it due to the combined weight of the cocaine and the fuel. Bad weather, such as a thunderstorm, could cause a heavy plane to stall. Pablo was making so much money that losing a plane was insignificant. Pilots arrested in Florida had usually performed dozens of trips. Already multimillionaires, they could hire the best lawyers.

On January 8, 1981, Lehder was indicted in Florida. In November 1981, members of a group based in Miami called Citizens Against Crime visited the White House to request help for the explosion of crime linked to the cocaine trade. In response, President Reagan authorised the South Florida Task Force, which became a vehicle for numerous photo opportunities, but did nothing to stop the flow of drugs. Ramping up the War on Drugs, the Reagan administration set its sights on Colombian super-villains.

CHAPTER 15

HIT MEN

Pablo hired a core team of gunmen from the Medellín slums with colourful nicknames, including:

Popeye – from the cartoon sailor, due to his service in the Navy

La Yuca – named after a root vegetable believed to provide strength

Pinina – a humorous name based on a blonde Argentinian telenovela starlet

Arete – meaning the Earring, infamous for organising the bombing of Avianca Airlines Flight 203

El Mugre – the Stain

Otto – short for Otoniel, whom Roberto referred to as Pablo's lucky charm because he spent so much time with El Patrón

El Chopo – Big Gun, infamous for organising the assassination of the justice minister

Tyson – due to his similarity to the boxer

El Negro – Blackie due to his dark skin, infamous for shooting the boss of the newspaper *The Spectator*

The inner circle felt like they belonged to a family – with El Patrón the father figure – with an inverted moral code. Pleasing the boss was good, which meant successfully murdering, kidnapping and bombing. Bad was when missions failed.

Completely illiterate, La Yuca came from a poor family that viewed killing as a career path to riches. Pablo called him the dreaded Yuca. After he started to make money, he locked himself away to binge on basuco, a kind of Creole crack. He found and killed people who had insulted him as a child. In an area Pablo controlled, La Yuca became a counsellor of the municipality. Knowing your place in the crime family was important to staying alive, a rule La Yuca ignored. By helping to coordinate the assassination of the justice minister, La Yuca was promoted, but he started to behave as if he were as powerful as a boss, so the bodyguards urged Pablo to have him killed, which he did.

By not showing fear in any situation, Pinina was rapidly promoted from a foot soldier to a military chief. Keeping his cool at all times, he didn't flinch at the most difficult assignments. Known as a friend of death, he demonstrated unlimited loyalty and organisational skills.

Before becoming one of El Patrón's most prolific hit men, Popeye had worked briefly as a cadet in the police and the Navy, only to grow disillusioned by the corruption. After he had quit the Navy, a female friend had remarked, "Popeye the sailor is back," hence the nickname. At an early age, he had grown accustomed to violence. He witnessed a machete fight, which ended after a man sliced the other's jugular vein. Spellbound, he watched the man die and remained gazing at the corpse, hypnotised by the blood. After that, he had no fear of death and was drawn to violence. Another time, he watched a government-sponsored death squad machine-gun five men in a shop until they lay in a pool of blood.

One of Pablo's administrators asked Popeye to accompany him to examine a mechanical bull. While the administrator checked the bull near a swimming pool, the surroundings impressed Popeye. On sofas, armed men were projecting strength, but disappointingly there was no sign of the boss. As they were leaving, Pablo appeared on a balcony, gazing at the horizon as if lost in thought. On the drive home, the two men sat in silence, relishing the afterglow from seeing El Patrón.

Popeye was offered a job transporting one of Pablo's girlfriends, a beauty queen. He took her to the most expensive stores, the hairdresser, the gym and to plastic surgeons. Patiently, he waited until daybreak for the end of the loud love-making sessions. He learned that Pablo sought beautiful women from modest neighbourhoods, some of whom had been schooled by their mothers in the art of sex in the hope of impressing him.

After ending his affair with the beauty queen, Pablo asked Popeye if he were willing to die with him. Popeye said that his boss would never die. Assigned to a gang run by Pablo's trusted bodyguard Pinina, Popeye quickly ascended the ranks and learned the business. Getting promoted into the Mafia was the most important day of his life. His hometown friends predicted that he would be dead within a few years.

Ill-tempered with a moustache and an eagle tattoo, Big Gun had spent his childhood in a reformatory. When he got excited, he stuttered. Pablo said: "Beware of Chopo when his stuttering is accelerating." When he couldn't talk with his mouth, he used his gun. People who had mocked him died. After a truck ran over his firstborn, he blamed his wife for being careless and shot her in the leg. When his wife and daughter were under police protection, he confronted the authorities and threatened to destroy the town unless they were released. The terrified mayor set them free. In his living room, he killed his ex-wife's boyfriend and dragged her around by the hair to prevent her from having another relationship.

Big Gun was vain. Arriving at a tavern, he found an associate dressed in new clothes. "I am your ally yet I look like your butler." He rushed out to an exclusive store and returned dressed from head to toe in Yves Saint Laurent. Swaggering over to his colleague, he said, "Now we can walk together, papacito." Sitting down to drink liquor, he listened to a salsa song which he said reflected his life: "Juanito Alimaña" by Willie Colón: "The street is a jungle of cement and wild beasts, of course! There is no longer a person going out mad in happiness, everywhere you go you expect the worst, Juanito Alimaña … is fine malice …"

Dealing directly with bodyguards insulated Pablo from the police. Issuing an order to a bodyguard made it impossible for the police to establish its origin. Each bodyguard controlled dozens of men, so combined they could rapidly raise an army. The bodyguards' base salary was approximately $1,500 a month, but the higher reward was the honour to be in the inner circle. With Pablo handing them lucrative contracts, they made quick cash by killing and kidnapping, with the highest profile victims offering the biggest fortunes. Ransoms of up to $5 million were paid by the family members of some of the people they kidnapped, a percentage of which went to the bodyguards assigned to the job. Despite the large sums, the bodyguards typically squandered the money on flash lives, helping out family members and friends, paying bribes, buying guns, prostitutes, fancy American clothes and cars, partying and gambling.

The candidates to become motorbike bodyguards were rigorously tested. They had to keep up with Pablo as he raced in the wrong direction down one-way streets and hit roundabouts at high speeds. The only person who succeeded was Crud, who the boss armed and gave a Honda motorbike. Bodyguards who successfully performed hits and kidnappings became overnight celebrities on the streets of Medellín. This, along with fast cash, attracted more job applicants, and so El Patrón built an army.

Pablo told a journalist that arming the bodyguards was easy: "We bought a lot of weapons: sometimes in a legal form through Indumil [an arms supplier run by the Colombian government] – while we bought the shotguns, that is, the cut-off shotgun and some pistols and revolvers and other [illegal guns] in the black market. Here in Colombia, we bought Browning pistols, Ingram submachine guns, R15s, AK-47 rifles, Soviets and lots of ammunition.

"The arms purchases made for a complete industry in itself, but hear this: drugs are an industry that must be defended with lead or with whatever means necessary. That's the fucked-up thing about drugs and contraband: they go hand in hand with violence. It's just that in this way it's the decent people rather than the assholes who either get ruined, end up in jail or dead. This stuff is like that. It is for people who have a lot of saliva. Better said: it's for warriors.

"These weapons were not to attack anyone but, at best, to make us be respected, not only from the bandits, but from the authorities. That's what the military calls deterrence. So, I said that our people should be better armed than the same authorities, because, man, when one gets all armed up like that, you get respected starting from the marshal down."

CHAPTER 16

HACIENDA NÁPOLES

Pablo started to search for a tract of land to establish a luxurious residence and business headquarters, which could be easily protected. In a helicopter, he looked for a place with water, mountains and jungle. A year later, he was still dissatisfied. Helping the search, one of Victoria's family members told him about a farm advertised in a newspaper: "They are beautiful new lands and soon they'll cross the highway and will be three hours from Medellín and about five hours from Bogotá."

Heading for the farm in 1978 – the year Pablo adopted his trademark moustache – El Patrón, Gustavo, Mario and four others set off on thunderous trail motorbikes, but monsoonal rain bombarded them. Without any protective clothing, they kept going, performing tricks and joking, attempting to knock each other down. Occasionally, they stopped to smoke weed and drink liquor.

Before midnight, they reached San Carlos, halfway to the farm. Lights came on in the sleepy town, as they went door-to-door with wads of cash to locate the owners of the restaurant, clothing store and hotel. After changing and devouring food, for which they paid up to five times the price, they slept.

Travelling on Sunday, their motorbikes upset a herder. "Slow down! The mules will get frightened!"

Roaring his motorbike, Pablo raced ahead and his men accelerated. The mules stampeded through a village. Some slipped on the pavement. One crashed into a ladder. While the herder stood shocked, Pablo and his men laughed.

After drinking and smoking, they left the town at high speed, challenging each other. Ahead of the rest of them, the guide was racing too fast on his motorbike to avoid a mule carrying wood, so he abandoned his bike, which broke the mule's legs. The animal fell. Pablo skidded to a stop and checked his guide, who was unhurt. A peasant was gazing at his animal, moaning, its blood spreading into the sand. The rest of the men stopped.

"Don't worry, old man. How much is your mule worth?" Pablo said.

"Thirty thousand pesos."

"I'll give you fifty thousand to keep quiet, but what do we do with the mule? We're not going to let it suffer." He turned to one of his men. "Shoot it." He handed him a gun. The first shots sent the animal into convulsions, which ended after two more to the head. "It was for a noble cause," Pablo said quietly.

Despite crashing their motorbikes on Sunday, they were still driveable. Eventually they reached Puerto Triunfo, where they stopped at a boardwalk by the slow-moving Magdalena River, the biggest river in Colombia, which flows north through the western half of the country.

Escorted by a realtor, Pablo was delighted by the land with its clear rivers and marble stone grounds. They were taken to a farm to meet a landowner, whom Pablo surprisingly recognised as a former neighbour from Envigado whom he had fought over a girl years ago. Leaving the dispute unmentioned, they went on horseback to assess the land and returned to the farm.

"The farm that I'd like to buy is this one," Pablo said.

"Pablo, this land is not for sale. It's an inheritance. All of my brothers have invested a lot of energy into it."

"In this life, everything has its price."

"No, not everything. It's not for sale."

"OK, then, tell me one thing. How much is it worth?"

"Thirty-five million pesos."

In the corner of the room, Gustavo laughed.

"I'll double that to seventy-five million," Pablo said.

"No. It's not for sale."

"Then name your price."

"Forgive me, but it's not for sale. Not everything has a price." Some of the men admired the resolve of the landowner, who wouldn't budge with his dignity at stake.

The following day, surveying more land, they found a 2,000-acre property called Valledupar, next to a smaller property. Impressed by the mountains, rivers, jungle and climate, Pablo offered to buy it. This time, the seller tried to weasel out of the deal by asking for too much money, but finally agreed to sell Valledupar for just under $1 million. Over four months, Pablo bought more land and nine other estates for almost $2.5 million, bringing the total acreage to 4,700.

Every weekend, his helicopter took him to his new land. Obsessed with Al Capone, he decided to rename the Valledupar estate Nápoles because Capone was born in Naples, Italy. The main house at Valledupar was improved and enlarged into a two-storey mansion by over 100 workers. He bought an early 1930s Cadillac that looked like the one driven by Al Capone. To make it seem as if Capone had actually owned it, he strafed it with gunfire. A professional cameraman who shot home movies filmed Pablo, Gustavo and their gang on motorbikes in front of the Cadillac.

Pablo's bedroom was smaller than the eight bedrooms on the first floor. His closet contained a safe for money and small arms, including the .38-calibre revolver he kept strapped to his ankle. Larger guns ended up in a secret compartment next to a 10-foot-deep closet only accessible through a tiny secret door. The godfathers of the Cali Cartel had a preference for such compartments, which they favoured hiding in rather than engaging in shootouts with the police. The anti-aircraft battery installed next to the swimming pool had a seat and cannons with buffers. The three garages at the back could hold up to five vehicles, but they were eventually converted into rooms with bunk beds and bathrooms.

By buying up more land, Pablo ended up with a 7,500-acre

luxury ranch-style resort with the Magdalena River running through it. Like Lehder on Norman's Cay, he presented himself to the locals as a legitimate businessman interested in buying their properties. To some who didn't want to sell, he gave a blank cheque for them to fill out, with the implication that if they exceeded the fair value there would be consequences.

According to General Maza years later, one completely refused to sell. After hearing that the man was a suspected snitch, Pablo invited his people to come and see what happens to informants. The man was tied up and rocks attached. Pablo set him on fire and threw him into the river. They extracted him, and lit him again. After three times, the man was still alive, so Pablo ordered the man's son – 10 years old – to shoot his father. His corpse ended up in the river, sunk by rocks.

Three security rings protected Hacienda Nápoles. The outer ring of armed guards monitored vehicles that had gone past the entrance. If any stopped or left the road, the guards would notify the main house. It took twenty minutes to drive to the next checkpoint, so if the authorities arrived, Pablo had plenty of time to escape. The inner ring encircled the main house and consisted of his most trusted men. Only people he had preapproved were allowed in after their invitations were double-checked by Pablo, who received them by fax from his sentries.

At the grand opening, Pablo and Victoria, a.k.a. Doña Tata, arrived in an orange and white striped helicopter. They were so well mannered and unassuming that some of the servants thought that their bodyguards were the bosses because of their commanding body language, loud chains and jewellery. The 300 relatives who arrived were no longer poor, but instead, lived in Medellín's most luxurious neighbourhoods.

Hacienda Nápoles had ten extravagant residences, swimming pools, twenty-seven artificial lakes, a road system, helicopter landing pads and runways, a petrol station, a car repair and painting shop, the largest motocross track in Latin America – which was opened with a race by the most famous motocross riders in

Colombia and Latin America – almost 2,000 staff and 100,000 fruit trees, all protected by mortar emplacements. With so many mango, guama, lemon and orange trees, Pablo used to joke that his goal was to be able to pick fruit without leaving his car. The suites sometimes housed over 100 guests. Hundreds of servants attended their needs and kept things running.

The guests enjoyed billiard tables, pinball machines, bars, jukeboxes, a bullfighting ring, outdoor dining areas, a games room, sightseeing helicopter flights and horse stables. The tennis courts were popular with Victoria and her friends, who organised tournaments. Helicopters brought tennis coaches from Medellín to teach the novices. Guests raced jet skis on the lakes. With the river so close, they sailed on boats and hovercraft. Pablo particularly enjoyed speeding on hovercraft, flying over the water as excited as a child. Whenever he crashed into the rocks, he had a helicopter take his hovercraft away and bring a new one. Downriver, he took Juan Pablo swimming with inner tubes. Depending upon what they wanted to do, Victoria and the kids were escorted around the estate on a golf cart.

He hosted parties, where he raffled valuable antiques, famous paintings and sculptures. Attendees ranged from politicians, business owners and artists to actors, models and beauty queens. The rich wanted to socialise with him as much as possible. They tried to sell the traffickers their overpriced properties and businesses or to get the traffickers to invest in stock-market schemes and near-bankrupt companies. They always wanted to be paid in dollars outside of Colombia. After they had developed strong friendships with the traffickers, the rich would request credit with zero interest and uncertain payback terms. Those who got drunk would whisper that they would like to be included in a shipment of cocaine, provided nobody found out and it was done quietly.

The first New Year celebration lasted for a month from the middle of December. The famous Venezuelan singer Pastor López and his group performed live for twelve hours from 9 PM for audiences of up to 1,000 people, many of whom Pablo didn't know. Guests arrived continuously, keeping the airstrip busy. Many brought gifts and alcohol. His pranks included paying cash to people to do outrageous things such as shaving off their eyebrows or sections of their hair.

The main house included a theatre, a disco and jacuzzis. The butler lived in another house nearby. Servants catered for every need, from providing swimwear to lobster, caviar and foreign sweets. Guests asking for cigarettes would receive whole cartons. Those requesting glasses of wine or champagne or a shot of liquor would receive bottles no matter how expensive. Observing the excesses, one of his advisers said to another, "Look and note well because this will not last long." Sometimes Hermilda brought teaching colleagues from a charity group called the Silver Ladies, and showed them the parts of the estate that she considered her own.

Up to thirty people could watch TV in a room next to the pool. If it malfunctioned, a new one was brought. In the poolside bar, guests played arcade games such as Pac-Man or socialised at one of ten tables adorned with giant whiskey bottles. Pablo used to climb a mamoncillo tree next to the pool, pick its fruit and pelt swimmers.

In the kitchen, guests browsed a menu. At Christmas, a helicopter delivered blood sausages, doughnuts and custard to Pablo's family. Gigantic pantries and refrigerators stored copious amounts of food. At the dining table with his family, guests and bodyguards, he recited poetry and sang tango music. He wrote poems for his kids. He always sang in the shower, and his towels were embroidered with the estate's name.

Pablo and Gustavo lived on the second floor. The rest of the family had the first. Family members from Medellín visited every weekend. To get there from the city, they were offered four modes of transport: aircraft, helicopter, SUV or motorbike. Secret meetings were held at the main house with guerrilla leaders, politicians, international traffickers, Mafia leaders and Medellín gangsters.

He loved spending time with his family. If his son or daughter needed his attention, he would halt business meetings. The police recorded a conversation between him and his wife. While they discussed family matters, someone being tortured started to scream in the background. El Patrón told the torturer to please keep the victim quiet because he was talking to his family on the phone.

He was often seen sat on his balcony, wearing blue jeans, light striped shirts and sneakers or boots, his hair combed sideways and displaying his distinct sideburns and moustache. Every day, he wore a brand-new shirt once and then donated it. Safe houses stocked emergency supplies of clothes. Ostentatious jewellery was absent, but he usually wore an expensive watch. Upon first glance his power was hidden, except to those who saw him adjust his jeans to access the gun on his ankle.

Some referred to Pablo and Gustavo as the Two Pablos because they behaved so similarly and copied each other. If one bought something for his estate, the other would have to have it. One helicopter delivered it for Pablo and a second for Gustavo. With the business needing constant attention, Pablo, Roberto and Gustavo worked different shifts. Gustavo and Roberto were early birds, whereas Pablo didn't usually wake up until noon, when he would eat a big breakfast in the dining room by the pool. At night, he would escape from his family to smoke cannabis and go to bed around dawn.

His brothers-in-law, Mario and Fernando, a.k.a. Weed because he always had a joint lit, were heavy partiers. El Patrón enjoyed the company of Mario, who was often drunk or high, and liked to hire vallenato musical orchestras and groups to follow him around. A prank they played was to extract all of the tobacco from cigarettes and replace it with weed, then offer them as normal cigarettes to tease those unwittingly stoned.

The other Mafia bosses, including Gacha and the Ochoas, frowned on pot smoking. If they detected the fumes, they would express displeasure. Nor did any of them smoke cigarettes. During lengthy meetings with the bosses, Pablo would retire at dawn to find a balcony, a garden or an open terrace to smoke cannabis and to allow the wind to carry away the evidence. He would bury the remaining stub in a pot and, feeling hungry, would raid the nearest kitchen and feast from a collection of bowls. Over time, his munchies increased his weight and made him appear fat compared to his athletically built associates. Although he didn't drink alcohol, he stocked entire cellars with non-alcoholic beers, which he particularly enjoyed while stoned when satisfying his munchies.

The parish priest of Puerto Triunfo would arrive at the gate of Hacienda Nápoles and insist on walking up the drive even though the workers offered him a ride. In a Nissan truck, Pablo would intercept him. The priest would leave with a donation, and in return he would put photos of Pablo and Gustavo under the altar and include them in his prayers.

One Hacienda Nápoles airstrip was disguised by a trailer home on a wheeled platform. If a truck pulled the home a short distance, planes could land on 1,000 yards. After take-off, the home was returned to its original position to prevent aircraft from detecting the airstrip.

Cocaine flights took off three or four times a day. The cash they brought was bulkier than the drugs, which presented a logistics problem. Pablo imported washing machines that had their insides removed, and the shells filled with cash. Money was hidden in machinery, new vehicles, stereos, TVs and appliances. Cash was invested into weapons. Bribes to Colombian airport officials ensured that the weapons would not be seized.

On New Year's Eve, 1981, Pablo drove his SUV to an airstrip to meet a flight from Mexico. To guide the plane, lanterns and torches were placed strategically, and diesel-fuel rings were lit. Gazing at the clear sky, the men watched the plane approach. Within fifteen minutes of it landing, it had been unloaded, and its flag and registration number altered. After take-off, the men re-joined the New Year's Eve festivities, including fireworks. Every year, fireworks from China were imported, each box costing

$50,000. He gave half to his men. The rest were enjoyed by his family, except for the unused boxes remaining.

He was honoured to host a 70-year-old guest from his past, Don Alberto Prieto, a.k.a. the Godfather. He told his son that he was going to introduce him to his only ever former boss. After shaking hands, Pablo asked the Godfather for permission to tell Juan Pablo about their past. With consent granted, he described the contraband days, and how the Godfather had enabled him to build a reputation in the underworld. It was the only night that El Patrón gave his bedroom to another guest.

Hector was the administrator at Nápoles. He ran things so smoothly that the kitchen was always open. If you wanted garlic lobster at 4 AM, it was never a problem. Pablo rewarded him with one of the runways at Nápoles. For each plane that used the runway, Hector got up to four million pesos, much more than the Medellín airport received. Becoming a multimillion-aire made him greedy. While he concentrated on selling drugs, the kitchen was closed. Pablo and his men arrived to no food, so Hector was killed.

CHAPTER 17

THE ZOO

As a child, Pablo sometimes wandered away from home. One day, Hermilda found him under a tree, with a stick, playing with a snake. "See, I'm not hurting you," he said to the snake. Gazing affectionately, she knew he was a sweet boy who loved animals – a passion that would motivate him to open Colombia's largest zoo.

Visiting the Ochoa brothers' Veracruz estate near the Caribbean coast reignited his childhood love of animals. From the Ochoas, he gleaned information about running a zoo. They advised him to find the correct habitat otherwise the animals would die. From the *National Geographic Encyclopedia*, he identified animals that would acclimatise to Hacienda Nápoles.

In 1981, Pablo located wildlife breeders in Dallas who imported animals from Africa. Taking his family to see them, he was welcomed by almost ten limos at the Dallas airport. In his own limo, Juan Pablo watched Tom and Jerry cartoons, while drinking chocolate milk. After riding on an elephant, El Patrón negotiated the price of the animals down to $2 million in cash. "I'll send for my animals soon," he told the owners.

To transport the first group, he rented a ship, which docked 250 miles from Medellín. The journey disturbed the animals, so he rented Hercules military transportation planes to import the rest. To anyone watching from the ground, the planes appeared to be a military invasion. They landed at Medellín's Olaya Herrera airport after 6 PM, when all scheduled flights were finished for the day, and the control tower and runway lights had been shut off. Security was minimal and he owned two hangars next to the main runway. The noisy dark planes kept their engines on while trucks, cranes and workers rushed from the hangars to collect the crates of animals. Alerted by the noise of the planes, the authorities arrived, but only found empty crates and feathers.

After one group was unloaded, an official arrived and ordered them to be quarantined at the zoo. "Fine. Let them go to the zoo," Pablo said, realising that the animals were about to be stolen from him. He sent his men to buy ducks, chickens, parrots and anything else they could lay their hands on. At night, his men went to the zoo, retrieved the exotic animals and left behind the local stock. To replace the zebras, they fetched donkeys and painted them before the zookeepers woke up.

His zoo was almost full and ready to open when he decided to buy a pair of rhinos. The pilot of a Douglas DC-3 agreed to land on a 3,000-foot runway at Hacienda Nápoles, much shorter than the 4,000 feet required. Coming in to land, it awed the spectators. Painted on its nose was a shark smoking a cigar. After touchdown, it spun on its rear wheel ten times and stopped just short of cascading into the Doradal River.

In 1984, Pablo told a journalist about the obstacles he had faced:

"[Officials] did not want to let me bring the animals: they said there was already a zoo in Medellín, there would be issues concerning the statutes of the Society of Improvements and Ornaments of Bogotá, and concern if there were diseases. Man, and I was paying a fortune in grains and grass in the US for the animals ... Until I ran out of patience or, rather, I got fucking pissed off. Hear that? Then I ordered my people up there to send the animals in a cargo jumbo jet. My Noah's ark.

"The plane landed a week later at the Medellín airport and of course, we were met by a toad [official] and behind him, another – supposedly from Customs, [demanding the] papers and permission. 'What permission?' 'Well, permission, sir. They are animals ...' I could not bribe them because the situation was obvious: the giraffe had been unloaded and was behind us, and on a forklift came the hippopotamus cage, with yet more animals coming behind the zebras.

"[They said] how one animal arrived ill and after two days, it died. 'It is the one that is hanging there in front.' So, already in full throng, I said to my man, 'Put together the six trucks, but put in front such and such ... and there, to the other side, such and such ... In those over there put the fat ones: the hippopotamus, elephants, giraffes, rhinoceroses ... and in these others, the birds, lighter animals, but carefully. You understand me?'

"They did it. When we finished loading the trucks, there were already people present from the mayor's office, health department, secret police, a delegate from the Army Brigade, another from the Medellín Fire Brigade, from the Grey Checkers ... 'What should I do?' I told my man. 'Make the trucks go out in a row and up in the roundabout. Make the three big ones figure out a way to sidetrack past the [official's] car to rush for Puerto Triunfo. Then make the other three head for the zoo of Medellín as ordered by the authority.'

"There they arrived with the birds and everything. I had already sent a boy with money to bribe somebody from the zoo. And so, we unloaded, leaving some [animals] for the gallery, others for a farm and others for the town. That same night we bought as many ducks, as many chickens, as many parrots and macaws and as many animals we could find. We even bought goats and sheep, and by three in the morning we arrived at the zoo and we took the antelopes, the black cockatoos from Indonesia, the hens from New Guinea, the white swans from Europe, the cassowaries, the pheasants, the mandarin duck, the royal cranes, some kangaroos, but left the national merchandise.

"In the midst of the mess, my man said, 'Boss, the zebras.' 'The what?' 'The zebras! They are in our minutes and must be replaced.' 'Well, bring four grey donkeys and have someone get a jar of black paint and a brush. Let the trucks with the zebras head for Puerto Triunfo and you wait for the donkeys to arrive, then make sure they are well-painted. Before dawn.'

"And, do you know what else happened to me that day? When I arrived at Puerto Triunfo, I started counting animals and seeing that they were taken care of, when suddenly my man told me, 'Boss, there's a hippopotamus missing.' 'A hippopotamus? You are right. There is only one.' We looked at the timetables and the papers and, of course, I had bought only the male. I was missing the female. 'Call Miami. We have to buy a hippo because Noah's ark is missing one.'

"They sent that one to [the town of] Turbo. There we unloaded it and put it to eat from a pasture in a paddock. It was a hippopotamus living in Turbo. Of course, the gossip took place and journalists from Teleantioquia arrived, and when I heard they had taken pictures, I quickly sent a truck with a container, and we loaded the hippopotamus into that hot son-of-a-bitch. That poor animal. And we brought it to Puerto Triunfo. Later, in Santa Fe de Antioquia, we came across a caravan of cars from the [officials] and the Red Cross, and a truck from the Army. Close call. Goodbye. Ciao. We succeeded!"

In Miami attempting to collect $7 million, Pablo postponed his meeting with the debtor to inspect a pair of black parrots. Paying $400,000 made them the priciest animals in his zoo. At Hacienda Nápoles, a vet noticed they had been neutered. Instead of having the seller murdered, Pablo just called and complained. He loved spending time with his parrots, which came in every colour. The final animals purchased were a pair of stinky pink dolphins from the Amazon, which ended up in a lake ten minutes from the main house. Juan Pablo played with them in the afternoon.

With almost 1,200 animals roaming around, the zoo needed a grand entrance. A giant white gate was built with "Nápoles" on its columns. On top of a cement entry way, Pablo mounted a Piper PA-18 plane, which one of his friends had crash-landed at Medellín's Olaya Herrera runway. The abandoned plane had been dismantled and restored without its engine, and its exterior covered in cloth. The plane welcomed visitors, who had to drive through the entrance and down long private roads lined with palm trees. Pablo created a myth that he had piloted his first shipment of cocaine to America in the plane.

At the entrance to the zoo's main areas, he decided to place a car assembled from parts. He combined the body of a vintage 1936 Ford and the chassis from the Toyota SUV his younger brother, Fernando, had died in. Toting a submachine gun, he ordered his men to draw their weapons and shoot the SUV to replicate the effect of the 167 bullets that had strafed Bonnie and Clyde's original car. He had watched every movie about the infamous couple. As bullets erupted, a voice from the car yelled, "Help!" Having fallen asleep inside, a worker was lucky to scramble out unharmed.

"Nápoles zoo belongs to the Colombian people," Pablo told a journalist. "We built it so that children and adults, rich and poor, can enjoy it, and owners cannot pay for what is already theirs." He announced that he would never charge an entrance fee as he wanted the poor to enjoy such a marvel of nature.

On one holiday weekend, the zoo received 25,000 vehicles from across Colombia. Due to the cars, the journey from the estate entrance to the main house expanded to two hours. Stuck in congestion, he decided to build a new highway. Visitors drove through the grounds to admire antelope, elephants, gazelles, water buffalo, zebras, giraffes, moose, hippos, ostriches, a soccer-playing kangaroo, an elephant that stole food from people's cars, thoroughbred horses, small horses, ponies, five life-size cement dinosaurs and a woolly mammoth that towered over the trees, and the biggest collection of exotic birds in Colombia, including black cockatoos, flamingos, mandarin duck and European black swans.

A lover of birds, he owned a parrot called Chinchon that recited the names of soccer players. Unfortunately, she fell asleep after drinking liquor from the men's glasses and was eaten by a cat. After that, he banned all cats from Hacienda Nápoles, including lions and tigers. Wanting his animals to be able to roam freely, he didn't want any dangerous cats.

The first ever birth in Colombia of an Arabian camel called a dromedary happened on his estate. He was proud until it died and he scolded the veterinarian. When deer started to destroy a garden, some workers caged them, but he ordered their release because, "Freedom is very nice." One emu became known as Shagger after trying to have sex with anything that moved. Remembering the luck that the rabbit had brought him in prison, he had his men fill helicopters and planes with rabbits, which formed a huge population on the ranch. Some of the monkeys had to be released onto a mountain because they stunk like demons.

The flamingos shed their pink colour and turned white. Blaming malnutrition, he consulted a vet who recommended feeding them shrimp for six months. Their colour didn't return. After the elephants grew disinterested in their food, they were offered a variety of grass and sugarcane. That didn't work, so he ordered three tons of carrots, which they also ignored. In late 1983, the six giraffes completely refused to eat, ignoring even their special feeders built into treetops, and they died.

Driving around in an open-topped SUV inspecting the health of the animals, Pablo had his son hold a submachine gun. Spotting a dear with a broken leg, lying near the road, he pulled over. With a bone jutting through its skin, the beautiful animal with yellow spots was wriggling and shivering.

"The only option is to kill it." From the SUV, he fetched his favourite gun, a black Sig Sauer pistol that never jammed or fired by accident. He asked whether his son would do it. Before Juan Pablo could respond, he thrust the gun at him. "Just aim at the deer's head and shoot." Juan Pablo was afraid and reluctant. "Wait in the car," Pablo said, disappointed.

"No. I can do it." Juan Pablo took the gun, and put fingers from both hands on the trigger. Less than three feet away, he missed the deer and hit the ground. On the third try, the deer died.

CHAPTER 18

CHARITY

Pablo despised elites who scorned the masses and politicians who spouted fake promises about helping the poor. Encouraged by his mother to be charitable, he could now make a difference in people's lives – something he knew would create powerful enemies.

In 1979, he started the social program *Civics on the March*. Poor neighbourhoods adopted trees in response to the UN having warned that industry was causing irreversible damage. Giving speeches, he encouraged people to join the efforts to preserve the environment. He extolled the value of planting trees and preserving green areas to improve the health of the community. According to Hermilda, Pablo the nature lover had wept whenever he had seen his father chop down a tree. In Antioquia, he planted over a million trees and publicly lambasted the lack of vision of men who tear down trees.

He offered sports to young people as an alternative to crime. Soccer was his favourite. As a child, he had made balls from old clothes wrapped in plastic bags and erected makeshift goalposts. Determined to provide better facilities, he built public areas with volleyball and basketball courts and soccer fields. He installed electric lights in dozens of pitches in the poorest neighbourhoods, so that kids could play at night. His investment in the professional soccer team, Deportivo Independiente Medellín, raised their status, which drew many kids into the game. Always performing pranks, he organised a game where a team of prostitutes played a team of transvestites.

Asked what motivated him, he said, "I felt anguish always in poor neighbourhoods, watching kids and young people exposing their lives when running behind a ball on streets full of crossing cars. I dreamed of the day in which this youth would have stadiums of their own to be able to play without humiliating themselves in front of anybody nor exposing themselves to accidents. That's how my vocation for the creation of sports fields was born. Today we are building fields for football, basketball, volleyball and multidisciplinary sports. Hopefully tomorrow, we might extend our action for baseball fields, to have lots of pools and gyms for the people."

He organised over 100 committees for community projects. Millions were invested in churches, street lights, road improvements and recreation centres. He sent doctors into neighbourhoods to heal the sick. Every Christmas, street kids received 5,000 toys, and Pablo and his son travelled in the back of a truck to give gifts to children in local villages.

"When we build schools," he said, "it seems that we re-encounter the nation that we long for. We have looked with pain upon children sitting on adobes, in ramshackle locales, and upon teachers living without protection before the indifference of the State. We love Colombia and now are capable of giving back some of what this beautiful nation has given us. We are doing it."

The poor knew that he was a criminal, but preferred him to a tyrannical government that protected the wealthy while allowing people to die of starvation and children to live at dumps. Until El Patrón, no one had dared to stand up to the criminals in power and attempt to give dignity back to the poor.

CHAPTER 19

DEATH SQUAD

In July 1981, a colonel gave Jorge Ochoa a recording of members of the M-19 guerrillas discussing a plan to kidnap a trafficker. With approximately 2,500 members, the M-19 was engaged in a war with the Army in the Valley of Cauca. Ochoa informed El Patrón, who admired the group because of its history of redistributing goods to the poor, including milk from hijacked trucks. "Those men are hard-working," he said out of admiration for their military tactics and daring. He liked that they had stolen the sword of the liberator Simón Bolívar from a museum and claimed it as a symbol of their struggle. Targeting traffickers for kidnapping, however, he viewed dimly.

After performing intelligence work, he had his men capture some M-19 guerrillas. Now that he had their attention, he arranged to release them at a meeting with more M-19 members at one of his offices. For propaganda purposes, he had invested in offices which hosted *Antioquia Today*, a TV programme with news. He used the rear offices for crime. On the night of the meeting, he had a small army of bodyguards.

"Keep your weapons on display at all times," he said. "I want the guerrillas scared, not killed, but anything could happen, so you need to remain vigilant in case there's a shootout."

Four members of the M-19 arrived, terrified of Pablo and his bodyguards. One entered the offices holding up a grenade with its safety pin removed as a strategy to protect himself – if he died, the grenade would explode.

After everybody calmed down and greetings were exchanged,

Pablo described the M-19's plan to kidnap a trafficker, which he advised against because the traffickers had built up their own power, which they could clearly see around them. He knew their plans before they had even been implemented, and it was best that neither side messed with the other. "It took me only three days to find some of you, so don't mess with us because you'll lose. I will not do anything to you because there is no need and above all because I am a leftist man." They hadn't done anything bad yet, but if they went behind his back, he would kill them. They may think that they could hide, but he would find them instantly. From a notebook, he read the names of the fourteen guerrillas in the Medellín chapter, the locations of their safe houses and all of their recent activity. Intimidated by his knowledge and show of force, the guerrillas agreed not to kidnap traffickers. As a goodwill gesture, he freed his hostages and gave them $15,000.

For months, the guerrillas visited him regularly. They played pool with his men, with whom they shared a warlike spirit. He even gave one a job at a Miami Beach petrol station. Shortages of oil had led to rationing. By investing in a petrol station, he ensured the smooth running of his cars distributing cocaine.

The M-19 was a by-product of The Violence that had almost consumed Pablo and his family. The battle for power between the Liberal and Conservative parties had ended in 1958 by each agreeing to rule for four-year terms. For sixteen years the power had shifted from one oligarchy to the other, with neither promoting social reform nor helping the millions of poor displaced from the countryside to the cities. Guerrilla groups gave the poor a voice in the struggle over inequality. They demanded democracy and land for the peasants.

After surrendering their arms to the government, some guerrilla leaders were shot in the streets. Feeling betrayed, some turned to communism. Government bombs forced them to hide in the jungle in south-east Colombia. For decades, they operated under the name of the FARC (Revolutionary Armed Forces of

Colombia), and promoted agrarianism and anti-imperialism. Kidnapping was a primary source of income until the cocaine boom, when the FARC imposed taxes on the coca farmers, which enabled the guerrillas to develop into a well-trained army that could challenge the government. Influenced by the Cuban Revolution, two other guerrilla groups emerged: the ELN (National Liberation Army) and the EPL (Popular Liberation Army). They were popular with university students and peasants.

In 1970, the M-19 emerged as a fourth group. On April 19, 1970, Pastrana, the traditionalist party candidate, competed against General Gustavo Rojas Pinilla, the candidate of the National Popular Alliance (ANAPO). After bitter and contested elections, the traditional parties handed power to Pastrana. Believing that electoral fraud had been committed on April 19, a revolutionary sector splintered from ANAPO, naming itself the M-19 after the unforgettable date.

Performing spectacular stunts brought the M-19 popularity. Through a tunnel they entered the Central Army Canton in Bogotá and stole thousands of weapons. Trucks transporting food were captured and the goods distributed in poor neighbourhoods.

President Turbay responded with mass arrests, torture and murder, until some of the M-19 leaders were captured. The attitude of the military was expressed by Colonel Ñungo: "It is better to condemn an innocent [person] than to release a guilty one."

The M-19 retaliated by shelling the Presidential Palace. On February 27, 1980, they stormed the Embassy of the Dominican Republic in Bogotá, where fifty-two people, including fifteen ambassadors, were celebrating the Dominican national holiday. The group called attention to human rights violations and demanded the fair treatment of their incarcerated colleagues. After sixty-one days, the hostages, including the American ambassador, were released after the majority of the guerrillas had flown to Cuba. The public cheered the guerrillas travelling on busses to the airport.

There was lots of infighting among the guerrilla leadership. Some wanted negotiations with the government, whereas others wanted war. By November 1981, their truce with Pablo had fallen apart. On November 12, 1981, a car stopped outside of the University of Antioquia in Medellín and two armed men emerged. One grabbed Marta Ochoa and forced her into the car, while the other shoved her friend onto the ground. The car sped away.

Jorge Ochoa immediately called El Patrón, who raced across Medellín to confer with the Ochoa patriarch, Fabio Sr. Not knowing who was responsible, Pablo offered to lead the investigation. Flicking through Marta's high-school yearbook, he recognised two faces in the photos: members of the M-19 who had showed up at his offices. Further investigation revealed that the Medellín chapter of the M-19 had sanctioned her kidnapping.

Pablo questioned the M-19 commander Elvencio Ruiz, who denied any responsibility, so he contacted the M-19 members in Bogotá's Picota prison: "Tell them that's it and that they won. Now how are we going to settle this situation?" After getting more denials, he announced, "This is now war."

Within a week, he used his contacts in the underworld and the intelligence community to identify and locate the fourteen main co-conspirators, some of whom were in a dilapidated hotel in Bogotá. He summoned four of them to a meeting.

Assuming that the guerrillas would demand millions for Marta's release, he contemplated his next move. Despite his show of force, the M-19 obviously still considered the traffickers as soft targets. They would have to be proven wrong, and the cost of their actions needed to be high.

On November 19, 1981, members of the M-19 tried to kidnap Carlos Lehder, who had been flaunting his millions in his Colombian hometown with a population of 180,000. He had announced his plans for Armenia: "I'm going to make this a real capital, so that the entire world can visit it and the fucking Yankees can finally appreciate what we have here."

At first, he donated – by way of a German with blond hair,

who didn't speak any Spanish – a Piper Navajo plane to the town. Although it impressed the locals, they were nonplussed. In a letter to the governor of Quindío province, he claimed that his company, Air Montes Company Ltd, which bought and sold planes, had a charity mission of donating planes to communities lacking air transport, hence the donation.

Adorned with fancy jewellery, clothes, cars and friends, he swaggered around, opening businesses and making pronouncements. He triggered a bubble in real estate that tripled prices. His new parent company, Cebu Quindio, planned to build an Alpine resort ten miles from Armenia that would accommodate world travellers. He gathered a following of young fans and lovers, several of whom ended up pregnant. Hailing him as Don Carlos, teenagers copied his haircut: tousled with a centre parting. His wealth, behaviour and celebrity status enticed the M-19.

In Lehder's own newspaper, *Quindio Libre*, the editor wrote, "Lehder, a man of a new era, captain of the seas and skies, landed in Quindio, home of the Indian chiefs, warriors and poets and idealists, at a time when dark clouds were hanging over the Republic."

He made public announcements to co-opt journalists: "It is unfair that journalists who represent the voice of reason and the flame of freedom in our democracy have to conduct their affairs in a place like this [with bad working conditions]." He donated $3,000 to the local press association's president for building improvements. After the refurbishment, a room was named in his honour: El Salon Bahamas.

In November 1981, Lehder got into a chauffeur-driven car and set off for the site of a future ranch. After eight miles, he spotted a car in the middle of the road with its hood up, the driver examining the engine as if the vehicle had stalled. The chauffeur stopped, left his gun on the front seat and both men got out to help. Two armed men appeared, dragged away the chauffeur and deposited him on the roadside. They tied Lehder's hands behind his back, threw him into the car and told him to stay there. They dropped the hood and sped off.

Due to his karate knowledge, he convinced himself that he could escape. He wriggled his bound hands free, kicked open the door and dived out. After rolling down a grassy slope, he ended up in a park. While he sprinted away, bullets whizzed by. Hit in the back, he fell.

"Let's go. The son of a bitch is gone," a kidnapper said, assuming he had died.

Ranchers discovered him and took him to a hospital. Radio programmes were interrupted with the breaking news of the assault on the German-Colombian investor. Outraged locals mobbed the hospital for updates. While he convalesced, a hunt proceeded for the kidnappers, who were traced back to the M-19, which surprised Lehder. Just a year earlier, he had boasted about his alliance with the revolutionaries. After two weeks, ten heavily armed bodyguards escorted him from the hospital. Resolved not to travel alone, he went everywhere with twenty-five armed ex-policemen.

In response, Pablo hosted a meeting at Hacienda Nápoles, which army officers and over 200 senior traffickers attended, including the entire Medellín group. With an air of royalty, they arrived in small planes and luxury cars. Recovering from his gunshot wound, Lehder came with a group from the coffee zone. The Cali group sent its delegates.

The Bogotá group was led by Rodríguez Gacha, a.k.a. the Mexican because of his love of mariachi music and all things Mexican. His affinity for wearing straw fedoras earned him another name: Big Hat. Short stubby Gacha named his ranches after Mexican cities. He was born in a small town, Pacho, north of Bogotá, to a poor family of pig farmers. As a young man, he developed a lethal reputation as a hit man. Executing even some of his business partners, he rose up in the emerald industry, which had a more violent reputation than cocaine. He owned seventeen haciendas in eastern Colombia near the Venezuelan border. Like most landowners, he was vehemently anti-Communist and anti-guerrilla. On his properties, he welcomed the Army with roasted veal and replaced their old boots.

At the meeting, the speeches given by Pablo and Lehder resonated, especially as Lehder described his own kidnapping experience. "We should attack the kidnappers ourselves," Pablo said, "and rescue Marta. If we pay for her to be set free, all our families will be targeted." Everyone agreed. He proposed the formation of an army, Muerte a Secuestradores, MAS, translated as Death to Kidnappers. Each trafficker donated money and hit men. Kiko Moncada contributed the use of one of his warehouses. After the MAS meeting and the drafting of a communiqué, the participants attended a picnic, where they discovered that they had lots in common. Never before had they gathered to form public policy.

Fidel Castaño told Pablo why he was so enthusiastic about the mission to save Marta. In the late 1970s, the FARC guerrilla group started gathering intelligence on his father, Jesus, a rancher in Segovia, Antioquia, who was a far-right conservative and an influential local politician. By 1980, Jesus had twelve children: eight boys and four girls. Ranchers bred large families for more hands to work the land. The family rose at dawn to milk the cows. Jesus made his own cheese, which he sold along with milk in the town of Amalfi.

On September 18, 1981, just two months before Marta was abducted, the FARC kidnapped Jesus and demanded fifty million pesos – a gross overestimation of the ten million pesos net worth of the Castaños. Aged 32, Fidel, the eldest son, tried to raise the money, but only came up with an additional six million.

When a guerrilla arrived for the cash, Fidel told him, "Believe me, I collected all the money possible and I have no way of getting any more."

"You are thirty-four million pesos short."

"If I could get more money," he said, "it would only be to fight you."

With the ransom only partially paid, the guerrillas tied Jesus to a tree and tortured him. Eventually, he died. The devastated siblings swore vengeance. Moved by Fidel's story, Pablo became much closer to the Castaños.

The relationships cemented at the MAS meeting gave birth to the Medellín Cartel. The four main factions identified by the US authorities were Pablo, the Ochoa brothers, Carlos Lehder and Gacha. The term Medellín Cartel came from American prosecutors looking to simplify their cases and obtain longer sentences. Cartels never existed until prosecutors introduced the term. They were collections of independent traffickers who sometimes collaborated.

Copies of the MAS communiqué were loaded onto a plane, which flew towards a Cali soccer stadium on a Sunday afternoon, before a match between Medellín and Cali. After the referee blew the starting whistle, leaflets fell from the sky onto the pitch. They described a general assembly, whose members would no longer tolerate kidnappings by guerrillas seeking to finance revolutions "through the sacrifices of people, who, like ourselves, have brought progress and employment to the country ... The basic objective will be the public and immediate execution of all those involved in kidnappings, beginning from the date of this communiqué."

It offered twenty million pesos for information leading to the capture of a kidnapper and guaranteed immediate retribution. The guilty parties "will be hung from the trees in public parks or shot and marked with the sign of our group – MAS." Kidnappers in jail would be murdered. If that was impossible then "our retribution will fall on their comrades in jail and on their closest family members."

More leaflets were dropped over a stadium in Medellín. Newspaper ads announced the formation of the MAS, who would not pay a single peso for Marta's release. The ads showed photos of Elvencio Ruiz and Jaime Bateman, M-19 commanders, with the title: "Fugitive kidnappers." Assuming the role of spokesman,

Lehder published the reasons why the MAS had been formed and its goal of preventing kidnappings:

"We have a beautiful, large, free, fertile and full-of-opportunities Colombia, for the just and hard working. When entrepreneurs and leaders are kidnapped, our economy collapses. These honourable and dedicated leaders have studied half of their lives to be useful to the great era that this republic and the world are living. We cannot think that the frightened Bateman [M-19 leader] is the one to manage large companies or universities because experience and knowledge have no substitutes. For the last ten years, hundreds of prestigious families have had to leave the country scared. Thousands of beautiful and productive estates have been abandoned, industrialists and builders have made businesses and walked away, and those who refused to be kidnapped were shot on the spot. With me, the kidnappers shot me with a revolver saying, 'We are from the M-19. You are now kidnapped.' I miraculously escaped.

"The decision taken by the Ochoa family was wise, after fifty days of expectation – receiving frosty calls by cynical murderers who demanded twelve million dollars in exchange for the life of a little sister, an angel just beginning to live. They have now said: 'Enough of the threats, we are going to look for our sister and we are going to reward the citizens that help us ensure that the guilty are brought before the military justice.' A response to kidnapping requires a faster, tactical and drastic treatment. We must unite and nullify this poisonous phenomenon, so that it does not contaminate future generations. We will overcome!

"What I propose is anti-kidnapping work similar to the Peace Commission, except that it is paramilitary. That this special anti-kidnapping commission assembles and instructs two forces: a team of judges and prosecutors specialised in kidnapping and terrorism, and the other tactical force formed by the prominent and fierce ex-soldiers and former agents, the most expert paramilitary civilians, civil defence forces, foreign mercenaries, the most excellent athletes and expert shooters, police, specialised police, intelligence of the DAS, the hawks of the Air Force and the sharks of the Navy.

"They would have a barracks academy, with a photo bank and a silver bank, a communications and information centre with special cars equipped with sophisticated surveillance and camouflage systems, helicopters, airplanes, amphibious vehicles and boats. A force of 2,000 men would be sufficient. A force that we would help to finance because we prefer to spend our fortunes defending our families and our people who are taken from us. For the new anti-kidnapping jail, the Americans will be asked for the latest and most powerful system of electric chairs with an incorporated incinerator. With the permission of the Tribunals, we will see what the Supreme Court says before the next Colombian solidarity petition asking for the death penalty for kidnapping. May God enlighten us! The MAS is a movement of faith and civic and physical consecration and should concern both the common kidnappers and the subversive kidnappers."

The MAS had approximately 1,000 troops, assisted by the military and police. In fatigues, Pablo hunted for guerrillas at night, typically arriving home to go to bed by 9 AM. With some of his best men such as Otto, La Yuca, Pinina and Chopo, he travelled in trucks from an infantry battalion headquarters, which hosted MAS meetings. The Cali godfather, Chepe Santacruz, participated in the hunt. Kiko Moncada's warehouse became a headquarters, where traffickers and members of the police and the Army discussed their progress. Protected by bodyguards, the Ochoas remained in their Envigado estate, where they recorded telephone conversations with the kidnappers. The police traced the calls and gave the information to Pablo.

He bought over 100 walkie-talkies for distribution in the Medellín slums. "Tell the young men with the walkie-talkies," he told his bodyguards, "to hang out near certain payphones and to report anyone who makes a call and mentions kidnapping. Have other young men with walkie-talkies wait in cars, and if they get a signal from the guys near the payphones, then they can capture the suspect."

When members of the M-19 tried to negotiate, their locations were traced and men nearby abducted the callers. Through this method, the MAS caught Pablo Catatumbo and Elvencio Ruiz in Bogotá. In Cali, they found Luis Gabriel Bernal and his wife. They sprayed the daughter with petrol and lit a match. "Speak or she burns!"

With pressure on the M-19, Pablo increased his home security. Around the clock, bodyguards protected his family. An armed Toyota Land Cruiser transported Juan Pablo to nursery school and bodyguards remained outside until he was taken home. Inside, the men played video games with Juan Pablo, whose classmates were under orders from their parents to avoid him. As Marta had been kidnapped from the University of Antioquia, Pablo had his sister, Alba Marina, quit teaching there.

With over 1,000 people hunting for the kidnappers and information pouring in from the Medellín slums, the M-19 started to learn about the steep price Pablo had in mind for them. Dozens of raids led to the capture of suspects, who were slowly tortured at the MAS headquarters, including with cattle prods and drowning tanks. While they were still alive, some had their eyeballs removed with hot spoons. Heated spikes were driven into skulls, which killed when they reached the brain. One hostage was tied to a tree with barbed wire, given a phone to explain his situation to his family, and tortured to death while they listened. While some confessed, others resisted and Pablo would say, "Kill that one on the spot. He's a stubborn one."

It was murder and torture on a level that exceeded anything previously organised by El Patrón. Men who had never killed were given the opportunity in a baptism of blood that bonded them together and accustomed them to extreme violence. It set the tone for what would happen to his future enemies and instilled fear in members of the criminal community, who heard what he was capable of. Within six weeks, over 100 of the M-19 had been dealt with, putting the Colombian army to shame as they hadn't apprehended that many since the M-19 had formed in 1974. The MAS treated informants the same as kidnappers. According to Brian Freemantle in *The Fix*, the informant who told the DEA about the first MAS meeting was captured. His hands were tied behind his back with barbed wire and his tongue cut out before he died.

Pablo told a journalist, "If there was not an immediate and strong response, the M-19 were going to continue screwing our own families ... We paid law enforcement eighty million pesos for the information they had at that moment and the next day, they began to fall. My soldiers took them to our secret houses, our secret ranches and people from law enforcement went there and hung them up and began to bust them up."

Distressed by the paramilitary activity, Victoria warned her husband that he would be killed. Having not seen him in a month, she feared that Christmas would come and go without him. Not spending time with his family showed a lack of commitment towards them. Trying to calm her down, Pablo said that if he didn't assist his friends, how could he ask for their help in the future. If the threat wasn't eliminated, his own family might be targeted.

On a raid in Medellín's San Javier neighbourhood, his men and soldiers surrounded a house. A car rammed down the garage door. During a shootout, two guerrillas were killed and a female captured. Searching the house produced Marta's ID and clues that she had been moved to another location, which was raided but found empty. Just five minutes before the MAS arrived, Marta had been evacuated. Pablo had reached a dead end.

Victoria's prediction of Pablo obsessing over the kidnapping throughout the Christmas holiday was fulfilled. To his disappointed family, he seemed to be exerting as much effort on Marta as if it were his own sibling. Not wanting the situation to drag out, he tried a new tactic.

On December 31, 1981, a terrified woman was discovered

chained to the gates of the newspaper *The Colombian* with a sign around her neck declaring that she was one of the kidnappers. Her kidnapped daughter had been returned to relatives because the MAS Constitution prohibited murdering innocent children.

The year ended with 400 dead guerrillas and associates. Pablo had wiped the guerrillas out of Medellín. Those hiding in other cities were caught and flown to the MAS headquarters to be tortured. In desperation, guerrillas hijacked an Avianca Airlines plane, which flew to Cali, from where they boarded a private plane to Cuba. Dismantling the M-19 isolated the cell holding Marta, so no matter how many people were captured, none knew the cell's location.

On New Year's Day, Pablo went to the Ochoas' estate. A newspaper ad was drafted stating that the family refused to negotiate or pay a ransom, but was willing to offer twenty-five million pesos to anyone with information about her location. It produced no results, so the Ochoas asked a Venezuelan ex-president to negotiate with the leaders of the M-19, who were hiding in Panama. They enlisted the aid of General Torrijos, a dictator with the title of the Commander of the Panamanian and National Guard.

The M-19 had chosen Panama because of its dictator's left-leaning stance. He had defied America by demanding the return of ownership of the Panama Canal. In a continent of right-wing dictatorships, Panama had become a safe haven for the left and a paradise for smugglers, arms dealers and traffickers, who travelled around Panama City in limos and stayed at plush hotels. Money-laundering was rife, and so much merchandise moved through the free port of Colón it was like a mini Hong Kong.

The dictator had his intelligence chief, General Noriega, contact the M-19, who was holding Marta in the coffee plantation zone in the middle of Colombia, at the same location they had intended to imprison Lehder. For a fee, Noriega brokered a peace deal whereby Marta would be released in exchange for $1.5 million and the MAS freeing twenty guerrillas. This was granted, so on February 16, 1982, Marta was released unharmed in Armenia, Colombia.

Despite her freedom, Pablo's relationship with the M-19 was far from over. During his first war with the government, they would make spectacular news headlines together. Upon seeing Pablo arrive at Panama City in his Cheyenne plane, the M-19 Commander Jaime Bateman told his assistant Yair, "You need to talk to that man. He is going to be very important." Bateman believed that Pablo's wealth, work with the poor and left-leaning stance would be useful.

El Patrón agreed to meet Yair, who arrived outside of his broadcasting headquarters, where he noticed a sign – CAUTION CHILDREN PLAYING IN THE STREET – and men practising martial arts in a garden. After walking around a pool, he met Pablo in an office.

"Jaime Bateman, our commander, sends you his greetings." After Pablo's welcome, Yair said, "You founded the MAS and I could be in the wrong place."

"You kidnapped the sister of a man I consider a brother of mine," Pablo said calmly. "We knew it was you and we said, 'They have already won and we have to pay, and that's it,' but there were no answers and we had to search. I founded the MAS and you already know the results: you won, we won, we rescued the girl even though we had to give a lot of money. We had to kill some people, and some of our people also lost their lives. But I assure you that once that was over I did not continue. Whatever you hear about the MAS, I assure you it's the Army using the acronym in their dirty work, so I propose to you a clean sweep. I'm interested in talking with you."

The discussion led to the organisation of a meeting with Bateman in Panama. While travelling to the meeting, Bateman's plane crashed on April 28, 1983, and his body was only recovered a year later. For the M-19, Yair continued to work with Pablo, for reasons Yair later explained:

"Pablo Escobar had the stature of a statesman. He ended a war in ten minutes. He seemed like a man who had the country first on his mind. Getting into Moravia, the famous hill where people lived on a garbage pile, to take them to a completely proper neighbourhood, was a political fact that the whole country had to know. Pablo did not have the appearance of the bad man: he seemed good-natured, and to say in the terms of that time, he was a cool guy. Usually a humble man, when he gets to have money and power, goes mad – he breaks up amidst pretentious and vulgar displays. But I did not see him wearing even a chain or a ring. He wore costly but discreet clothes. It caught my attention and I laughed at the importance he gave to his hairstyle. I found it funny that he cared so much for his look.

"Thousands attended his speaking events. We were interested in taking advantage of this platform so that people would know our project even if it was presented by another person. He would say, 'I rode a bus for twenty-eight years and therefore I am one of you. I am from here, accept me as one of you. I come here because economic conditions have changed and I come to share with you what is mine, to share with you the right that Colombians have to live with dignity. That we do everything that we can do so that youth will not get into the vice of drugs, etc.'

"I'm not saying it was not as bad as the press described, but the Pablo I knew had other facets. I even took him to today's cardinal and candidate for Pope, Monsignor Darío Castrillón, because I knew about Pablo's religious thought, and I thought that not only from the point of view of politics and social issues, but from the Christian point of view, he could rally all that power to do things beneficial to the country.

"In a war, if an ideology does not unite, then objectives must get united. Our project needed someone, from a revolutionary political perspective, to take advantage of it. The interests that Pablo Escobar could handle were contrary to ours, but at a given moment they could also find commonalities – without the illusion of turning him into a revolutionary overnight. I knew that this relationship was transitory, but I considered my stay there important in a way that was never explicit but was about political advice. Pablo the drug trafficker, the bandit, always had a criterion in favour of a revolutionary process in Colombia and was an ally, an admirer of the M-19."

Through his relationship with Yair, Pablo provided the M-19 with cash and resources. He gave them sanctuary at Nápoles and used his military contacts to find out which members were at risk of capture. The highly sought target, Commander Iván Marino, often sheltered among his men.

Although the kidnapping of Marta was resolved, the after-effects would leave their mark on Colombian history. The formation of the MAS introduced paramilitaries to Colombia and brought together the Medellín Cartel. It was the start of the military allying with traffickers to form illegal death squads to torture and murder guerrillas.

The MAS campaign caused the different trafficking groups to see the benefits of working together. If they pooled their resources to ship cocaine to America, they would make more money. Independent operators put aside their differences and started cooperating in the manufacturing, distribution and marketing of cocaine, while continuing to run their own enterprises.

In future meetings, trafficking methods were streamlined. They offered government officials "plata o plomo" – silver or lead – meaning they could either accept a generous bribe or be killed. Their network had access to anyone in Colombia, so officials knew they couldn't avoid the death penalty. With the guerrillas tamed and officials accepting bribes, the cocaine business flourished out of Medellín. If the cartel leaders called a meeting, traffickers from across Colombia attended. The American market was mostly divided up between the Medellín and Cali Cartels. Cali had New York. Medellín had Miami. Los Angeles was split between the two.

The success of the MAS elevated Pablo's power status, which was publicly acknowledged at a party at La Rinconada, a stable with a bullring and horse track in southern Medellín. While an orchestra played at 9 PM, young people lit flares and gunpowder in a makeshift fireworks display. At 10 PM, Pablo arrived,

SHAUN ATTWOOD

simply dressed as usual, to a crowd yelling, "El Patrón! El Patrón!"
Everyone stood to applaud him. Overwhelmed, he signalled for
everybody to sit and he settled in a corner with the other bosses:
Gustavo Gaviria, Pablo Correa, the Ochoa brothers, Griselda
Blanco, Fidel Castaño, Gacha and the King of Marlboro. Seated
nearby were what the public referred to as the Cream: industrialists, journalists, bankers, models, civil and military authorities,
priests, artists and politicians. Further away, young bodyguards,
mostly uneducated and from the peasant class, lined the corridors,
talking loudly.

Gacha became a conduit between the Emerald Mafia and the
Medellín traffickers. The FARC raided one of his biggest labs and
stole cash and cocaine. After he complained to their commanders,
they demanded taxes. Enraged, he vowed to annihilate them
and engaged in a long and costly war. With guerrillas launching
assaults on his cocaine labs in the east, he moved his operations
to the Middle Magdalena Basin, where he opened forty facilities,
which produced up to two tons of cocaine weekly. He brokered
deals with paramilitary forces, whereby he provided them arms in
exchange for protecting his labs. Suppressing the guerrillas caused
violence to surge in Colombia. Hiring foreign mercenaries from
the UK added to the mayhem. Unlike Pablo, who sympathised
with left-wing ideals, Gacha was a staunch Conservative. His
alliance with the anti-Communist Emerald Mafia and the paramilitaries provided a safe trafficking route from the Middle Magdalena Basin to the coast. Coca paste travelled inland from eastern
Colombia through the emerald district. After getting turned
into cocaine, it was exported through the lower Caucau region
of Antioquia. Gacha also pioneered trafficking routes through
Mexico into the US. Between Gacha's paramilitary forces and the
thousands of hit men Pablo controlled in Medellín, the two most
psychopathic members of the Medellín Cartel controlled plenty
of firepower. According to Popeye, they were a war committee of
two. They made the big decisions, which the rest financed.

In his hometown, Lehder bragged about his leadership role in the MAS and his contributions to the Liberal Party. He wanted to be a senator in order "to represent the kidnappables and extraditables of Colombia. I want to represent unions, and I want to represent the poorest of the poor." In private, Pablo started to refer to Lehder as Big Mouth. He disliked Lehder's cocaine habit and viewed his openness about their activity as a liability.

Inspired by Pablo's Hacienda Nápoles, Lehder set about constructing Posada Alemana, a giant convention centre nestled into green hills fifteen miles north of Armenia, with clubhouses, restaurants, discos, exotic-bird aviaries, beautiful gardens, gazebos and stucco bungalows with thatched roofs. By the entrance was a nude statue of John Lennon, holding a guitar, with a bullet hole in his chest and back, and a dedication: TO THE GREATEST MUSICIAN OF THE CENTURY.

With the goal of getting rid of Colombia's extradition treaty with America, Lehder started the National Latin Movement Party, with green and white colours and its own brand of Hitler Youth called Woodchoppers, young people toting clubs who policed his Saturday afternoon rallies. The podium included a twelve-foot poster of Lehder speaking. Many of the attendees were hoping to get their hands on the $5 bills he distributed at his events. To crowds of up to 10,000, he claimed that Adolf Hitler – whom he referred to as Adolfo – had been misunderstood, and that international Zionism was the root of terrorism in Central America.

He preached that everyone had the right to hold a small amount of cannabis. "Marijuana is for the people!" Not shy about his trafficking, he declared that, "Cocaine is for milking the rich!" He backed up his claim in a radio interview by stating that cocaine profits were funnelled to the people, and that's what had upset the oligarchy. He publicly echoed Pablo's belief that the cocaine traffickers were akin to the Kennedy family, who had profited from alcohol prohibition. He wanted his critics to examine the source of the wealth of Colombia's elites before lambasting him. He claimed his priority was the welfare of the people and denied being materialistic.

With business forever expanding, new methods of outsmarting the authorities were required. Massive cocaine labs were built in the most inaccessible parts of the jungle. They grew into towns with their own housing, schools, dining facilities and satellite TV. Houses on wheels were used to disguise jungle runways. Cocaine was shipped in refrigerators and TVs with hollow insides. Electrical industrial transformers weighing more than 8,000 pounds were gutted and filled with up to 4,000 kilos. A 23,000-kilo shipment was mixed with dried fish. European and American chemists blended cocaine into items made out of plastic, metals or liquid, and other chemists separated the cocaine out at the destination. Cocaine was mixed with fruit pulp, flowers, cocoa and wine. Liquid cocaine ended up in all kinds of drinks. It was soaked into lumber and clothes such as jeans. Cocaine was turned black and mixed into black paint. It was chemically blended into PVC, religious statues and the fibreglass shells of boats. All of these methods were tested by drug-sniffing dogs.

Pablo bought planes to transport cocaine and cash, including DC-3s – fixed-wing propeller-driven airliners. He decided to invest in submarines. As buying a sub would have attracted attention, he commissioned his brother to build two, with the help of Russian and English engineers. The manufacturing was done in a quiet shipyard. The subs carried around 1,000 kilos. Unable to come close to the shore, they were met by divers who loaded the cocaine onto boats.

By 1982, Pablo was making $500,000 a day, rising to $1 million a day by the mid-80s. Millions were buried underground, but each year ten per cent was lost due to rats and water damage. He paid people to live in houses and apartments with up to $5 million stored in the walls, protected by Styrofoam. Using wooden cases wrapped in Styrofoam, millions were stashed below swimming pools in storage chests. Accountants in ten separate offices kept track of the money, some of which was invested in property worldwide, famous paintings and antique cars. Refrigerators containing $7 million intended for Colombia were accidentally shipped to

Panama. The money disappeared. Pablo calmly responded that sometimes he won, sometimes he lost. A plane with $15 million crashed in the jungle and exploded, turning the money into a bonfire. Workers who lost drugs or cash were given more drugs to make up for the loss. If they messed up again, they were killed.

CHAPTER 20

ENTERING POLITICS

In the election campaign of 1978, the Conservative Party printed a poster of the Liberal candidate, Julio César Turbay, looking like a Mafia don, accompanied by the slogan: DO NOT LET HIM BUY THE PRESIDENCY. Even though they emphasised his links to the traffickers, he won the election. In America, the widely watched TV show *60 Minutes* exposed his relationship with the traffickers.

To obtain power, presidential candidates often took money from the traffickers. Those who didn't found themselves left behind financially, and were unable to compete. In return, the traffickers expected immunity from prosecution and government protection of their enterprises. The dilemma leaders faced once in power was that billions of dollars of aid from America were contingent on the country being compliant in the War on Drugs. To achieve this, the leaders protected some traffickers while arresting others.

After becoming the president with the help of drug money, Turbay attempted to appease America by clamping down on the exportation of weed. Harvests were destroyed with toxic chemicals from the USA, which supplied helicopters, planes and weapons to attack the smugglers. In 1979, almost in secret from the public, Turbay signed an extradition treaty with America, which meant that Colombian citizens indicted for crimes by American prosecutors would be handed over to the US authorities and processed in America's justice system – a fate the traffickers feared worse than death. Eventually, extradition would become the crux of the traffickers' war with the government, provoke record levels of violence and ultimately lead to the downfall of most of the senior members of the cartel.

With so many powerful politicians taking drug money, few dared to denounce it. An exception was the young Liberal leader, Luis Carlos Galán. After the murder of an ally in 1976, Galán wrote:

"The horrible death of Rubio Pupo makes him a symbol that claims from the government, from the parties and from all key institutions of society, a unified front, intransitive against the sombre coalition of the three mafias willing to impose their laws in Colombia, to the service of drug trafficking, of smuggling and to the illegal business of emeralds, and they have even placed their agents among the management of the State itself and in the Congress."

With an aquiline nose, an intense gaze and curly hair, Galán gave anticorruption speeches that mesmerised the masses. At 27 years old, he had joined the Ministry of Education and become a senator. In 1978, running for Bogotá's council, he formed an alliance with his brother-in-law, Alberto Villamizar – who would become entangled in Pablo schemes almost until the boss's death. As a sales manager for a tyre factory, Villamizar brought strategy to Galán's electoral campaign in Bogotá.

Once elected to the council, Galán proposed challenging the two dominant parties, Liberal and Conservative, for corruption, including receiving hot money. As his New Liberalism philosophy spread, he appointed regional leaders including Rodrigo Lara Bonilla and Enrique Parejo, both of whom would clash with Pablo. With the traditional members of the Liberal and Conservative parties having a stranglehold on power dating back to the 1800s, no one could have anticipated that Galán's new movement was on a collision course with the traffickers that would devastate Colombia.

In early 1982, Pablo and Lehder joined some of Pablo's family members and the Mayor of Envigado at the dinner table. They conversed about the upcoming elections. "There are open seats," the mayor said. "Pablo should run for election. The masses would support him."

With so many of them on his payroll, Pablo was no stranger to politicians. Cartel members competed to own the most powerful ones, just like they outdid each other with luxury cars, homes and zoos. Politicians were approached by cartel lawyers with brown envelopes full of cash. If they declined the bribe, they would receive a call asking if they would prefer to be killed. With so many of their peers taking money, and the cocaine business bringing so much prosperity to Colombia, it was easy to say yes. Many of them felt that cocaine was America's problem because that was where it was mostly consumed. If they didn't want it, Colombia wouldn't produce it. Due to America's history in Central and South America, the US was viewed dimly by many Colombians. Some saw cocaine as the lesser-developed world's weapon against the US and believed that imperialism would be destroyed from within by its own excesses.

Besides wealth, Pablo was driven by a hunger for power. He believed that political power would legitimise him as a leader of society. As a politician, he would be protected by certain laws and ineligible for extradition. Trafficking was only a means through which he would become a man of history, whose legend and glory would live on.

Watching Pablo's face light up at the mayor's suggestions, his mother-in-law, Nora, stood up and chastised him for forgetting who he was and what he did. If he entered politics, there would be no sewer in the world where he could hide. They would all be endangered. He would hurt all of their lives. He needed to think about his son and his family. In deep contemplation, Pablo stood and paced. He told Nora not to worry because he always did things correctly, and he had paid the secret police to destroy his criminal record.

"Look at all of his charity projects," the mayor said. "This will bring in a lot of votes. All of the soccer fields and sports facilities. Thousands of trees planted in the poor areas."

After two hours of discussion, he agreed to run as an alternate for the Renewal Movement, which was supporting the presidential candidacy of Luis Carlos Galán. As Pablo approved of Galán's powerful speeches in support of the people, he had no problem with joining the Renewal Movement.

In 1982, the presidential candidates included the Liberal Party's Alfonso López Michelsen. The front runner for the Conservative Party was Belisario Betancur. New Liberalism's Galán was a rising star whom the major parties viewed with suspicion. The lawyer Jairo Ortega founded the Renewal Movement, which backed Galán. Wanting to keep his decision secret for the moment, Pablo became a substitute for the list Ortega would lead for the House of Representatives.

In Antioquia, Galán's followers initially campaigned with Jairo Ortega, but objected to his trafficker connections. "I have no concrete reasons to expel him from the campaign," Galán told them.

Three days later, Pablo got on the hood of a Mercedes-Benz and gave a speech to 1,000 people in the La Paz neighbourhood. "I promise to work from Congress for the poor of Envigado and Antioquia. I'll always have a special affection for this neighbourhood."

At another rally, a drunk yelled, "What about politicians who don't keep their promises?" He pointed at Pablo, who scowled and watched the police remove the drunk. The police took him to a neighbourhood where El Patrón's men shot him.

Giving speeches, Pablo wore chino trousers, polo shirts and sneakers. He spoke politely and softly at the openings of soccer pitches, roller-skating rinks, hospitals and schools he had financed. Eight weeks of events increased his confidence. At a rally in a town square, he denounced extradition and demanded a repeal of the American extradition agreement. He believed that Colombia's subservience to the USA had humiliated his country. He said that extradition was barbaric because it distorted the concept of a person's territory and an immense burden fell on the family members of the extradited, especially innocent children who knew nothing of their fathers' illegal activities.

Behind the patriotic rhetoric, the traffickers feared extradition because they were masters at playing the Colombian justice system, whereas in America, they were portrayed as murderous narco-terrorists and the judges would swiftly dispatch life sentences. They were terrified of getting tried in a foreign country where everybody spoke English, hardly any time was spent investigating cases and judges and prosecutors competed for big-name trials. The risks associated with prosecuting traffickers in Colombia were so high that few prosecutors wanted those cases.

Registering its list of candidates for the House of Representatives, the Renewal Movement finally publicly documented Pablo as an alternative. In a meeting with his advisers, Galán assessed the risk of his alliance with Pablo and Ortega. He decided to announce their expulsion at an event scheduled in Medellín's Bolívar Park, where the speakers included Galán's second in command, Rodrigo Lara Bonilla, and Jairo Ortega.

A journalist travelling with Galán asked how things were in Antioquia. "They are entangled," Galán said.

"With the Liberals?"

"No, with the Mafia. It seems that Pablo Escobar wants to sneak into our lists and I am worried. If you join us this afternoon in Medellín, you'll probably be able to confirm it."

Despite the rain, the event was crowded and Galán was cheered. During his speech, he called Pablo and his ally Ortega undesirable people. He ordered the closure of the Renewal Movement's campaign office in Envigado and the destruction of their publicity material. Pablo was forced to close his political headquarters. In a note to Ortega, Galán wrote: "We cannot accept the inclusion of people whose activities are in contradiction with the moral and political restoration of this country. If you do not accept my conditions, I cannot allow any attachment of your movements list with my presidential campaign."

Suspicious of Galán's motivation, Pablo learned that a doctor had disclosed his cocaine trafficking to the candidate. It was the same doctor who had performed the autopsy on Pablo's brother Fernando. The doctor was at his office in Envigado when Shooter arrived and executed him.

Ortega arranged a meeting with Pablo and Alberto Santofimio Botero, a.k.a. Santo by the traffickers, the stocky leader of the Liberal Alternative, a small party nominating candidates for Congress. While incarcerated, Pablo had previously seen Santo visit his cellmate the Godfather. Santo had even served time himself for using death certificates to appropriate state resources, but through his brilliant oratory skills, family connections and plenty of cunning and deceit, he had become a powerful presidential candidate. Santo stroked Pablo's ego by telling him that through his money and intelligence he would definitely become the president.

One of Pablo's lawyers, Humberto Buítrago, warned him, "This path can only lead to perdition because the Colombian political class is fucked up."

Pablo gave his usual response: "We already have financial power, now we go for political power."

Impressed by Pablo's wealth, Santo accepted Ortega and Pablo into the Liberal Alternative. Pablo enjoyed Santo's eloquence in political debate and conversation, which he peppered with quotes from philosophers, authors and political leaders. He told Pablo: "An intelligent man is one who is so intelligent as to hire those more intelligent than him." Behind his well-polished façade, Santo had no qualms about eliminating anyone in his way.

At Hacienda Nápoles, Santo schooled Pablo. "Alberto, do you believe that I have what it takes for politics?" Pablo asked.

"I don't know if you have what it takes, but you have plenty of money. In this country, money runs politics."

"How are votes won?"

"In the councils, you buy councilmen. In the assemblies, you buy deputies. These guys have the votes, which gets you to the mayor, the government departments, the House of Representatives and the Senate. That way, you get to the decentralised establishments and to the state budget. There it is, my dear Pablo, the contracts and therefore the money."

"If I already have money, why would I want more, Alberto?"

"Pablo, politics brings not only money, but also power. With that power, you could name the director of civil aeronautics, who will allow your aircraft to enter and leave as you wish. You could choose the director of customs, so that your goods are not searched. You can control the director of the DAS, the generals of the Republic, the police commanders et cetera. That's what politics can give you, Pablo. Power! You'll see what we do together when I become president of Colombia."

At an event in Medellín, Pablo, Santo and Ortega got on the stage, the politicians wearing suits, ties and red carnations in their lapels, Pablo in short sleeves with a carnation. They criticised Galán and urged people not to vote for him.

The Liberal Alternative put an ad in the newspapers: "We support Pablo Escobar's candidacy for the Chamber of Representatives because his youth, his intelligence and his love for the most vulnerable make him deserving of the envy of cocktail politicians. He has the support of all the liberals and conservatives in Magdalena Medio, as he has been the saviour of this region."

Approaching Medellín's Moravia neighbourhood, the stench suggested that Pablo and his men were getting near to the garbage mountain. A combination of putrefying human waste, vegetation and chemicals released a unique gas that assaulted their senses as they ascended a narrow road used by garbage trucks. At the mountaintop, below swarms of vultures and buzzards flying in a grey sky, the enormity of the dump was revealed. Packs of malnourished dogs with patches of fur missing were scavenging, as well as cats, rats, mice, flies and mosquitoes. Grimy emaciated people emerged, curious and desperate, including some young pregnant women. Rapidly, they multiplied, surrounding the visitors.

Displaced from rural areas, they had built makeshift shacks on the dump, which had grown into the most densely populated community in Colombia. They survived by sifting through the trash and finding items that could be recycled, and a reliance on transportation links such as the train station. In this hellish environment, almost five lived in each room and almost a third of the residents were children. It was characterised as "children fighting with buzzards for leftovers." Thirty per cent of the shacks had been deemed too dangerous to occupy.

"I can't conceive that human beings live in these conditions," Pablo told his men, while inhaling fume. Explaining why he felt committed to the poor, he told the slum dwellers, "I joined the Civic Board of my neighbourhood in 1968. Many times, I have performed work with a pick and shovel, happy and sweaty. From an early age, I had an obsession with schools, maybe because I am the son of a self-sacrificing educator who loves her profession. Building schools seems to reunite us with the homeland we long for, and we have seen with pain, many children sitting on tiles in dilapidated premises, and teachers living without any protection against the indifference of the State. To give back something of what this beautiful country has given us, we are doing just that. I rode a bus for 28 years, and because of that, I am one of you. I am from here. Consider me one of your own. I come here because the economic conditions have changed. I come to share with you what is mine, to share with you the right we Colombians had to live a dignified life."

Days after his visit, a fire spread through the neighbourhood, devouring shacks, especially those constructed with cardboard. "We are returning there," he announced upon seeing the news. Walking along lanes used by the garbage trucks, he was saddened by the destruction. He donated blankets, mattresses and other essentials. No one in power seemed to care. In the evening, he hosted a meeting with his advisers. In between playing with a piece of paper he kept putting in his mouth, he said, "How much does it cost to build a simple house?"

He started a programme called Medellín Without Slums, a.k.a. Barrio Pablo Escobar, with a goal of providing free housing.

Using his resources and by soliciting donations from traffickers, he calculated that he could build 5,000 houses within two years. To finance the first 500, he organised a bullfight with famous matadors, bulls imported from Spain, Miss Colombia 1982 and other beauty queens. Traffickers visiting his office were asked how many houses for the poor they could afford. He wrote down the numbers. The total soon came to 300. He returned to Moravia with Father Elias Lopera, who gave the official Catholic blessing.

Two Catholic priests were board members of Medellín Without Slums. They introduced him at public events, accompanied him in the slums and blessed a charity art auction he hosted at the Intercontinental Hotel, which was called Paintbrush of Stars. At the opening of soccer stadiums, huge crowds yelled his name.

"Man of the people! Man of action! A man of his word!" was his catchphrase, capitalising on the public's resentment of politicians who always reneged on their promises. Wherever he arrived, he would organise a team to take action. It usually included a local priest, an action-committee president, a sports coordinator and other community representatives. They would prioritise the area's needs and present them to Pablo. After promising to fund certain projects such as floodlighting a soccer field or painting a school, the work would start immediately.

He started a radio show called Civics on the March and hired publicists and journalists to boost his man-of-the-poor image. They claimed his fortune had come from used-car sales, renting bicycles and real-estate deals. A column in the newspaper owned by his uncle Hernando Gaviria, *Medellín Cívico*, lavished him with praise: "Yes, I remember him … his hands, almost priest-like, growing parabolas of friendship and generosity in the air. Yes, I know him, his eyes weeping because there is not enough bread for all of the nation's dinner tables. I have watched his tortured feelings when he sees street children – angels without toys, without a present, without a future."

He organised events, where famous people added to the praise. His own chief of propaganda Édgar Escobar, a.k.a. the

Poet, would also take the stage. Here's one of Édgar's speeches:

"Today Pablo Escobar Gavira visits us. Born in a Catholic home in the beautiful plateau of Rionegro, where he grew up dreaming and forging a future between hardships, games, letters, numbers and juvenile mischief. Whose streets he ran in his youth as he became a traveller selling hope, loaded with the Christian faith received from his mother and teacher – mother Hermilda – he acquired the ideas, principles and his nerve as a leader.

"He has ingeniously worked to harness a significant fortune and now, he offers a new style of being rich: simple and generous. He feels himself the administrator of the goods of a people. He is already an unquestionable idol in Envigado and Sabanera and goes into Medellín and the Valle de Aburrá with a new form of doing politics: it is no longer the blah, blah, blah of promises.

"From his mind of genius is born a Medellín Without Slums, a corporation whose objective is to eradicate homes made out of tin and cardboard. The first and only company of this type started in the world by one person. A work applauded by Tyrians and Trojans. The mere cry of a Medellín Without Slums can be an emblem of change and of the motto of a government of the people and of a revolution. He yearns and plans a change for Colombia: that the wealthy enjoy full freedom and guarantees for their investments and their businesses, but that they do not continue using the State to subsidise their investments. That the State dedicates itself with priority in its interventionism to promote the development of the poor people, to be the solution of their problems and the satisfaction of their needs."

Due to his stance against extradition, the Conservative Party's Betancur entered the 1982 campaign aided by money from the traffickers. From 1978, the Ochoas had donated to Betancur through Jesús Valderrama, a manager of their livestock companies. Gustavo Gaviria supported the Conservative campaign in 1982 by participating in an auction at El Castillo Museum. The Medellín Cartel lent Betancur a plane, which he demanded be painted the blue colour of the Conservatives. Although Gacha considered the request brazen, the plane was painted – and years later it would be seized in an anti-trafficking operation.

The Liberal Party's official candidate was Alfonso López Michelsen, the ex-president from 1974 to 1978. He was supported by Santo, now the head of the Medellín Cartel's political division, with Ernesto Samper heading the campaign. After hearing that the traffickers had contributed to the Conservatives, the Liberals wanted to get in on the action. At the Intercontinental Hotel, López and Samper met the traffickers and took money. To minimise his risk, López was advised to only stay briefly and to let Samper stay for the duration – which ended up four hours – to conclude everything with the traffickers. One method employed to accept hot money without having to register it was to have the traffickers purchase raffle tickets for the prize of a car. Having placed bets on both sides, the traffickers hoped to win favours in return for their donations regardless of which party came to power.

After details of the meeting were leaked, López and Samper claimed they had fallen into a trap. López stated, "I was in a hurry. I went in for a moment and I did not even sit down. I shook hands with some guys I did not even know, and then in the course of later episodes, I discovered that they were the Ochoas, Pablo Escobar and, probably, Carlos Lehder and Rodríguez Gacha."

While his associates preferred to control the politicians from behind the scenes, Pablo had become obsessed with his public image. He would joke, "What have they mentioned about President Reagan and me today?" He collected newspaper articles about himself from around the world in all languages. Journalists were invited to Nápoles, where he spent hours cultivating relationships. During those times, the politicians visiting him tried to avoid the journalists to prevent the documentation of their sins. On one occasion, he was on a boat with some politicians and a journalist from *The Time*, whom he asked to photograph them all together. Pictures were published of Pablo with Santo, Ernesto Lucena Quevedo, David Turbay and William Jaramillo.

Having created a power base in the barrios of Medellín with non-stop exhausting speeches railing against the oligarchy who never helped the poor, he spent the day of the election results, March 14, 1982, at the Liberal Renewal Movement's headquarters with his wife, Ortega and Santo. The vote counting was taking so long that Victoria grew bored and went home. He called her with updates.

He was so pleased with the result that he wanted to tell Victoria in person. He entered his house, grinning, and advised his wife to get ready to be the First Lady of Colombia. For hours he talked about his plans for the country, including building free hospitals and universities.

"I need to get a new outfit for your inauguration," Victoria said. "I'll start planning it right away."

"I'm not going to wear a suit," he said. "I'll enter Congress in my shirtsleeves."

He received a certificate from the minister of the interior, which verified his position as an alternate representative to Congress, a status that gave him parliamentary immunity from criminal prosecution and extradition to America. To celebrate, he took twenty family members to Rio de Janeiro. They were bussed around the city to restaurants and shows. At night, the men went to strip clubs, which upset the women so much that all of the family members were fighting on the way home.

With the presidential campaign heating up among the four main candidates, including Galán, Pablo and his associates continued to back López the Liberal and Betancur the Conservative. As well as contributing money and loaning aircraft, Pablo bussed liberals to the voting stations, enabling some to vote twice at separate locations. With Galán's support cannibalising the Liberals' voter base, Betancur won in a landslide on May 30, 1982.

In a letter published in *Medellín Cívico*, Betancur thanked Pablo's uncle, Hernando Gaviria:

"Receive my voice of thanks for your decisive contribution to the National Movement that has led me to the Presidency of Colombia. This great crusade, of which you have been a part, pledges its gratitude. I have summoned all my effort to achieve it in the four-year period in which the changes that the country is claiming began. I use this opportunity to exhort you to embrace the task of government that we will undertake. The country can rest assured that I will link to this work all my effort and my care to build a better homeland, with opportunities for all, under the rule of peace and social justice.

Yours truly, very cordially, your compatriot and friend
Belisario Betancur"

The famous Colombian author, Gabriel García Márquez, received a guarantee from Betancur that under his rule, no Colombian would be extradited to America, so the Nobel Prize winner wrote a column: "A treaty to treat us badly." Supporting non-extradition, he pointed out that as a matter of principle, Colombia should not send its citizens to be tried abroad, just like no mother sends her children to the neighbour's house to be punished. Before publishing the article, he again called Betancur: "President, I have written a column where I maintain that I'm sure that under your government no Colombian will be extradited. Can I leave it like that?"

"You can leave it like that," Betancur said.

Pablo's inauguration was on July 20. In a red and black velvet dress by Valentino, Victoria accompanied him in a military-green Mercedes-Benz limo borrowed from Lehder. Dressed in a cream suit, El Patrón emerged from the limo and was stopped at the door to Congress for not wearing a tie. He insisted on being allowed in, but the doorman objected. Eventually, his cameraman handed him a tie with a floral design, and he went in. People were photographed taking the "oath of possession" with an open palm lifted, whereas his right hand was displaying a V for victory. At 32 years old, he looked triumphant and confident, with many of Colombia's most powerful ready to do his bidding. That evening, Ortega and Santo joined his family for a celebratory dinner.

On August 7, Betancur was inaugurated. His main goals

included making peace with the guerrillas and improving housing and education. Drugs seemed to be off his agenda. With the majority of politicians taking donations from the traffickers, why ruffle any feathers? Besides, many previous presidents had taken drug money. Those who hadn't didn't stay in office for long. When the president announced that he was philosophically opposed to the extradition of Colombian nationals, the traffickers were delighted enough to celebrate in Brazil again, but without their women imposing constraints.

In August, two Learjets flew Pablo and his associates, including Jorge and Fabio Ochoa, Gustavo, Fernando Galeano, Otto, Shooter and Pablo's brother-in-law Mario, to Rio de Janeiro. Each took $100,000, which they agreed to spend entirely in Brazil. At the priciest hotel in Copacabana, the Meridian, they occupied an entire floor and lavished the staff with $100 tips. Daily, up to forty prostitutes and dancers arrived. In rented Rolls-Royces, they drove onto a soccer field, which the media later reported as a visit from Colombian politicians and prominent businessmen.

Always on the lookout for exotic animals, he found a blue parrot with yellow eyes, the only one in existence. Although Brazilian law protected it from being exported, he paid $100,000 and it was flown out of the country in his private plane.

They paid to be an exclusive audience at one of the most popular shows. Watching the samba-dancing women shimmy their shoulders and shake their hips increased their lust, so they arranged a yacht trip with striptease dancers. Before they had set sail, the media found out about the yacht, which spooked Gustavo. "I ain't going there. If someone makes an attack on us, they'll end the Colombian Mafia."

"But everything is already paid for," Pablo said.

"It doesn't matter. Let's not risk it. We should go back to Colombia."

Back in Nápoles, he started to reminisce about the dancing girls of Brazil, so he summoned his pilot. "Bring me some mulattos from Brazil's cabaret."

The pilot checked his watch. "I'll be back in fifteen hours." The plane returned on time, and the dancing girls performed in the house.

Pablo was mesmerised by their movements when a message arrived: "Your wife is on her way by helicopter." He ordered the women back into the plane, which took off and circled the estate. Noticing nothing amiss, Victoria stayed for three hours, after which the plane landed and the party resumed.

A few weeks later, the Chamber of Representatives assigned him to an official committee destined for Spain to independently monitor the general election. Delighted, he packed his usual luggage with the addition of hidden-heel shoes to increase his height from 5 foot 5. With Ortega and Santo, he flew first class and watched the Socialist Workers' Party win the election. He attended the presidential ceremony for Felipe González, whose popularity amazed him. At a private meeting in Spain, he acted subserviently to Santo, who even had him fetch whiskeys. When a journalist asked him for cocaine, he responded, "I'm a healthy man. I don't put that in my body."

CHAPTER 21

TV STAR MISTRESS

In the middle of 1982, Virginia Vallejo boarded a small plane to Hacienda Nápoles, with her wealthy fiancé, the nephew of ex-president Turbay, who had signed the extradition treaty. As detailed in her book, *Loving Pablo, Hating Escobar*, they were accompanied by her fiancé's two children and some friends including a model called Angela. The plane landing roused Virginia from slumber. With a concerned expression, her fiancé pointed at over twenty hit men outside, pointing machine guns at the plane, wearing polo shirts, blue jeans, sneakers and sunglasses. Anticipating getting kidnapped, the passengers started to panic. Virginia was blaming her fiancé's cocaine habit for dimming his wits sufficiently to blind him to the trap that they had fallen into when the aircraft door opened, allowing warm air inside.

The two armed men who entered the plane frowned upon seeing the passengers and apologised for the mix-up. They had been expecting more zoo animals, not guests. They prayed that the boss would not find out because he would kill them.

Getting transported in jeeps, the guests were spellbound by the expanse of land, water and sky. At the ranch house, Virginia assumed that the boss was a crafty old politician with a king-of-the-town complex, who treated his staff well because they all had a certain confidence and pride. The property manager apologised for the boss's absence, but a last-minute problem had detained him. At a giant wooden dining table, the guests received the Antioquian food that El Patrón preferred, including rice, beans, ground meat, fried egg and avocado.

In the morning, the guests sped across miles of grassland on dune buggies, two-seaters on low-level frames, with the engines roaring, leaving smoke and dust in their trails. By noon, they headed for shelter in the jungle. Approaching the vegetation at high speed, Virginia's fiancé crashed into a long thick stick, which ended up inches from her eye. While a flock of colourful birds squawked and flew away, the guests were relieved that nobody was injured. Back at the ranch's medical building, she received a tetanus shot, while her fiancé fretted over the cost of replacing the buggy, which would have to be imported from America.

Having been told that the boss had arrived in a helicopter, the guests gathered in a salon. While he beamed at their astonishment over his young age, she admired his mischievous smile. A dismissive hand gesture swept away their concerns about the buggy. After explaining that they had plenty of spare buggies, he greeted each guest individually in a calm friendly tone and announced that he would like to show them the zoo. She noticed that his eyes lingered on her model friend Angela.

Jeeps transported the guests, one driven by Pablo accompanied by two Brazilian women in thongs. "The three elephants are Asian," he said. "The larger ones and those in danger of becoming extinct have two or more females, and some of the other animals such as the zebras, camels and kangaroos have more. It keeps them happy and prevents violence."

As she liked to poke fun at sex-obsessed men, Virginia said that the animals were happy because the estate was as gorgeous as the African plains. Pointing at the hippos, she said they looked right at home. Baffled as to how he had imported giraffes due to their size, she fired off questions and offered her own theory about the route they had taken and the officials he had bribed. After scolding her for having knowledge of international crime, he asked whether she would give him lessons. He said they were all imported legally with their vaccinations and paperwork in order.

Pablo took them speed-boating across the river, dodging every rock and fallen tree as if he knew every inch of the water.

After an hour, the boat stopped so that they could have lunch on the riverbank. While fumes wafted from a barbecue, Virginia attempted to relax by entering the river and floating on her back, failing to notice a whirlpool. As the water trapped her legs, she waved for help, but the bodyguards and guests were so far away, they laughed, waved back and continued to drink and eat soup. With her lower half paralysed, she feared drowning.

While giving orders, Pablo gazed at Virginia. Realising that she was in trouble, he jumped into the water, told her to remain calm and in a swift strong motion with his arms, extracted her from the whirlpool. Clinging to his body, watched by her perplexed fiancé, she was carried to the shore.

"Out of all of the people watching, why were you the only one to realise I could have drowned?" she said. Pablo said he had noticed the desperation in her eyes, while the rest were focussed on her arms. "It's not just that. You're the only one who saw my anguish and cares about my life." With the shock wearing off, but still trembling, she managed to smile. She warned that he was now responsible for her as long as he were alive. He objected that she should not assume that he would die first, so she changed it to be for as long as she were alive, in which case he could pay for her funeral.

He laughed. "Surely that will take a century. Today has proven that you have more lives than a cat."

At the shore, her fiancé handed her a large towel. She noticed the hurt in his eyes. After eating grilled beef, she withdrew from the group. Full of appreciation of life, she admired the river, the sunlight on the trees on the opposite bank and even the butterflies.

Pablo entertained the guests with Rolligons, massive tractors that held fifteen people with wheels larger than humans. The passengers challenged him to knock down trees. "Anything that can't resist my attack doesn't deserve to live," he said after demolishing one. "It needs to return to the earth to become food."

Rumbling back to the ranch house, they passed the vintage

1936 Ford he and his men had riddled with bullet holes. "It's Bonnie and Clyde's!" he lied.

"The real couple's or from the movie about them?" Virginia said.

"It's the original. I don't buy fakes."

"But it looks like someone shot it with a machine gun."

"The six cops who caught Bonnie and Clyde were so desperate to claim the reward that they shot the car for over an hour with automatic rifles. They left over 100 bullet cartridges at the scene."

The Rolligons stopped at the Hacienda Nápoles entrance crowned by the small plane. While he reached up for a hatch, the passengers rapidly slid to the sides, except for Virginia, who ended up with gallons of cold water falling on her. Frozen in place, she struggled to breathe. When she could finally speak, she asked sarcastically which famous person had previously owned the small plane perched over the entrance – perhaps Charles Lindbergh? Pablo claimed that it was a plane that had brought him good luck, similar to the luck she had received when he had saved her from drowning. He congratulated her on being baptised and laughed hysterically.

In the evening, Virginia was getting dressed in a turquoise silk tunic when Pablo knocked on her door. "Come in."

Without releasing the doorknob, he leaned his head inside. "I apologise for earlier. How are you feeling?"

"Having taken five baths at various temperatures in the last twelve hours, I'm cleaner than ever." He smiled. "How come there are no wildcats in your zoo?"

He explained that carnivorous animals would eat the others and are difficult to import legally. After adding that he recently saw an angry wet panther shivering under a plane, he laughed and disappeared, leaving her admiring his playful nature. At dinner-time, the guests praised her outfit. Catching Pablo admiring her, she lowered her gaze.

Afterwards in her room, her fiancé explained that Pablo was

the king of cocaine and that he would soon be the richest man in the world. "I thought politics financed his lifestyle," she said.

With his eyes bloodshot from snorting cocaine, he said that it was the other way around. "He gave me a fifty-gram cocaine rock." He displayed a white stone.

A few weeks after the visit to Hacienda Nápoles, Virginia, her fiancé and the model Angela were invited to Jorge Ochoa's La Veracruz ranch on the Caribbean coast. Pablo's plane transported them to an airport, where he was waiting in a jeep. Driving under a blinding sun, he slowed down for a tollbooth. Rather than pay $3, he smiled at the toll boy and drove on, which in Colombia is called "blowing the toll." Waving at them to stop, the boy chased them, but eventually stopped. Asked why he hadn't paid, he said that he had no respect for authority unless it was armed. When there were no police in the booth, he didn't pay.

They arrived at an impressive house on a ranch where the Ochoas bred fighting bulls. Parked outside were Ferraris and Mercedes in loud red and yellow colours. Although the zoo was smaller than Pablo's, Virginia was impressed by how well the property had been decorated. Pablo introduced her to Jorge Ochoa and his wife Maria Lia, a tall beautiful woman. The guests ate and toured the estate, with Pablo paying special attention to Angela.

"I'd love to see your famous champion horses," Virginia said when they were about to leave.

"I promise to plan something soon," Pablo said. "You won't be disappointed."

Pablo flew them back to Medellín, where they stayed at the Intercontinental Hotel, by his large offices, situated amid curvy streets and hills covered with semitropical vegetation. He said that everybody would be in bed early because it was Sunday, so at midnight he was going to take them on a thrill ride in James Bond's car.

Even though it had numerous buttons on its dashboard, the car looked unimpressive. He explained each button's function: to release a smoke cloud to envelop your pursuers, to spray tear gas at your pursuers, to pour oil onto the road so your pursuers slide off a cliff, to drop hundreds of nails to destroy your pursuers' tyres, to spray petrol, to activate a flamethrower to light the petrol, to detonate explosives, to emit a high frequency that destroys eardrums. He admitted that the machine guns on either side of the car had been removed to avoid them falling into the hands of a vengeful panther. Angela would co-pilot the demonstration, while the rest raced him in their cars.

Allowing the guests and bodyguards to forge ahead, he drove slowly at first, but after several minutes, he floored the accelerator until he was in the lead. One minute they caught sight of him on a bend, and the next he disappeared. After an hour, the James Bond car screeched into view, and emitted a cloud that forced the guests to stop. Trapped, they suffered blurred vision and a burning sensation in their throats. They coughed, but each intake of air felt as if it were setting fire to their lungs. Racing away, Pablo and Angela laughed, leaving the rest fighting over access to a roadside water spigot. Waiting behind the bodyguards for the spigot, some of whom were crying, Virginia placed her hands on her hips and yelled at them to act like men instead of little girls.

Pablo returned. "My co-pilot was to blame. I'd only authorised her to press the button for the smoke, but she pushed the tear gas by mistake." He ordered his men to show dignity, stop crying like little girls and to let Virginia access the spigot.

Virginia stopped coughing. "I'll let the girls drink. I can get water back at the hotel." Before leaving, she called his car a bucket of bolts and a stinking skunk.

Visiting in late 1982, Virginia learned from other guests the origin of Pablo's entrepreneurial skills. "He started out as a gravestone thief. They filed off the names of the dead, and sold them as new, not just once, but several times." She chuckled. "They moved on to stealing cars, which they dismantled within hours and sold the parts. Then he became a triggerman during the Marlboro War."

She asked for an explanation, but no one would elaborate. She assumed it meant he had stolen large quantities of cigarettes.

Perplexed by the origin of his wealth, she waited until she was alone with her fiancé to say, "How come he has his own fleet of planes and landing strips? How can he ship tons of cocaine and smuggle into Colombia African elephants and giraffes, Rolligons and boats?" He said that Pablo was the wealthiest because he had no competition, he had bribed a person high up in the Civil Aviation Agency, a cousin of the Ochoas and that he and his associates had financed the campaigns of the two presidential candidates.

With Pablo providing free cocaine, Virginia's fiancé's addiction spiralled. After they argued, he would go on the rampage and disappear for days, having sex with ex-girlfriends, flamenco dancers and mud wrestlers. Then he would return offering bouquets of roses. After he pulled a gun in a restaurant and pointed it at two of Virginia's fans, she warned that if he didn't quit cocaine she would leave him. He chose cocaine, so she ended their relationship.

In 1983, her TV company was floundering. After consulting her business partner Margot, she contacted Pablo in the hope that he would advertise with them or invest in the company. In Medellín, he agreed to run advertisements for his brother's company, Osito Bicycles. The money would cover all the company's debts.

"As a condition to accept the advertising, I'd like to put you on TV," she said, "to film you giving away the houses to the people who live at the dump and in the slums."

"OK, but I would only need a five-minute segment."

"I'm so grateful to you and I have so much admiration for you helping people with Medellín Without Slums, I'd like to dedicate the entire hour of my Monday show. In three weeks, it will air at 6 PM."

Back in Bogotá, she told a friend about his help. He said that Pablo was falling in love with her, which was great because it would help her company and career. She denied that would happen because he fancied Angela, and she was still heartbroken over losing her fiancé to cocaine. At 32 years old, she was not the young-model type he liked. He pointed out that Pablo needed a powerful woman at his side to achieve his goal of becoming the president, not a model or a woman from his own class. Finally, he warned her not to wear any designer clothes at the dump because they would retain the foul smell.

At the dump, she and her assistant braced for up to five hours of filming in the toxic environment. Recognising Pablo and Virginia, the people rejoiced and began to hug and touch the boss. Pulling on Virginia's blouse, a girl urged her to see her Christmas tree. Expecting the girl to produce a twig, she was surprised when she displayed an almost new Made-in-America frosted Christmas tree.

"Christmas gets here two weeks late," Pablo said. "That's when the trash from the rich gets dumped here. The poor convert it into construction material and treasure."

A girl showed a Nativity scene, including a giant baby Jesus with one eye and one leg, a tiny Joseph, a medium-sized Virgin Mary and a plastic donkey and an ox. A woman invited them to see her house made from bricks cemented together and a plastic-tile roof. Old furniture lay around the kitchen and two bedrooms. Her son was doing homework at a table.

"Where do you get your food from?" Virginia asked. The woman said that they used money from recycling to buy food from the market, only animals ate the food at the dump.

With children following her and Pablo around, Virginia asked what had been the strangest thing ever found there. They said they had found rats eating a dead baby and the corpse of a young girl, who had been raped outside of the dump because the people who lived in there were good. Pablo confirmed that they were the best in the world.

Still gagging on the stench and with sweat streaming down her face, Virginia was ready to perform Pablo's first ever interview for the national media. With enthusiasm and concern, he talked about the 2,500 families struggling to survive there. The residents described their meagre possessions and told stories of what they had found in the dump. In a country where the government had treated them like dirt, they were eternally grateful for Pablo providing them houses, where their children could grow up in a more normal fashion and have better prospects. They trusted Pablo as an honest politician who followed through on his word. Everybody's faces glowed as if Pablo's presence had transformed the energy of the dump. By the end of the filming, Virginia no longer cared about the smell as the experience had opened her heart to suffering and to Pablo's compassion. As he guided her away, holding her hand, he made her feel safe and she knew that she loved him.

Walking to the car, he asked for her thoughts. She said she was deeply moved and thanked him for humanising people forced to live like animals. Meeting them had revealed that they were angels. After contemplating her answer, he put his hand around her shoulders and told her that nobody had ever said things like that to him. She was different. Would she have dinner with him? He had a beauty salon on standby to remove the skunk stench from her hair. She called him a zorillo – a tree that emits a skunk-like odour. More like the swordsman Zorro, he said.

Entering the restaurant, the politician and famous TV presenter drew all eyes. They were seated at the furthest table from the door. "I've never dated an interviewee nor a politician," she said.

"There's a first time for everything." He said that when he was sad or worried, he remembered her scolding the bodyguards jostling for water in the tear-gas cloud. Thinking about her as Napoleon at Waterloo was an endless source of amusement, and equally funny was the time he baptised her in freezing water and with her tunic clinging to her body, and she turned into a panther. He admired her bravery and gratitude, which many beautiful women lacked.

"I have extra gratitude because no one has ever given me anything or acknowledged my talents," she said, feeling appreciated.

She added that she didn't consider herself beautiful and her defects would become apparent over time.

"Why did you start your own TV company?"

As the host of the 7 PM news programme *24 Horas*, she had fallen out with her director, who had insisted that she describe the M-19 as a criminal band. After she had continued to refer to them as guerrillas, insurgents, rebels or a subversive group, the director had threatened to fire her from the best paid job in TV. She had exploded on him, mocked his family's political connections, including him being the grandson of an ex-president, and quit. Afterwards, she realised she had made a mistake, but refused to admit it to anyone.

"I'm grateful that you confide in me." He asked whether the M-19 knew that she had defended them.

"I've no idea. I don't know any of them. I didn't quit out of sympathy, but from journalistic and linguistic integrity."

He acknowledged that he knew them well, they had kidnapped Marta Ochoa, and now they knew him well, too. He explained how 800 men positioned at payphones had waited for the guerrillas to make a call and his men had tracked and kidnapped some of the leaders and their families."

"How did you find 800 trustworthy men?"

He offered to show her their neighbourhoods and his other social projects. He asked why she had split with her fiancé. She refused to live with an addict, and generally, she didn't like to talk about her exes. "Are you still married to the Argentinian director in his 50s?" With despair, she said he had refused to sign divorce papers to prevent her from remarrying. Pablo said her lawyer needed to call her ex-husband and tell him to sign or face the consequences.

"Will Zorro murder the ogre who has locked the princess in a tower?"

He said he only killed brave ogres to prevent wasting bullets on cowards and that she was worth dying for. His response affirmed the love she felt.

After the ex-husband refused to sign, Pablo said he would remedy the situation if she would have dinner with him again in the capacity of being a free woman. She doubted she would be free anytime soon. El Patrón assured her that she would be free within two days and they would be having dinner on Friday.

On Friday, after editing the video of Pablo, she received a call from her lawyer, who revealed that her ex-husband had called in a frantic state, claiming that if he didn't sign the papers by noon he would be dead. After he had arrived drained of colour, he trembled so much he could barely hold a pen.

In the afternoon, her housekeeper said that six deliverymen had brought too many flowers to fit in the elevator and were seeking permission to use the stairs. Suspecting a crime was underhand, she wanted to know what to do. Virginia told her to go down and determine who had sent them. The housekeeper returned with a note from El Zorro. P. to his freed Panther Queen. After receiving 1,000 of Colombia's national flower and orchids in various colours, the housekeeper said that she didn't like the deliverymen and the flowers were ostentatious. Delighted with the flowers, Virginia said they must have been arranged by the famous artists of the Flower Festival.

At 3 PM, her phone rang. Knowing who it was, she asked whether he had pulled a gun on her ex-husband. He laughed. "I've no idea what you're talking about. What time would you like me to pick you up for dinner?"

"At 6 PM, the Medellín airport closes and Friday's last flight probably has twenty on its waiting list." After protesting that he hadn't realised, he said he would arrange dinner in the year 2000 and hung up. Five minutes later, her phone rang. Without asking who it was, she said that the flowers were flowing out of the windows and they were the most beautiful thing she'd ever seen. "How long did it take to pick them?" He said they were just like her and he had commissioned people to start collecting them the day he had seen her with cuts on her face and knees. His Learjet Pegasus and three pilots were expecting her.

Embracing Virginia in Hacienda Nápoles, he said that when he had first held onto her in the river, he knew he had not saved her for another man, but for himself. He offered to give her anything in the world. She said that he was not God, therefore he could not prolong their golden moments by freezing time. While he slept, she admired the stars from the balcony, giddy with love.

After that night, she worked in Bogotá on the weekdays and spent most weekends in Medellín – a schedule that would last for fifteen months. His eleven planes and two helicopters transported her. On his planes, she met important people from all over the world, including political leaders, a diplomat sent to speak to the ruler of North Korea, the founder of the German Green party, a friend of Yasser Arafat's, members of the Colombian special police, Mexican generals and Israeli arms dealers.

He kept insisting on giving her anything she wanted and claimed that she was the only woman who hadn't asked him for anything in the first week. How about a Mercedes or a penthouse in Bogotá? She protested that she didn't want to be perceived as a kept woman and such luxuries would attract the attention of the tax authorities and kidnappers. With him insisting, she gave him a choice of gifts: a plane or a million kisses. After laughing, he picked the kisses.

"What can I give you back?" she said.

"Teach me how to give interviews because it's inevitable that I'll end up doing more than a few. I admire your skills. What's your secret?"

"I have three secrets. Firstly, say something original, interesting, important or witty. Everyone enjoys laughing." She refused to divulge the second and third in the first week of dating because she preferred to take things slow.

He smiled. "If you teach me your secrets, I'll share some of my own."

"Number two is not to answer every question, but instead to state what you want. To pull it off requires years of practice and fame. Beware of who you give interviews to. Ideally, they should be friendly media editors, directors and journalists." He should only grant interviews to a person who knew his secrets and loved him with all her heart. She wanted to know how he went from stealing gravestones and selling car parts to exporting cocaine. With him lowering his gaze, a familiar trait, she realised she had found a weakness.

As politicians come under unrelenting journalistic scrutiny, she said he needed to get serious about his answers and always emphasise his social projects. After her TV programme about him was broadcast, all of Colombia would be wondering how he had made his money and why he was so generous. His benevolence would threaten the elites who preyed off the masses, and they would target him for character assassination. Journalists contacting Medellín could learn his secrets instantly. On the plus side, none of the elites would ever entirely reveal the origin of their own fortunes, and his mental agility would help him. There were reasons the superrich never granted interviews.

Excited by their collaboration, he said that as a boy he had headed a fundraiser to build a school in La Paz for 800 students. Money from renting bicycles and selling used cars was parlayed into land speculation. "Do you think I'm lying?"

"It sounds true, but it couldn't possibly be the source of your fortune. What did your parents do?"

"My father worked on the land of an industrial leader. My mother was a rural school teacher." She urged him to start by referencing his father as an honest Antioquian peasant who taught him hard work, and how he learned to care for the weak from his teacher mother. "Would you have fallen in love with me if we had met when I was poor?"

"Absolutely not!" Neither would any of her friends have introduced her to a married man who was removing names from gravestones. While he was poor, she had been dating Gabriel Echavarría, the son of one of the ten richest in Colombia, and then Julio Mario Santo Domingo, the handsome heir to the country's largest fortune. Smiling, he said that if they were her previous standards, she really must love him. "It's why I love you so much," she said.

"You're the most generous and brutally honest woman I've ever met. That's why you make me so happy."

She schooled him on responses, some serious, others witty, and advised him to rephrase land speculation in Colombia to Florida real-estate investment. She wondered why he didn't want to operate from behind-the-scenes, like a traditional boss of bosses. Besides, fame only created envy in Colombia. She refused to believe his previous explanation of Marta Ochoa being rescued through exhaustive tracking.

"I'll explain that on another day," he said.

"What is the MAS?"

After lowering his eyes, he described the formation of Death to Kidnappers in 1981 by the big traffickers, with the support of wealthy landowners, the military and the DAS. Kidnappers would be caught by the MAS army of approximately 2,500 men and handed over to the military.

"From now on, refer to your associates as professional colleagues, after all they are farmers, industrialists, businessmen and exporters."

Reluctant to probe further into his ability to execute operations with results that would have required extreme force, she pointed out that there are approximately 3,000 kidnappings a year and to stop them would require the elimination of several groups with more than 30,000 guerrillas, something the Army had failed to achieve because no matter how many were arrested or killed, even more were recruited. She cautioned him that even though the wealthy appreciated the MAS because they were not risking any money or their own lives, he would ultimately pay a price for the murders by the MAS and the enemies it created.

He shrugged. "I don't care. My only interest is to be the leader of my profession and to have the support of my colleagues to get a president elected who will end extradition." He wanted her to rest before meeting some of his friends that night, including his cousin Gustavo and his brother-in-law Mario. Gustavo was like a brother to him. With his intelligence, he practically ran their business, which allowed him to concentrate on what mattered the most, including his social projects and Virginia's lessons.

She wanted to know what his goal was for after the Senate, but he cut her off. He said they would need 1,001 nights for him to give her the million kisses she had offered. Listening to him leave in a helicopter, she wondered how he would achieve his lofty goals amid Colombia's powerful contradictory forces and interests. She sensed that he would be a formidable leader, but worried that he would divide the country. By teaching him everything she had learned, she hoped to make herself indispensable.

She learned that he justified trafficking in terms of providing pleasure. Cocaine had been subjected to the same moralism as alcohol during prohibition, which increased violence and murder, including more dead police. If his business were legalised, he would pay his taxes, the Americans would have no problems with Colombians, murder and violence would plummet and there would be less prisoners.

At Hacienda Nápoles, Mafia bosses and their associates occupied over twenty tables, including the Moncada and Galeano factions of the Medellín Cartel. They referred to themselves as The Group (El Grupo) and Us (Nosotros). He introduced Virginia to the other bosses individually, lavishing them with praise and respectful tones that exceeded formality and were based in caution because they all had the power to kill each other and would do so if a slight was perceived.

"Here is Gonzalo, a loyal man, who likes to eat and enjoy good things," he said, referring to Gacha, who was wearing a hairy hat with a snake's head, a heavy chain with an ornament of Christ, an emerald ring and a bracelet. "Here is Jorge Luis Ochoa, whom you already know." He turned to Kiko Moncada, who was small, thin and not well dressed, perhaps downplaying his importance even though he had arrived in a $500,000 Ferrari. He next introduced

Fernando Galeano, a trusted friend who accompanied Pablo to many meetings. Finally, he introduced Carlos Lehder and Fidel Castaño.

She learned that his brother-in-law Mario was a fanatical fan of the opera, a subject that bored Pablo and Gustavo. She found Gustavo quiet, impenetrable and more mature than Pablo. He was a listener who absorbed information, while remaining secretive about his business interests. As a Conservative, he frowned on Pablo's lavish spending on social projects. Both cousins hardly touched alcohol and refrained from dancing, while remaining alert and in control. Gustavo opened up when talking about racing cars. She won him over by listening for hours. She concluded that it was in the cousins' DNA to win at all costs and to crush any competitors. She felt that the majority of the men in his family bored him as they were too conventional, except for Gustavo and Roberto. He much preferred the company of the other bosses with whom he had more in common, including wealth, a lack of scruples, aggression and risk-taking.

Near midnight, two young bodyguards toting rifles rushed inside and announced that the wife of a boss had arrived, and she was aware that he was inside Hacienda Nápoles with his mistress. With two of her friends, she was insisting on gatecrashing. Pablo ordered that they tell her to act like a lady, as no self-respecting woman goes out at night to hunt down her partner. She needed to wait at home with a frying pan and a rolling pin, but she was not coming inside. The bodyguards disappeared and returned even more sweaty and distraught. The women claimed Pablo knew them and he should let them in. After acknowledging that he was familiar with that kind of wild women, he ordered that they fire two shots over their car and if they attempted entry to aim directly at them, and if they didn't stop, to kill them without hesitation.

Twenty minutes later, four shots were fired. Covered in scratches, the bodyguards admitted to fighting the women. With the assistance of other bodyguards, they had marched the women away at gunpoint. They feared the drunken boss would suffer when he returned home, so to prevent a funeral, Pablo organised a room for him at the estate.

Boarding his Learjet, he told Virginia that he had a goal to run his business from a jumbo jet, a flying office with all of the rooms you would find in a house, while having the safety of the sky where nobody could bother him.

"How would you be able to fly around secretly like that?" she said.

"You'll find out when we return. From now on, whenever we meet, I'm always going to have an unforgettable surprise for you ... For the first surprise, I'm going to blindfold and possibly handcuff you."

"Are you the kind of sadist portrayed in the movies?" Smiling, he acknowledged that he was the worst kind of depraved sadist from horror films. "As I'm a masochist, we're the perfect couple."

He kissed her. "I've always known that."

At 10 PM on the day of the surprise, he collected her in a car, followed by four bodyguards in another. Speeding away, he mocked her for being unable to drive. She said bad eyesight prevented her from driving, but she had an IQ of 146, which helped her memorise thirty minutes of programme content because she was unable to read the teleprompter. "What do you think my IQ is?" he said.

"Around 126." He protested that his confirmed minimum was 156, so she needed to stop being so cocky. "Then prove it. Slow down. Driving over 100 mph, we'll soon be two dead geniuses."

He said neither of them were afraid of death. Bored of his bodyguards following them, he told her to check her seatbelt because he was about to flip onto the other side of the highway ten feet below. He turned the car so sharply, it rolled over and spun three times. She kept quiet about her head injury, while he raced towards his penthouse. Within minutes, he was in a garage, with its door closing behind them. He'd lost his bodyguards so easily, he said he might have to fire them.

Inside in pain, she sat in a chair with a low back in a bedroom with a camera by the door. Standing with his arms folded, he said he had demonstrated his high IQ and big balls. If she made a false move or complained, he would tear her dress in half and film what happened next. While singing "The 59th Street Bridge Song (Feelin' Groovy)" by Simon & Garfunkel, he placed a black blindfold on her and said that he should probably use handcuffs and duct tape. She protested that only a blindfold had been agreed. As he had just nearly broken her neck in the car, he needed to show some restraint. He agreed, but threatened to use the handcuffs if she attempted to jump away like a panther with delusions of genius. She said she wasn't in the habit of leaping away from criminals with delusions of schizophrenia.

She heard him walk on the carpet, open a combination safe, chamber six bullets into a gun and turn off its safety switch. Whispering in her ear, he grabbed her hair and circled the gun's barrel on her neck. He explained that traffickers were known as magicians because they worked miracles. As the king of the magicians, he knew a secret formula to reattach her head to her body by using a diamond necklace. She objected that the diamonds were cold, painful, too small, not what he had promised and since he was improvising, they didn't count. He said everything counted, especially the gun on her skin. She warned him not to allow the blindfold to come off or the surprise of the century would be ruined. Having been trained to shoot with a Smith & Wesson by the police, she had a better aim than officers with perfect vision. He pointed out that having a gun in her hand was a lot different from having a murderer point it at her temple, a situation which he had been on the receiving end of – a reference to the deceased DAS agents who had made the mistake of holding him and Gustavo at gunpoint.

She leaned back, sighed theatrically and said nothing could be more sublime. He opened the buttons of her dress and lowered the gun from her throat to her heart. She pointed out that he wasn't a murderer, just a sadist. He said he was a serial killer, and wanted to know why she liked the gun. She said it was a temptation, it provided an option out of life. He told her to talk until she was permitted to stop and kissed the nape of her neck. While she talked, he touched her with one hand while lowering the gun until it reached her belly. She warned him not to go any lower or he would never see her again. He threatened to use the duct tape. She said the surprise better be good, it was probably his gun collection, and she wanted to remove the blindfold. He said she'd better continue to follow orders from the murderer holding the gun and not a poor little woman who weighed 120 pounds and possessed an inferior IQ. She asked whether the surprise was diamonds or kilos of coke. He said she lacked imagination and gave permission to remove the blindfold.

Able to see, she attempted to examine the passports in various colours, when a leg cuff closed around her ankle, almost tripping her over. He jumped, caught and kissed her. He demanded her to say how much she loved and adored him if she wanted to see the passports with duct tape covering the countries. Smiling, she said he was the biggest genius of the underworld ever and the cuffs were hurting. Still cuffed, she watched him get on his knees and open the passports, revealing pictures of him in disguises. She laughed at the variety and praised him for being the world's biggest bandit. Uncuffed, she got on the bed, where he massaged her sore ankle and head.

After he fell asleep, she checked the gun, which had six live rounds. From the terrace, she gazed at four cars full of bodyguards. Like them, she believed she would give her life for him – a man who considered himself a stud but made love like a peasant, but who adored her tremendously – and that he was the most exciting and fun person in the world. By the time she woke up, he was gone. She felt concern about the enemies he would make by implementing his enormous social projects. He wanted to give thousands of houses to the homeless and to end hunger in Medellín.

Joining him for the opening of a basketball court, she met his family, including Victoria and Juan Pablo. While she appraised them, they treated her with suspicion. Victoria seemed uneasy in the crowd, despite the loving smiles she exchanged with Pablo, which did not render jealousy in Virginia because she understood that her passion for him was not exclusive. She believed that he had classified the opposite sex into three categories: family members whom he loved even though they bored him, glamorous women whom he paid for one-night stands with and those who were unattractive to whom he was indifferent. She saw herself outside these three and as a strong female character who could speak his language and make him laugh.

Observing him besieged by people thanking him for his benevolence, and behind the façade of the balloons, fireworks and musical band, she sensed that his family lived in fear of things exploding at any moment. His preoccupation with admiration from the crowd she viewed as naive because she had been performing on the stage since childhood. She hoped to add polish to his methods so that his message would reach beyond Antioquia.

Her TV broadcast of the dump received national attention. He was inundated with interview requests, but she said he wasn't ready and needed more training. Obsessed with controlling his image and encouraged to use television by Virginia, he tried to fine-tune his responses by subjecting himself on camera to hours of questions on hot issues. Watching the recordings with his advisers, he blushed while they targeted nervous movements, including scratching his ear, rubbing his head and a habit picked up from the labour class of scratching his balls. Cameramen were told not to record him doing that.

He created a regional TV show called *Antioquía Everyday*, which broadcast daily at 12:30 PM. After his staff interviewed Pablo Peláez, a mayor from the aristocracy who lambasted the traffickers, Pablo said, "Do not give screen time to my enemies," and ordered the mayor's execution. He funded a children's programme called *Small People*, which emphasised education, ecology and social commitment. Gustavo's teenage son introduced the show, which gave away prizes such as bicycles from Roberto's factory.

The producer of *Antioquía Everyday* brought the most advanced technology to Nápoles. "Can you organise the equipment a little bit so I can see it working?" Pablo said. The producer recorded the animals and landscape around Nápoles. After watching the beautiful scenes, Pablo said, "We should make a documentary series about the flora and fauna of the region."

"But who will be our guide?"

"I will," he said. "Let's start tomorrow at 4 AM, so no partying tonight." After going to bed uncharacteristically early, he was ready at 4 AM. With ease and without bodyguards, he led the producer and an assistant on a labyrinthine journey through the jungle. When the nature documentary was finished, he proudly showed it to his friends.

In early 1983, Pablo invited Virginia to two anti-extradition meetings. The first was at Kevin's Disco in Medellín, and at the second in Barranquilla she would meet some of his most important associates and supporters, who were presently the richest men in Colombia. Combined, they would defeat extradition even if they had to use force. She told him to read I *Art of War* by Sun Tzu because he was impatient and had a tendency to attack uphill.

"When it comes to strategy, I adapt to the moment," he said. After asking her to guess the alias he had instructed his men to use for her, he revealed it was President Belisario Betancur and laughed.

At the first Forum Against Extradition, he sat at the main table next to a priest and Virginia. As if rousing the audience to go to war, he attacked Galán for removing him from his movement and pushing for extradition. Magistrates were present and an ex-Supreme Court judge lambasted the treaty signed by President Turbay. Anti-extradition graffiti appeared in the cities. In Bogotá, there was a big demonstration in the Plaza de Bolívar.

The media published photos of Pablo and Virginia at the

meeting. In April 1983, *Semana* used one in an article that branded him as "A Paisa Robin Hood." It stated: "Just saying his name produces a mix of reactions ranging from explosive joy to deep fear, from great admiration to cautious contempt. But no one is indifferent to the name Pablo Escobar." After reading it, he told his wife that he wished he were Robin Hood, so that he could do even more for the poor.

After discussing the article with his advisers, he left the room and one said, "Definitely he thinks he will be the president of the republic." He told one of his military chiefs that he would appoint him as the Minister of Defence.

He told *Semana*, "When I was sixteen, I owned a bicycle-rental business ... then I started buying and selling automobiles, and finally I got involved in real estate ... I didn't have any money, but as a community action member in my barrio, I promoted the construction of a school and the creation of a fund for indigent students."

The media published a survey of the three most famous people in the world: Pope John Paul II, President Ronald Reagan and Pablo Escobar.

The media was not invited to the second Forum Against Extradition in Barranquilla. Pablo and Virginia stayed in a presidential suite and travelled to the mansion hosting the meeting. He told her that most of the attendees were MAS members. "The poorest have only $10 million." He boasted that his combine controlled several billion and she was about to witness a war declaration.

At the mansion, he offered to sit her at the main table overlooking 400 men on the verge of bathing the country in blood. She agreed, hoping to gauge their opinion of Pablo from their faces. The aggressive speeches and reactions disturbed Virginia, who feared for Colombia. After he had spoken, many congratulated Pablo.

Some questioned Virginia disparagingly and joked about using cocaine money to get a TV star. An old cowboy said that as a conservative he would never vote for Santo and that Pablo was a Johnny-come-lately who shouldn't be issuing orders. One said that she was unaware of his history as a triggerman with over 200 murders.

After the dissenters had dispersed, an old man praised Pablo and Lehder for going after the guerrillas because the FARC still had his son, whom they had kidnapped over three years previously. Virginia saw Gacha amid his emerald associates, whom the majority of the attendees praised and congratulated.

Back at the presidential suite, she said, "The right-wingers don't trust a Liberal like Santo." He responded that they would all run to him in the event their family members were kidnapped.

Pablo finally visited Virginia at her apartment in Bogotá. Unfortunately, he brought more bodyguards than her elevator could hold, so several elevator trips were required. Upset by the presence of so many strangers, she set a precedent whereby he could only enter her house on his own. He agreed and at other locations, he ordered his bodyguards to disappear before she arrived.

While Pablo's star was rising with Virginia's media assistance, the reign of the old bosses ended abruptly. The Godfather was walking down a street in Medellín when he had a heart attack and died. The King of Marlboro was flying over his farm in Caucasia when his plane exploded. Arrested in America, Griselda Blanco would end up serving almost twenty years.

With the demand for cocaine increasing, Pablo employed new methods to increase productivity. Installing dryers in Bolivia helped to reduce the bulk so that more could be transported. After cocaine base became harder to source from Peru and Bolivia, the crop was planted in the Colombian Amazon and Orinoquía natural region. The unemployed flocked to the jungles to make fortunes from cocaine, including peasant farmers who had gone bankrupt after the collapse of the coffee market and the poor from the cities who were tired of living at subsistence level. The traffickers gave them technical advice, credit and marketing systems.

New towns and settlements flourished in areas over which the central powers had no control, and the guerrillas operated as the local government.

As the cocaine economy spread throughout the jungles, more labs were introduced, including Tranquilandia, the largest and most sophisticated complex of labs so far, financed by Gacha, the Ochoas, Pablo Correa and other traffickers. The initial workforce arrived in helicopters on a small area cleared of jungle. When they had sufficient equipment, a landing strip was made for small planes. The lab employed a massive workforce ranging from cocaine cooks to kitchen staff, and required vast quantities of chemicals, including ether. The traffickers hoped that the Tranquilandia would produce a chunk of the tons of cocaine consumed yearly by approximately five million Americans.

CHAPTER 22

POLITICAL ENEMIES

At a meeting, Virginia overheard Pablo and Santo discussing getting Galán out of the way of their rise to power. They viewed Galán as a traitor willing to hand over Colombians to imperialist America. Still aggrieved by Galán, Pablo sought to undermine the charismatic founder of New Liberalism and his ally, Senator Lara Bonilla. With Galán gone, Santo could be the president in 1986 and Pablo in 1990.

One of Pablo's associates, Evaristo Porras – who had been incarcerated for trafficking – led Lara into believing that he was a legitimate businessman who supported Galán. Armed with a recording device, he met Lara in a room at the Bogotá Hilton, where he wrote a cheque. Although the conversation hadn't been recorded properly, Lara had taken drug money. Anticipating that Lara and Galán would obstruct his rise, Pablo kept the incident a secret for future use.

At Pablo's house, Virginia met Evaristo Porras, who was so high on cocaine that his rapidly moving jaw had taken on a life of its own. In private, Porras handed Pablo a tape recording. The boss reprimanded him for being too high and instructed him to return to his hotel room.

"We need to watch this video together," Pablo told Virginia. "I'm going to need an urgent favour from you." They went to his study. "Evaristo Porras is protecting our interests in Leticia by the Amazon River, which has become increasingly important as a transshipment point for paste coming from Peru and Bolivia. Evaristo has won the lottery three times and is known as the world's luckiest man. At least, that's where he tells the taxman his wealth came from."

The dark blurred video showed Porras with a young man talking incoherently about agriculture. "That's Rodrigo Lara Bonilla, Luis Carlos Galán's right-hand man. Bonilla is taking a cheque for a million pesos as a bribe. This is a carefully arranged trap I coordinated with Porras and the cameraman." After the tape had finished, he said, "I need you to denounce Lara Bonilla on TV."

"I absolutely and categorically cannot do that!" She said that Santo had received even more money from him, so she would have to denounce Santo and the rest of his cronies in Congress, including Jairo Ortega. Having received so much slander over the years, she would never use her platform to hurt anybody. She couldn't tell from the video that Lara had been bribed because it didn't show whether he had a legitimate business relationship with Porras. She had no problem promoting his social projects, but he needed to find somebody else to do his dirty work. If everybody obsessed about eliminating their enemies, there would be nobody left in the world. His quest for vengeance would destroy his soul.

Pablo had been gazing down in silence for a long time, a trait that was starting to perplex and disturb Virginia, who often worried that she may have crossed a line. Snapping out of his trance, he jumped up, grabbed Virginia, kissed her forehead and rubbed her back. "I need you at my side for so many things. I don't want to lose you." He apologised and said she was right.

Downstairs, they found Santo and a woman reciting love poetry. Virginia made up a poem about using Pablo for the twenty-four wings on his aircraft. He responded by writing a poem about when he didn't call her or see her, he hoped she would know he was missing her. Disturbed by his overuse of the word don't, she smiled and thanked him.

He said he had to depart for a meeting with ex-president Alfonso López Michelsen. He showed her a cheque for $600,000 payable to Ernesto Samper Pizano, the head of the presidential campaign for López. He said that was the price for the country's most powerful, intelligent and experienced president, who was opposed to extradition. She said that López should have asked for $3 million. He responded that $600,000 was just a down payment, and that he was also backing Ernesto Samper Pizano as a future president.

Pablo introduced Virginia to Alvaro Uribe Velez, who as the director of the Civil Aviation Agency, obtained licences for El Patrón and his associates to build landing strips, without which they would have been stuck smuggling cocaine in car tyres. He predicted that the 31-year-old would eventually make it to the Senate, and that if he or Santo failed to become the president, they would both back Alvaro Uribe Velez. His prophecy came true after his death: Alvaro Uribe Velez became the Colombian president on August 7, 2002.

In June 1983, the FARC targeted the family of Alvaro Uribe Velez for kidnapping. During the attempt, his father died and his brother was injured. Pablo's helicopter transported the corpse back to Medellín. Saddened by his friend's loss, Pablo admitted to Virginia that although trafficking was a gold mine, only tough guys could handle the business because it produced so many corpses. If anything happened to him, he wanted her to tell his story.

He set her literary challenges, including writing about what she saw and felt at the dump, to describe how she felt when they were making love and to write how she would feel if he died. Her six pages on the first were so visceral that he was nauseated. The five and a half pages on the second almost made him want to be a woman. He believed that the seven pages on the third would make his mother weep until she died.

She advised him to listen to speeches by Jorge Eliécer Gaitán, the presidential candidate whose assassination had sparked The Violence. She believed the content and tone would help him. Her great uncle had been next to Gaitán during the assassination. She asked Gaitán's daughter Gloria for the speeches for Pablo and explained why. Gloria travelled to Medellín and chatted with Virginia and Pablo for hours, mostly about politics and the absence of a real leader to fill her father's shoes.

"What do you think of Pablo?" Virginia asked on the flight back to Bogotá. Gloria disliked his habit of gazing at the floor while talking to you, which meant he was lying or hiding something. When asked by Pablo what Gloria thought of him, Virginia lied in the hope of keeping him inspired.

While Pablo continued to make public appearances – at a soccer game, he performed the opening kick in front of 12,000 people – he had underestimated the growing threat from the Reagan-Bush administration.

In 1982, President Reagan announced, "My very reason for being here this afternoon is not to announce another short-term government offensive, but to call instead for a national crusade against drugs, a sustained relentless effort to rid America of this scourge by mobilising every segment of our society against drug abuse."

The Reagan-Bush administration tried to link the FARC guerrillas with cannabis trafficking and called them narco-terrorists, but the Colombians were sceptical. President Betancur was upset with the Americans for disturbing the peace negotiations with the guerrillas. The Americans changed their strategy: they searched for a politician amenable to their foreign-policy goals. They settled on Lara Bonilla, the new justice minister. By offering help and support, the DEA in Colombia encouraged him to pursue the traffickers.

Before Lara's appointment, the traffickers believed that nationalism and fear would prevent extradition from being applied. In his opening speech as the justice minister – an appointment that was viewed as a betrayal of the traffickers by Betancur – Lara criticised Pablo and his associates, who were laundering money through soccer clubs. Having decided that it was almost time to reveal the cheque that Lara had accepted, Pablo challenged the justice minister to a debate on dirty money.

On the day of the debate, copies of the cheque were circulated throughout the Chamber of Representatives, which was packed with spectators, reporters and photographers. Even the hallways were crowded with people hyped-up about a confrontation between Lara and the traffickers. Having spent the night in the presidential suite at the Tequendama Hotel in Bogotá, Lehder arrived with his ex-police bodyguards. Denied access to the floor of Congress, they went upstairs to the press gallery.

Having spent the night in the presidential suite at the Hilton Hotel, El Patrón arrived. People watched closely as he sat quietly in a swivel leather chair at the side of the oval room. The house president requested the removal of his bodyguards. Pablo gave a nod and they left. His ally, Ortega, started to address the allegations of taking hot money from the traffickers. He asked Lara if he knew Evaristo Porras.

"No," Lara said, shaking his head.

Ortega said that Evaristo Porras – a resident of the Amazon border town of Leticia – had been incarcerated in Peru for drug trafficking. In April, Porras had written a cheque for one million pesos to Lara as a campaign contribution. Holding up the cheque, he added that Lara had thanked Porras for the cheque in a phone call. Ortega produced a tape recorder and played the unintelligible conversation.

"Let the Congress analyse the minister's conduct with this person who offered him a million pesos. Mr Porras is a recognised international drug trafficker, according to Peruvian police. But far be it from me to try to detain the minister of justice's brilliant political career. I only want him to tell us what kind of morality he is going to require of the rest of us. Relax, Minister, just let the country know that your morality can't be any different from that of Jairo Ortega and the rest of us."

Cheering erupted in the gallery from Lehder and his men, who mocked and cast murderous gazes at the journalists attempting to hush them. Pablo watched quietly, occasionally picking his teeth or forcing an uncomfortable smile.

Thirty-five-year-old Lara stood to respond in a business suit and tie, his thick dark hair swept aside, his charming face clean-shaven. Not in the habit of scrutinising the origin of incoming donations, he'd never heard of Mr Porras, nor could he recall any such conversation. "My life is an open book." He said that he was and always had been blameless, rendering him impervious to his enemies' claims. He would resign any moment that suspicion fell upon him, "knowing that I will not be followed by complacent ministers affected by the blackmail and the extortion being perpetrated against Colombia's political class." He damned the act of casting suspicion on the alleged recipients of the money as opposed to its senders, including "those, who, yes, have to explain here or anywhere else in this country where their fortunes have come from ... Morality is one thing, but there are levels: one thing is the cheques ... that they use to throw mud at politicians. But it's another thing when somebody runs a campaign exclusively with these funds." He pointed an accusatory finger.

"[We have] a congressman [Pablo] who was born in a very poor area, himself very, very poor, and afterwards, through astute business deals in bicycles and other things, appears with a gigantic fortune, with nine planes, three hangars at the Medellín airport, and creates the movement Death to Kidnappers, while on the other hand, he creates charitable organisations with which he tries to bribe a needy and unprotected people. And there are investigations going on in the US, of which I cannot inform you here tonight in the House, on the criminal conduct of Mr Ortega's alternate."

Claiming that all of them were guilty of receiving tainted contributions, some of the respondents defended Pablo, whom they said had been attacked for the sole purpose of providing Lara with political capital. "It was only when Representative Escobar joined our movement that all kinds of suspicion were thrown on the sources of his wealth," a congressman said. "I, as a politician, lack the ability to investigate the origin of any assets ... Representative Escobar has no need to rely on others to defend his personal conduct, which, on the other hand, and as far as I know, has not been subjected to any action by the law or the government."

Simmering inside, Pablo kept quiet. Re-joining his body-guards, he left the Chamber and walked into a swarm of report-ers, whom he tried to dodge. At home, his mother-in-law Nora criticised him for swishing a tail made of straw by a candle. His reassurances that nothing bad would happen failed to convince her. She said that he was too hard-headed and had failed to prioritise his family. Lara appeared on the news criticising Pablo, who yelled at the TV.

"The country must know the reality," he said, surrounded by journalists thrusting microphones at his face, "about certain pow-erful capitalists who thought that patrimonial amnesty implied the pardon of the felonies they have committed to make their fantastic fortunes."

Responding on TV, Pablo said, "I want to inform the public ... that [Lara] has twenty-four hours to present concrete evidence that supports the accusations made yesterday in the Chamber of Representatives ... I'm not looking for a confrontation among the Colombian people. I seek peace and I've always wanted peace."

Lara was notified that he had a day to back up his claims or else be sued. While he set about gathering evidence, he issued statements criticising drug trafficking, which necessitated "a frontal fight, clear, open, without fear or retreat, running all the necessary risks." He classified the allegations of the cheque he'd received from Porras as a smokescreen.

Pablo arrived home to find Victoria watching Lara on the news: "My accusers could not forgive the clarity of my denun-ciation of Pablo Escobar, who through clever business deals has manufactured an enormous fortune ... This is an economic power concentrated in a few hands and in criminal minds. What they cannot obtain by blackmail, they get by murder."

"Don't watch this!" He marched to the TV and turned it off.

The media contacted Porras, who acknowledged donating a million pesos to Lara and admitted that he had been indicted by the Peruvian police for trafficking, which he blamed on a youthful indiscretion. Working in the coca-leaf business for Pablo, Porras claimed that his wealth had originated from winning the lottery three times. Faced with Porras's testimony, Lara admitted receiving the cheque, which he said had been for a family debt. At Pablo's request, a judge initiated an investigation into the cheque. Lara was on the verge of losing his job.

"[Lara] has lied to the country about six times," Pablo said on TV. "First, he lied when he said he didn't know Evaristo Porras. Second, he lied when he said he hadn't received any cheques from Evaristo Porras. Third, he lied when he said Pablo Escobar was the founder of the MAS. Fourth, he lied when he said Pablo Escobar had a criminal record in the US. He also lied when he used Mr Bahamón's letter, a naïve letter that has weak arguments. You get a cheque for one million pesos, and you don't know it's written in your name. It's a weak argument. And finally, [Lara] lied when he said he wasn't going to quit. We'll see what happens in the next few days."

Confident of discrediting the justice minister, Pablo granted an interview with the journalist and author Germán Castro Caycedo, who arrived one sunny morning at a villa in El Poblado, with an indoor meadow surrounding a pool, a TV studio and a room with video-editing equipment. The several minutes of news produced at the villa was broadcast in Telediario, the newscast of Arturo Abella. To soften the light, the journalist and his cameraman set up their equipment under vegetation. Pablo arrived smiling slyly and dressed casually, wearing long white socks and dark shoes with one shoelace brown and the other black. After the interview, he told the journalist to stay in Medellín because he wanted to show him something that the country had not seen. If staying in Medellín disrupted his travel plans, Pablo's personal planes would be at his service the next day.

In a green Renault 18, Pablo collected the journalist from his hotel at 7 PM. The driver took them to a poor neighbourhood in north-eastern Medellín. Entering an unlit football stadium packed with young people, Pablo said, "The capacity is 6,000."

When the journalist was ready to film, a speaker announced the arrival of "El Patrón," who in the unlit stadium had walked through darkness to the middle of the pitch. Fireworks exploded and powerful lamps started to blanket the sides of the stadium with white light, until the whole area was radiantly clear and the crowd was yelling with all of its might, "*Paaaablo! Paaaablo! Paaaablo!*"

A few hours later, Pablo told the journalist, "This is the tenth pitch I've brought real stadium lighting. I give the plans, calculations, sand, cement, iron, towers, reflectors, drainage, grass and they do the work."

"How do the authorities react to this?"

"They don't say anything. I imagine they're happy because I'm doing part of their work."

Pablo told Virginia to go on a shopping spree in New York, but she was nervous about transporting cash. He said that Uncle Sam always welcomed money entering America and only restricted money going out. Having flown to Washington with $1 million in a briefcase, the US authorities had assigned him a police escort to get him safely to a bank to make a deposit; however, if you tried to take money out of the country, you would end up with a life sentence because it was considered more serious than trafficking.

She travelled with four Kleenex boxes containing $10,000, each in a separate piece of luggage or carry-on. When Customs asked whether she had robbed a bank, she said she had bought the dollars on the black market, which is customary in Latin America, and pointed out that she was a famous TV journalist on numerous magazine covers. They let her through.

In July, Lehder gave a radio interview. He said he had bought Norman's Cay for over $1 million, which had benefited the

Colombian bonanza – his euphemism for the billions in drug money that had flown back to Colombia. Due to his land next to America, he had become a transportation specialist. He claimed to have spent time in an American prison for being a Latin neighbourhood leader, who had defended his race, principles and country. He aimed to become a senator to represent the poorest of the poor, unions and Colombians at risk of extradition.

Pablo visited his men in La Estrella, who were waiting to play football with him. As a forward, he kept leaving the pitch for business phone calls, and the game lasted for three hours. After the game, prostitutes arrived and a party began. Sitting in a corner, he observed his subjects like a king until one of them announced that ABC News had broadcast a TV programme about Colombia's biggest traffickers, and claimed that he was a drug lord with a net worth over $2 billion. With men gathering around, he said, "There are many bastards who are talking bad about us. They better expect consequences."

The following day, he announced that he would sue the TV network: "We will end once and for all the slander they are doing, not only in Colombia, but also abroad. I have no records of any drug trafficking, not in the US nor in this country."

In late August 1983, Guillermo Cano, the stately grey-haired son of the founder of the newspaper *The Spectator*, saw Pablo on TV and said to his staff, "I know that guy. I've seen a mugshot of him. He was in prison. He was involved in drug trafficking. Let's look into it." Delving into the newspaper's archive produced a story about his arrest for cocaine in 1976, including his mugshot. Cano called Lara, and said that he was going to publish the story the next day.

On August 25, *The Spectator* ran the story and printed mugshots of Gustavo and Pablo – with his infamous smile. Next to the photo it read: "This is Pablo Escobar with cocaine! And this same person is in Congress?" Cano wrote: "The substitute representative to the Chamber for [Santo], Pablo Escobar Gaviria, is among the six individuals captured on June 9, 1976 in the Antioquia town of Itagui with a shipment of 39 pounds of cocaine as the culmination of an operation set up by the DAS section of Antioquia."

Seeing his mugshot, El Patrón dropped his usual calm and grimaced. The destruction of his criminal record by the secret police and the murders of the policemen investigating the case were meant to have prevented his cocaine arrest from resurfacing, but he had forgotten about the newspaper's archive. Enraged and after being chastised by his mother, he told his men, "Whatever it takes, leave not a single copy." A flyer was distributed that read: "If you love Magdalena Medio do not buy *The Spectator*." But his men racing around in vans buying copies only attracted more attention.

The fiasco reminded Pablo of Judge Espinosa, whom he had condemned to walk to work by destroying any car that she purchased. Her courtroom in the National Palace was firebombed and reduced to ashes.

To capitalise on the buzz, *The Spectator* published daily stories about him and the rest of the media joined in. They described how he had played the system by having his case transferred to various courts and judges, and how all of his criminal records had disappeared. The exposure led to an investigation into the murders of the policemen.

When Virginia's business partner at the TV company learned about Pablo's murderous past, she destroyed the film of the dump, had her boyfriend purchase the production company and ostracised Pablo and Virginia.

In his editorials, Cano relentlessly attacked the traffickers:

"We are facing an open challenge where drugs – cocaine and cannabis and their juicy economic dividends – are trying to convert themselves into the opium of Colombian politics."

"How shameful! It terrifies us to think that the country has been degraded to the point that in a much-needed debate in defence of morality and democratic institutions, the conclusion is not the unmasking of the sinister criminals, so they receive the punishment their evil deeds deserve, but they end up being the good guys of the movie and the others the bad guys."

Lara obtained a recording of the DEA-assisted ABC News documentary and played it in Congress. While casting Lara a death stare, Pablo accused the justice minister of slander and demanded proof of the allegations. Rebutting Lara's accusations in an interview, Pablo said that his money came from construction. While denying that he was a trafficker, he extolled the benefits that trafficking had brought Colombia, such as creating jobs and providing capital for numerous projects that had contributed to economic growth. He lambasted Lara for becoming an instrument of US foreign policy. Lara held his ground. He detailed how the traffickers had financed Colombia's main soccer teams. He tried to cancel the licences for 300 small planes they owned. He attempted to confiscate Pablo's zoo animals and named thirty politicians he believed had taken drug money.

Due to the proliferation of the accusations against him, Pablo had to hide and was wary of talking on telephone lines that had been bugged. Only able to see Virginia less frequently and with complex planning, he told her that his life had been full of challenges, so recent events were normal. His relaxed nature, his ability to strategise and his unlimited resources instilled her with confidence.

Eavesdropping on conversations, she learned about Santo's power over Pablo. The politician was urging the boss to sever the heads of his most visible enemies. El Patrón responded that he was going to give them a lot of lead until they learned to respect him. Speaking in private, Santo urged Virginia to have Pablo increase his political contributions because their level was insufficient to gain the presidency, and only with him in power would extradition and Pablo's past be suppressed. She held a cocktail fundraiser for Santo in Bogotá, which the politician only attended briefly without even thanking her. She complained to Pablo that Santo was classless, ungrateful and was taking advantage of his idealism. On tour in the Department of Tolima, the politician had embraced Virginia in a sleazy way to show off to his local leaders. She felt that he didn't have the best interests of the country at heart and would double-cross Pablo. Her image had been damaged enough because she was helping Pablo.

Pablo stood silent, sat down and rested his head in his hands with his elbows on his knees. Gazing at the floor, he spoke slowly and dispassionately about how upset he was by what Virginia had said, but that Santo was his bridge to the political class, including ex-president López, and sections of the Army and security organisations. That Santo lacked scruples made him invaluable.

His answer shattered Virginia and she sobbed. She wanted to know if Santo's sleazy embrace meant it was time for her to consider other options. Pablo said they were both free to consider any options they wanted. Seized by jealousy, she lost control and started punching the air, while yelling at him for being a scoundrel. When she decided to trade him in, she said it wouldn't be for an ungrateful pig like Santo. She had dated the wealthiest and handsomest men in Colombia. She would trade him in for a president or a dictator.

He laughed hysterically, grabbed her arms to prevent her punches from landing, wrapped them around her neck and grabbed her waist. He said her future husband would inevitably need him to bankroll his presidential campaign, and when she collected the cash from him they would have endless sex. Also, there were only two Colombians as wealthy as him: Jorge Ochoa and Gacha. He was her only option, and she was his because nobody could make him laugh hysterically. He didn't believe she would abandon him when powerful interests had started a hunt that could end with his death. If she loved him, she would not trade him in for 100 years or at least seventy. Wiping tears away, she pledged to trade him in within ten and on her next shopping trip she would buy everything on Fifth Avenue. After hearing that she would never help Santo campaign again, he said that was fine as long as she was never absent from his bed.

In September 1983, Victoria told Pablo that she was pregnant. After six years of trying for a second child – that included three miscarriages and an ectopic pregnancy – the news was welcomed by Pablo, who was still under political attack. His spirits soon fell after the media reported his affair with Virginia, even claiming that he intended to marry her. After hearing this, Victoria grew hysterical. Yelling, she banished Pablo from the house.

For three weeks, Pablo sent her flowers and called every day, insisting that she was the only woman he loved. Jealous people were out to destroy their marriage. He wanted to go home and spend the rest of his life with her. In a card, he wrote that he would never trade her for anybody. "Don't worry," Victoria said on the phone. "I'm not the only mother without a husband by her side. I think we should go our separate ways." On a Sunday night, he showed up with a sad expression and they reunited.

Lehder continued to challenge the authorities: "They say I conspired against the US. I would say not only did I conspire, I will also conspire until the extradition treaty is cancelled." He said that a government official had requested $380,000 to get rid of his extradition request. The next day, the corpse of the official was discovered, and the cause of death determined as poisoning.

On a mission to clear his name after the cheque scandal, Lara pursued the traffickers with a suicidal zeal. "I know what awaits me when I denounce the gangsters, but that does not scare me and if I have to pay with my life, so be it. My mission is to help the country to have prompt and effective justice and not let myself get entangled in nonsense. It has happened that those individuals are enriching themselves overnight, claiming that there is no proof, but dare to come to Congress. This is unacceptable and it is my duty to inform if this happens."

Although Lara wanted to get an extradition order issued for Lehder, the attorney general had prevented it by classifying the extradition treaty as unconstitutional, and Betancur had agreed with his attorney general. But on September 2, 1983, the Supreme

Court ruled in favour of extradition, and an arrest warrant for Lehder was issued.

Having disappeared, Lehder claimed he had seen it coming, "because my friends in the Ministry of Justice alerted me regarding Lara Bonilla's intentions." He told reporters that the only way he would be extradited was over his dead body.

His extradition order was signed by Lara, who forwarded it to Betancur for approval. Having been indicted in Florida, Lehder was at risk if he left Colombia and ended up in a country with a bilateral extradition treaty with America. Aware of the trouble brewing, Lehder had tried to broker a deal with America, whereby he had offered to sell Norman's Cay for $5 million to the US for the purposes of building a military base provided that his Florida indictment was dropped. The US rejected the deal.

With his problems multiplying, and after consulting an adviser, Pablo told the media that he had no problems with the US justice system. Proudly, he displayed his passport with a visa he had recently obtained from the US Embassy. On September 8, the US Embassy cancelled his visa and the Tenth Superior Judge of Medellín issued an arrest warrant for him for conspiracy to murder the DAS agents who had arrested him in 1976. As well as the two shot in the head by him in 1977, the officer in charge had been assassinated by men on motorbikes in 1981. In his early 40s, bespectacled Judge Zuluaga was a fierce opponent of corruption, who had difficulty walking due to physical weakness. He told his secretary about indicting Pablo, "I just signed this. I put myself in the hands of God because I may be signing my own death sentence, but justice is above men."

Arriving at the court to be notified of the judicial decision, Pablo had so many bodyguards and supporters that Carabobo Street had to be closed. It was a show of strength to the judge, but Lara had guaranteed Zuluaga the government's full support and encouraged him to demonstrate a patriotic spirit. Pablo left the courtroom convinced that the judge's decision was based on currying favour with Lara in the hope of receiving a promotion.

With his association with Pablo harming his presidential prospects, Santo decided that it was best to only work with him in private, while giving the impression that they had parted ways. On September 10, Pablo was removed from his list of supporters and he made a public statement requesting that Pablo retire from politics, forsake his parliamentary immunity, respond to the charges against him and clear up the controversy. Santo travelled from Bogotá to Medellín to ask him to sign a letter of resignation from his movement. Finding the letter already written, Pablo yelled, "I'm the one who writes the letters, Dr Santo!"

On September 11, Pablo announced that his association with Santo had ended and that he had only entered politics eighteen months ago because inside of the government was the best place to serve the community. If the community was turning its back on him, he would return the favour. He refused to forsake his parliamentary immunity and congressional seat. Lara demanded that Congress remove Pablo's immunity from extradition.

The newspapers reported his 1974 car-theft indictment, while championing Lara. *The Time* quoted the US ambassador to Colombia: "How is democracy going to continue in Colombia if it is managed and manipulated by these criminals?" He praised Lara and criticised the penetration of narcotics money into politics.

With the media spotlight on their activity, the traffickers, including Pablo and Gacha, showed up at the attorney general's office and demanded to see Carlos Jiménez Gómez. They asked whether peace could be achieved by the government allowing them to reintegrate into civil life. After a series of meetings, *Semana* reported:

"The Procurator General of the Nation, Carlos Jiménez Gómez, recently carried out intense efforts in the name of peace, in front of the country's great narco-traffickers. The result of these interviews was a kind of 'agreed peace' in which the total withdrawal of drug traffickers from political activity was agreed, starting with the dismantling of the civic movements of Pablo Escobar …"

Over lunch, President Betancur told the author Gabriel García Márquez, "We are not only going to negotiate peace with the guerrillas, but also with the drug traffickers. They themselves are proposing it."

But as negotiations progressed, Lara was relentless. In October, he claimed that the traffickers owned six of the nine professional soccer teams, and named Gacha, Hernan Botero, and the Cali godfather Gilberto. *The Spectator* printed a complete list with more names. The Supreme Court ruled in favour of the extradition of two cannabis traffickers. Lara signed the paperwork, but the president referred it to the Colombian courts. Lehder's extradition order remained unsigned. On November 17, 1983, Lara fined Pablo 450,000 pesos for the illegal importation of eighty-five animals, including camels, elephants, elk and a large Amazonian rodent called a capybara.

The evidence against Pablo was so overwhelming that there was nothing he could do to salvage his political career. In early January 1984, he asked Virginia for advice about retiring from politics. She said that would be like surrendering to Lara. He should attack extradition head on and start to finance social projects in Bogotá to raise his popularity in the capital.

He explained that although his public support of Santo was over, they were still working together behind the scenes. To bring down extradition, Santo was more indispensable than ever. With Lehder getting addicted to cocaine, Norman's Cay and the Bahamian president were in jeopardy. With so many problems, Pablo needed to milk his business dry and only then could he think about retiring. After weathering the storm, he could return to Congress. Due to his foresight, he knew which problems were coming months in advance, which enabled him to prepare solutions. Money could fix anything in the world except for his own death.

On January 20, 1984, he submitted a letter of resignation:

"I make public my definitive and total withdrawal from politics, a decision that I adopted since September last year, which is unchangeable and I ratify it despite the large votes of solidarity that have come to me from all the municipalities and neighbourhoods. I will continue in a frank struggle against the oligarchies and injustice, and against the partisan councils, authors of the eternal drama of ridicule to the people – and the politicians: indolent in essence before the pain of the neighbour and always careerists when it is about their bureaucracies, which is why I feel the depressing contrast of those who have nothing compared to those who only understand an exclusive currency of their lives through the accumulation of capital opportunities and cannot see the fulfilling of any social function. There is an enormous difference between my seventeen years of hard and relentless civic struggle compared to the months of my active participation in politics, to which I gave myself fully thinking that through it could be channelled many factors and resources in favour of the people. And so I have finally concluded that the popular constraints and ailments [of the people] are disconnected from the priorities of politicians whose selfish views are only fixed on retouching their deteriorated narcissistic images and increasing their rotten feuds."

Regrouping at Hacienda Nápoles, he assumed that his resignation would reduce the backlash against him, but things had misfired so badly that the media was exposing his cocaine business. He couldn't understand why he had been declared an outlaw while those with official power, also full of sins, had nothing to fear. He blamed Lara's stubbornness and the evil spirit of the politicians who had taken his money and betrayed him. He would never trust them again.

Santo suggested that Pablo help him progress, so that the power could be shared. "Don't you worry, Pablo," he said. "I'll be in charge of politics and you'll get the benefits."

According to Popeye, who was present at meetings, Santo wanted Pablo to eliminate his competition by any means, including murder. If Santo became the president, the traffickers' best interests would be served, including non-extradition.

On February 9, 1984, Kevin's Disco hosted the baptism party

for the son of one of Jorge Ochoa's cocaine distributors. With plenty of champagne and quail eggs dipped in honey, the cartel leaders and 2,000 guests celebrated Jorge becoming the child's godfather. Over the course of the week, the bosses discussed their problems.

Jorge Ochoa stated that kilos of cocaine airdropped onto the water for speedboat collection were getting wet and ruined, which required new waterproof packaging. With record amounts of cocaine getting produced by the jungle labs, almost 4,000 kilos a month, he suggested that they adopt better transportation methods. He wanted to transport 2,000 kilos weekly.

On February 13, 1984, after an arrest warrant for Pablo was withdrawn, he stated that unless extradition was abolished, he and Lehder would close 1,500 businesses, which would create 20,000 unemployed. On March 2, he publicly criticised Lara for working for the US, and he blamed the Medellín municipal government for turning off the lights in his soccer stadiums.

While Lara was in a meeting with the DEA, one of his aides interrupted because there was so much whistling on his telephone he could not be heard. The aide claimed that not only was his office phone bugged, but also his home.

After a politician pushing for Pablo's extradition was murdered, Lara made an announcement that upset the traffickers: "The more I learn, the more I know of the damage that the narcos are causing this country. I will never again refuse the extradition of one of these dogs. So long as Colombian judges fear drug traffickers, the narcos will only fear judges in the US."

Lara suspected that he was being shadowed. When he answered his phone, his own conversations were played back. He rebuffed offers of large sums of money. The death threats increased. He hit back by having his friend and colleague, Colonel Ramírez, the head of anti-narcotics, go after the traffickers. He told Ramírez that he wanted to know everything about the traffickers because they were capable of doing anything. Ramírez launched raids across the country. As many of Lara's previous attacks on the traffickers had been fuelled with information provided by Ramírez, the colonel was starting to appear on Pablo's radar as a threat.

CHAPTER 23

SIGNS OF WAR

Pablo and Virginia's relationship entered a blissful period, but a threat arose when the Cali godfather Gilberto expressed interest in her. The two bosses shared similar backgrounds. The Violence that had consumed Colombia had displaced not only Pablo's family, but also Gilberto's. Raised in Tolima, a coffee and rice area, his family had fled to the Valle del Cauca, a sugar area. Both bosses had parlayed money from kidnapping into cocaine. In his region, Gilberto controlled all of the authorities, from the police to the Army.

Known as the Chess Player due to his long-range strategic thinking, Gilberto was the Cali Cartel's mastermind, which was run by four bosses, including his brother Miguel, and also Chepe and Pacho. With Cali just over seventy miles from the western port of Buenaventura, it was ideally placed to ship cocaine north to America. As well as having a geographic advantage, Gilberto preferred bribery over bullets. His business empire included hundreds of drugstores, which camouflaged the illegal activity. For money-laundering, he owned and invested in banks.

Many reasons have been cited for the war between the Medellín and Cali Cartels. With business and egos expanding, Gilberto's attempt to romance Virginia would aggravate Pablo, and send a signal about his rival's self-confidence. It was the beginning of a chain of events that would culminate with them attempting to kill each other.

Virginia worked for a radio station owned by the Orejuela brothers, Gilberto and Miguel. Meeting Gilberto and his present

175

wife, she found the boss to be polite, sophisticated and unimposing, whereas his tall wife with eagle eyes was bossy and jealous. In contrast to Pablo's deadly aura, Gilberto had the air of a professor.

On a phone call, Gilberto asked Virginia to join him at a bullfight, after which, his wife called Virginia demanding an explanation. She said she had attended in her official capacity as a sports commentator and international editor for the radio station, and the next time this happened, she should remind her husband to invite his wife, too. She stopped short of rubbing in Pablo's dominance in the cocaine business.

Her TV shows were drawing record viewers. *Show of the Stars* went out at 8 PM on Saturdays and was broadcast in several countries. Her other main programme *Monday Magazine* was the biggest competitor of the news show hosted by Andres Pastrana, whom Pablo would eventually kidnap. A rumour that Andres was losing viewers because Virginia crossed her legs in a seductive fashion prompted Di Lido Stockings to ask her to do a second commercial in Venice.

When Pablo showed up unannounced at her apartment, she was alarmed. Due to the raids by Colonel Ramírez, he said he had to leave the country in a hurry to make arrangements in Panama and Nicaragua. He hoped to be gone for a week, and when he returned, he'd take her to Cuba to meet Fidel Castro. He told her not to be sad and to go shopping in New York.

He did not reveal that he had drawn up a hit list. After its implementation, the government's response would exceed anything previously experienced by the traffickers. To protect his business from getting dismantled, he aimed to diversify the production of cocaine into countries such as Panama, Cuba and Nicaragua by leveraging relationships he had established with powerful people in those countries through his contacts with the M-19.

After he returned, one of Virginia's friends joked that she should have a child with him. After hearing the joke, he sat quietly and decided to tell her the story of Wendy Chavarriaga, the woman he loved before he had met Virginia. Whenever Wendy suspected he had been with another woman, she crashed her car into his, cut down doors with a chainsaw, attacked him with a hammer and threatened to kill him. As he idolised her, he tolerated her behaviour. She went on trips to New York with a dozen girlfriends, which he funded.

The only thing he prohibited was to have a baby with him. When she got pregnant, she stormed into the beauty salon that serviced his wife and yelled that her child had been conceived out of love, not duty like hers. Four of Pablo's men abducted her and dragged her into a veterinarian's clinic. An abortion was done without any anaesthetic, after which he never saw her again. He thanked God that he now had Virginia, who, even though she threw tantrums, was his princess and his oasis.

Pablo withheld the truth about Wendy's fate. Following the abortion, he had assigned Popeye to keep an eye on Wendy, but the hit man had fallen in love with her. While they were in bed, the phone had rung. Popeye had answered to Pablo, who played a recording of Wendy speaking to the DEA. El Patrón told his hit man to murder her without hesitation or to die himself. It was love or death, and he needed to hurry because the boss was waiting. In a rage, Popeye grabbed his gun and shot her twice in the forehead.

The abortion story alone nauseated Virginia and crushed her adoration for him. Hiding her reaction, she wondered whether he would do anything so evil to her. She tried to convince herself that it wouldn't happen because she was his sweet panther and the opposite of Wendy Chavarriaga.

After Pablo said that he had hidden a present on his body, she searched his hair and removed his shirt, belt and trousers. In his sock, she found a fully loaded 9-mm Beretta gun with a marble handle engraved with his initials. She grabbed the gun and threatened to get revenge for the night he had held a gun to her. Instantly, he disarmed her and put the gun into her mouth. He said this time was no game, the gun was licensed in his name and he was loaning it to her because she might need it due to his coming war with the government. If the authorities captured her, she would be raped and tortured. He would teach her how to shoot herself to die immediately. She needed to remove her dress before he ripped it off and stand naked in the bathroom in front of the full-length mirrors. She relented to his forceful attitude and to save a $3,000 dress.

He unloaded the gun and stood behind her. "If you pull a gun and intend to kill, you need to remain completely calm and know you're in control." He showed her how to stand if she were facing multiple assailants, the correct body language, thoughts and feelings. He frightened her and tried to bring her mind back into control. He advised her which assailants to kill first in different scenarios, ranging from two to four at various distances, some armed, others unarmed. "When surrounded by five or more armed who are closing in, you need to shoot yourself before they capture you." She should shoot herself under the ear so that the bullet would go directly into the brain.

They practised wrestling for the gun until she was in too much pain. He threw the gun on the floor, grabbed her hair and described the most horrific forms of torture. Terrified, she attempted to cover her ears, so he restrained her arms. "What I've described is only a fraction of what they'll do to you if you don't learn to defend yourself," he whispered in her ear. "You must hate them like I do and be ready to kill without pausing. When they come for you to find me, you must have no doubts about pulling the trigger."

She asked how he had learned such horrific things. He said because he had squeezed many people, including kidnappers. When asked how many, he said about 200 had died, but a lot more had lived. When asked what had happened to those who had lived, he didn't answer.

She collected the bullets and the gun and gave him a key to her apartment that he could use if he needed to hide. She gave him a golden heart locket containing the combination to her safe, which would store her gun when she was out of the city. Silently, he held her with an increasingly common sadness in his eyes. After he left, she tried not to imagine the fates of the 200.

CHAPTER 24

JUNGLE LABS RAIDED

With the help of the DEA, the authorities located a complex of jungle labs including Tranquilandia. The police had heard about the complex, but had been reluctant or unable to find it 250 miles from the nearest road.

In 1981, a DEA analyst had written a report based on the Colombian importation of acetone and ether from January 1, 1978 to June 30, 1981:

"A major vulnerability to Colombia's traditional status in the world cocaine trafficking community is its dependence on the importation both of acetone and ether, neither of which is produced in appreciable quantity internally. While acetone has fairly wide industrial application in Colombia, ether does not, with perhaps as much as ninety-eight per cent of the latter believed to be destined for illicit users." With the USA and West Germany producing ninety per cent of the ether, the analyst identified JT Baker Chemical Supply Company of Phillipsburg, New Jersey as the largest supplier to the traffickers, having exported 758.8 tons of ether to highly suspect users.

The report concluded, "The Drug Enforcement Administration can effect major damage to the Colombian cocaine processing industry through the denial of selected precursors namely acetone and ether. Of the two, ether by far is the most vulnerable … If the Drug Enforcement Administration can successfully cut the availability of these precursor substances through timely coordinated action, the coca processing industry in Colombia could founder."

The analyst recommended that the DEA should force

companies to decline exports ordered by suspicious buyers, or to at least limit the quantities to half a metric ton with a maximum of twelve tons a year and to report suspicious orders to the DEA. Agents could set up false companies to sell barrels of ether with tracking devices. With the DEA applying pressure on the Colombian government to limit ether importation, the domestic stock dwindled and the black-market price climbed. In America, JT Baker agreed to work with the DEA.

On November 22, 1983, a Colombian offered $400,000 in cash for 1,300 fifty-five-gallon drums of ether from JT Baker. "I want the drums unlabelled. I'll take delivery anywhere in the US and I'll take care of the shipping to Colombia myself." The order of 200 metric tons exceeded the biggest order in the DEA study, which was seventy.

After contacting the DEA, the salesman stalled the Colombian. The large order would take time to fill. A week later, the Colombian received a call from a DEA agent pretending to work for North Central Industrial Chemicals in Chicago. Having heard about the delay in his order, he offered to supply any amount of ether. Falling for the trap, the Colombian went to a hotel in Miami to meet two undercover agents posing as sellers from Chicago. The next week, the Colombian was filmed in Chicago making a down payment of $15,000.

Before the first seventy-six barrels of ether left for Colombia, DEA technicians cut two open and inserted battery-powered transponders. The traffickers had no idea that when the ether left the plant it could be traced all the way to Colombia. Signals from the transponders were picked up by a spy satellite as the ether moved south through New Orleans and Panama to Colombia. The signals indicated a spot near the Yarí River, part of the Amazon River basin, deep in the densest part of the jungle.

On March 7, 1984, the DEA agent in charge of the operation went to police headquarters and entered the office of Colonel Ramírez, whom he visited regularly. Feisty and proud of his country, Ramírez was clean-shaven with a square solid face and thick lips. The agent found the colonel writing reports, while listening to radio conversations. Whether in his car, office or home, Ramírez was always attuned to the radio frequencies used by the authorities and the traffickers. Told there was a lab in the jungle, Ramírez asked the agent to pinpoint it on a map. With a finger, the agent identified a spot by the equator, where the Yarí and Mesay rivers merged.

Reluctant to daunt the colonel, the agent withheld the size of the ether shipment because he believed the Colombians lacked the resources to deal with such a large and inaccessible complex. Viewing the location as a logistical nightmare, Ramírez said it would take a few days to get planes and helicopters. The aircraft would need bladder tanks for extra fuel and by virtue of the long flight, the operation would be at risk of failure because the traffickers would receive reports of military aircraft in the air. Smiling, Ramírez said, "Hell let's do it!"

By March 10, 1984, everything was prepared. Out of fear that the traffickers would receive inside information about the raid, the men in green military garb didn't know the nature of the operation until airborne. Helicopters took off from Bogotá at 6 AM. An hour later, they started monitoring the transceiver, homing in on its tones. By noon, they were skimming jungle foliage and almost out of fuel when they spotted smoke rising from the dense green vegetation and an airstrip littered with debris, including tree branches and 55-gallon drums. A helicopter attempted to land, covered by another. Armed with submachine guns, the troops getting off the helicopter came under a small amount of fire, but the shooters fled, and everything was quiet. Only tiny gnats and mosquitoes attacked the troops. The other helicopters circling took turns to land. More troops positioned themselves for combat, but there was no resistance.

According to Jorge Ochoa, the bosses had ordered the workers to surrender peacefully: "In 1984, the police took over Tranquilandia. A lot of people were working there … Security agents arrived by air … We could have defended Tranquilandia at that moment with violence, but we said, 'No, no, there should be no violence.' So police took over the place with no violence. They didn't fire a single bullet at anyone."

The official report later stated that the traffickers and 100 guerrillas had fled along trails and rafts on the Yarí River. Based on the report, the US ambassador coined the term narco-guerrilla. The small amount of gunfire had actually come from guards paid by the traffickers to defend against guerrilla attacks.

Dozens of low-level poorly dressed workers milled around, waiting to be arrested. Some fled into the jungle. Hired from the Medellín slums, they were known as dog washers. Most were young men hired to stir the containers where the alkaloid was processed. Some were female kitchen staff. The police organised them into a group. They were asked for ID, searched and ordered to clear the runway.

While the helicopters refuelled, a small plane landed. To prevent the return of the shooters, the helicopters took off and circled the area. Towards the west side, the troops found ten makeshift warehouses with plastic-covered zinc roofs, raised wooden floors and some with clapperboard sides. One was a dorm for 100 people. Some of the others housed offices. Towards the north end of the runway were sixteen large huts. The troops saw a modern cocaine lab in one, with a helicopter nearby. They found four small aircraft on the eastern side of the airstrip.

Realising they had never encountered anything so big, the troops felt a sense of accomplishment as they combed the area and found washing machines, dryers, showers, cots, mattresses, generators, electric pumps, bulldozers, four-wheel-drive vehicles, bedding, food and assorted machinery. Chickens, turkeys and pigs were foraging at a garbage dump. Khaki uniforms and automatic rifles had been abandoned at the edge of the jungle. A stash of weapons was found with cloth to make uniforms. The camp consisted of corridors raised on large cylinders and gigantic plants to generate energy. It had a small medical centre and a drug store stocked with malaria medicine. They found canned food from Brazil and Peru.

From the prisoners, the authorities learned that they had received delicacies on Sundays and were treated to canned beer. To minimise the harmful effects of the chemical vapours, the workers were flown home periodically, otherwise they would lose their appetites and energy, their moods would sour and their skin dullen.

By counting the 55-gallon drums and jugs, the lone DEA agent who had filmed the stinking plastic trash cans containing wet cocaine hydrochloride was able to estimate the size of the operation. The troops found 363 drums of ether, 305 drums of acetone, 133 jugs of aviation fuel and 482 jugs of red gasoline. A logbook revealed that the complex had received 15.539 metric tons of cocaine paste from December 15, 1983 until February 2, 1984. The DEA agent realised that it was the biggest manufacturing plant ever busted in world history.

Worried about retaliation and the return of the shooters, the officer in charge called Ramírez in Bogotá. "We need immediate reinforcements. Can you arrange a second expedition immediately? We need to get the prisoners out and to search more of the area. The helicopter pilots have located more airstrips, but we need backup to perform the searches. Some of the prisoners have confirmed that there are more complexes with the other airstrips and this complex is called Tranquilandia."

At 9 AM the next day, March 11, a car parked on a street in Bogotá. Four men got out and approached the house of Ramírez's younger brother. After hearing his bell ring, the ex-policeman Francisco opened the door and went outside to talk to the men, who came across as soft-spoken and well mannered.

"Tell your brother he can have $400,000 to stop what he's doing and to forget about it. We can deposit it in America, Panama or wherever he wants it." After confirming that he would relay the offer, he was told that the message was from Los Pablos.

After the men left, Francisco called his brother, described the incident and asked what had happened. Ramírez told him not to mess with the situation. It was so dangerous, his brother needed to get lost for a while. If the men returned, he should tell them that the colonel had no idea what they were talking about.

When the men reappeared, Francisco gave his brother's response. "We understand of course," one said. "Remind him again about the $400,000." Unable to reach his brother, Francisco turned on the news, which showed the colonel at Tranquilandia, surrounded by troops, inspecting the cocaine, the labs and blue industrial drums.

On March 13, investigating an airstrip sixteen miles north, Ramírez found an abandoned complex. Aware of the activity at Tranquilandia, the workers had fled. The complex was littered with test tubes, pipettes, thermometers, plastic bags, tape, paper, presses, bags of lye and heaters. A ton of cocaine had been stashed in fifty massive ceramic jugs. They found a milling machine, boats, earthmoving equipment and chainsaws. The complex was called Cocalandia. By an airstrip, they found 140 pails of cocaine, equivalent to 500 kilos. Following a path led to another complex called Cocalandia 2.

The cocaine was moved to the huts with the mattresses, chainsaws and machinery. Making his response to the offer by the traffickers clear, Ramírez ordered the destruction of the cocaine and chemicals. Ether was thrown into each hut, many of which contained chemical barrels. When the soldiers lit the ether, it exploded, almost setting them on fire and burning the trees. Multiple explosions sent dense black plumes through the jungle and into the sky.

On March 14, over the river from Tranquilandia, the police found four metric tons of cocaine in drums at Tranquilandia 2. The DEA filmed it getting burned and the destruction of the site. The victories were daily. On March 15, half a ton of cocaine was destroyed at The Diamond. On March 16, they seized Tranquilandia 3, Palmeras and an anonymous site with an airfield, cocaine testing facilities and a boat ramp. On March 17, they moved on to

Pascualandia, where they confiscated a plane and burned another. They found a camp with a dorm, a kitchen, a communication centre, weapons and a tailor shop for manufacturing military gear.

From the raids, the police estimated that the traffickers had lost almost fourteen tons of cocaine, seven planes, fourteen labs and encampments and almost 12,000 drums of chemicals. The DEA labelled it the Silicon Valley of cocaine, a cocaine industrial park, and reported to Washington that Ramírez had established a record in the quantity of assets, cocaine (worth $1.2 billion) and money seized or destroyed. Over two years, the complex of labs would have generated $12 billion in revenue for the Medellín Cartel.

Paperwork found at the site – waybills, receipts and accounts – indicated which bosses owned the complex. It appeared that several had combined raw materials. A crashed plane registered in the name of Gacha's brother suggested that Gacha was a senior partner. A letter from a police chief based in an Amazon River town where coca leaves were traded confirmed that Gacha had suffered a loss due to the raid, and that since December 1983, Gacha had been coordinating flights of paste and base to Tranquilandia. The DEA had previously assumed that Gacha worked under Pablo, but now they believed he was an independent boss with his own power base.

As the plane carrying the transponder in the ether drum had refuelled at Hacienda Veracruz, the authorities knew that the Ochoas were involved. At Tranquilandia, the general manager's diary was found, which contained a warning: "This is the property of Guillermo Leon Ochoa. Don't steal it and don't pretend that it has been lost. Thank you." The authorities assumed that it had referenced a member of the Ochoa family. Having revoked the licences for a fleet of the Ochoas' planes, Lara launched an investigation into the Ochoas' ownership of Hacienda Veracruz. For eight years, the Americans had been lobbying Colombia to spray cannabis fields with glyphosate. On April 6, 1984, Lara announced that would start on a trial basis in the north coast.

The raid forced the DEA to revise its view of cocaine production. The cartels had gone from pooling the output from numerous small labs to operating at the level of a giant corporation. The success of the bust earned Ramírez a promotion, but put him in the crosshairs. With the goal of becoming the police chief, he aimed to find other jungle complexes. Unaware of the tracking device in the drum of ether, he assumed that the DEA had an informant or had found the lab using satellite technology. While basking in the media spotlight, he was aware of the danger to himself and his family. With his children guarding their house with submachine guns, he resolved to follow up with more blows against the traffickers.

Pablo issued a statement to the US ambassador denying any role: "I can only characterise your statements as tendentious, irresponsible and ill-intentioned without any basis in reality; they denigrate the good faith of public opinion. My conscience is clear." He accused Lara of being "the representative of your government in the Colombian cabinet."

The raid manifested an even deadlier nemesis for Pablo, General Miguel Maza Márquez, a bulldog of a man who was the head of the Central Directorate of the Judicial Police and Intelligence, a.k.a. the DIJIN. To eliminate Pablo, he had far more resources than other officials because he had allied himself with the Cali Cartel.

Maza stated, "There was talk of a congressman whom his colleagues called Pablito, who on weekends invited people from the national stage to celebrate at his hacienda in Nápoles. He gave them shows with international artists, with beautiful ladies and excellent drinks. The congressman was number one, the most famous guy around for being the best host of the time. Anyone would be pleased to be invited to his home."

After the jungle raid, Colonel Ramírez called Maza: "Pablo and his associates are more irritated than ever, they have cornered the minister, they control the house and the office. All the phones are intercepted." Maza feared the worst for the justice minister.

He saw Lara walking towards his death as if sacrificing his life would cleanse the stain of his alleged links with drug money.

Hearing details of the raid on a radio, El Patrón remained calm as the authorities announced that tons of cocaine had been destroyed. Years later, Jorge Ochoa told the author Dominic Streatfeild – documented in *Cocaine* – that the quantities were embellished for PR purposes, and that only chemicals were found because word about the raid had reached Medellín and the traffickers had removed the most valuable stuff. Whether tons of finished product were seized or not, the complex had required a multimillion-dollar investment and the potential lost revenue was in the billions. Someone was going to have to pay. The government braced for retaliation.

CHAPTER 25
KILLING THE JUSTICE MINISTER

El Patrón had assumed that his retreat from politics would reduce the attacks by Lara, but they had only escalated, so he needed a new strategy. Aware that there would be severe repercussions for killing a justice minister – a first in Colombia – he decided to do it anyway to set an example because Lara had gotten away with too much. Pablo saw himself as stronger than the weak government. He assumed that Lara's death would destabilise Colombia and he would ultimately be invited to participate in the resolution of the crisis he had created. He offered the M-19 150 million pesos to kill Lara. They said no, and warned him against attacking Galán's friend, because they were the most progressive politicians.

He instructed some of his top hit men – including Pinina and Otto – to coordinate an assassination attempt from an ambulance. They altered a van by adding metal panels to make it bulletproof, while allowing gaps to fire through. They painted it to look like an ambulance, including red crosses.

In Bogotá, hit men spread out in dingy hotels and began to shadow Lara, who took various routes from home to work in a white Mercedes-Benz guarded by two vans. In April 1984, Pablo authorised the kill, but due to the ineptitude of the ambulance driver the attempt failed three times. Fearful that the ambulance had been noticed, Pablo converted it into a flower delivery van and added two hit men on a motorbike.

Fearful of the repercussions, members of the Cali Cartel tried to steer him away from killing the justice minister. Aware that Lara was going to be moved to an embassy, they suggested that the assassination be postponed until Lara became an ambassador. But Pablo was adamant that Lara had to go.

"We have to kill him any way possible," he told Pinina and Big Gun.

Paid $500,000, Pinina recruited a hit team from his own Medellín neighbourhood, Lovaina. Iván Dario Guisado, a.k.a. Narices, a 31-year-old, had a history of murder, robbery and assault. Eighteen-year-old Byron Velasquez, a.k.a. Quesito, was gaunt, curly haired and looking to earn a reputation. Initially, Byron was only involved in paying the hit team until Pinina, whom he trusted like a brother, asked him to participate by providing cover for the lead assassins.

Before travelling to Bogotá, Byron went to mass at the Shrine of the Blessed Virgin Mary Helper of Christians in Sabaneta. The parish priest, Father Ramón Arcila, was revered by the public and traffickers due to some remarkable occurrences. While travelling at high speed, he had been ejected from a car after its door had opened. His prayers to the Virgin were answered instantly, as he landed on the roadside unharmed as if Mary had placed a pile of fluffy cushions below his posterior. On another occasion, he was delivering mass when the parishioners saw the Virgin's face in the pulpit. Always humble, he gave full credit to Mary, for whom he was only a mediator. The miracles multiplied his followers, who received a sprinkling of holy water. Those receiving his blessings rejoiced as cancer was healed, stuttering stopped, paralysed limbs reactivated and even bankrupts became wealthy.

As his popularity soared, requests poured in for drug shipments to arrive safely in America, for bullets to hit their targets, for hit men to remain courageous and for criminal enterprises to be successful. Based on these demands, Mary was renamed the "Virgin of the Assassins." The criminals' religious donations expanded with the drug trade. They prayed, wrote letters, confessed and communed. In the Aburrá Valley, sixty-seven parishes devoted themselves to the Virgin of the Assassins, leaving only thirty-two to Jesus Christ.

Father Ramón Arcila offered a motorbike-blessing service. Byron parked his next to a few dozen owned by young people desperate to get rich with Mary's divine inoculation against death. They had their own slang and habits, with a preference for religious images, rumba music and Western materialism. Always ready to pull a trigger, they fought each other and fired at passers-by and animals. For those who died, there was a carnival atmosphere at their funerals. With Mary loving all of her children and protecting their homes, the young people carried her image on their motorbikes, on scapulars tied to the right foot or on their jackets. Byron asked for success on his motorbike, and if the assassination went well and he emerged unscathed, he promised to return every Tuesday to pray to Mary.

Some members of the hit team settled in the Victoria Hotel in front of the Ministry of Justice. From a room, they observed Lara's movements. Another group shadowed his car to learn his routes. On a map, they drew the two routes he used to get to his house in Los Frailes, north of Bogotá. They decided where to situate the assassins and mapped their escape routes. In their spare time, they drove around in green Renault 12s, splurged on food and liquor and harassed waitresses.

The flower delivery van transported men with AR-15 rifles to a vantage point by Lara's work. The plan was to follow Lara, pull up next to his car and open fire. The motorbike duo would fire at the bodyguards. The justice minister's bodyguards emerged from the building, walked up to the van and leaned against it, unaware. The hit was postponed.

The US emissaries encouraging Lara to extradite Pablo had grown concerned by President Betancur's lack of action to protect him. The president had made no public statements in support of his justice minister nor taken any action on extradition. Betancur seemed to be distancing himself from Lara. Having learned that people working with Lara were passing information to the traffickers, US agents brought him a bulletproof vest. "You should be more concerned. You should take more precautions." He declined the vest, but they left it with him.

Aware of the threat to him, his wife and three little children, he requested more security. "I am a dangerous minister for those who act outside the law. I only hope that they don't take me by surprise." Despite the tough talk, he called the US Embassy and excitedly revealed that he was getting transferred overseas as the ambassador to Czechoslovakia.

"You'll be safe there," the US ambassador said. "All the terrorists are in the government."

As the transfer would take thirty days, he needed a place for him and his family to hide at because the Colombian government couldn't protect them. The US Embassy offered to put him in a Texas safe house owned by a rich businessman, but the plan was not adopted. Receiving threats by telephone, he kept changing his number, but they kept coming.

Hoping to perform the mission under the cover of darkness, Byron adjusted two motorbikes so that one switch would turn off their lights. With two motorbikes and two cars, the assassins hoped to surprise the bodyguards. They anticipated that Lara would be travelling with six bodyguards in two cars, one car in front of his vehicle and the other behind. Byron was told to wait for the signal and to provide cover for the other hit men, including Iván, who would be the primary shooter on the other motorbike. Eight blocks away, Pinina would be waiting in a getaway car.

On April 30, 1984, Lara thanked a journalist for publishing an article about his work. "I am going to be killed today, but that article can be my will for the Justice Department." After playing his friend some samples of the fifty death threats received that morning, he said, "If I don't answer this phone, it will be because I am dead."

Byron kissed an image of Mary the Helper of Christians. "The wait is over, Mama, protect me." He followed Iván. At 7 PM, they got on two motorbikes and headed to Bogotá, armed with grenades and submachine guns. Heavy traffic prevented the assassins' cars from keeping up with Lara's transportation. Only the motorbikes made progress. On the first attempt, Iván lost his nerve and didn't draw his gun. He told Pinina that Lara went by as he was struggling to get the gun from his bag. By the time he had retrieved it, the opportunity had passed. Byron found Pinina in a rage, so Iván offered to go back and complete the mission.

"OK. Let's do it," Pinina said, "because Pablo is going to be furious that we've lost so much time."

Byron was ready to provide cover again for the other motorbike by shooting at the bodyguards, but Iván decided to switch motorbikes because Byron was a better driver who would take more risks. In a backup car, La Yuca got stuck in traffic, so the pressure intensified on Iván and Byron to proceed without the original backup.

Sitting on a back seat, Lara was travelling slowly with his bulletproof vest and some history books next to him. Around dusk, Byron spotted Lara, but the second backup motorbike had disappeared.

"We're on our own," Byron said.

"Let's do it and get the hell out of here," Iván said.

Weaving around cars, the motorbike homed in from the rear and slowed down towards the right side of the Mercedes-Benz. After extracting the submachine gun from his jacket, Iván took aim at the figure on the back seat. Within seconds, it emptied its magazine, exploding the windows, hitting Lara in the head, chest, arm and neck.

Gunfire flashed from the cars with the bodyguards, who gave chase as the motorbike with its lights off raced away. Iván turned to fire at his pursuers, but had difficulty aiming due to Byron's manoeuvres. He threw a grenade, which exploded. Fifteen blocks later, rain had turned the road dangerously wet and Byron almost crashed, which allowed the bodyguards to catch up.

"They got me," Iván said, hit by a bullet.

"I think they got me, too," Byron said.

By chance, a bullet hit the tyre of the motorbike, which crashed into a curb. Bullets exploded Iván's head. Next to the motorbike, he flopped down. Hit in the arm, Byron was arrested. The hit men in the van returned to Medellín.

Iván was found dead in grey trousers, black shoes, a white T-shirt, a blue waterproof sweater and a plastic print of the Virgin attached to his underwear by a hook. His sweater contained eleven $500 bills, two $20 bills, a $1 coin, a pack of cigarettes and five lottery tickets with the numbers 6924. The official report stated that both of the hit men were wearing bulletproof vests, two MK-2 grenades, a long .38 revolver and a Belgian-made Ingram machine gun with fifty bullets.

At 7:40 PM at Shaio Clinic, Lara was pronounced dead. The gangsters in Los Trece Botones tavern in La Estrella celebrated the news and hailed Big Gun for coordinating one of the highest profile hits in Colombian history and for proving El Patrón's trust in him.

After fishing in the La Miel River, Pablo returned to his estate. Informed about the assassination, he displayed quiet satisfaction. Anyone who dared to challenge him now would understand the consequences. Immediately, he travelled to a jungle hideout.

Watching the news, Pablo's family saw officials in white doctors' coats examining and photographing Lara's Mercedes-Benz with its windows shot out and blood splattered on the back seat, which was light blue, Pablo's favourite colour. It showed Byron getting arrested and bundled into the back of a van. "A gunman riding a red motorcycle pulled the trigger of an Ingram machine gun and murdered [Lara] … Colombia has no doubts about the masterminds behind the job, and the objections against the extradition treaty …" Holding each other in front of the TV, Victoria and Nora sobbed. Juan Pablo asked why they were crying. Eight months pregnant, Victoria ordered him to gather his belongings. They fled to a relative's house.

Expecting to give birth to a boy, Victoria packed baby clothes into a small suitcase and boarded a helicopter with Juan Pablo and a doctor in case she went into labour mid-flight. It took almost three hours to reach Panama's border, where the helicopter landed in a jungle clearing. After changing into beach clothing as a disguise, they got into a van, which took them to Panama City. For three nights, they slept on mats in an apartment.

A group of the co-conspirators, including Pinina and Otto, travelled in the early morning to the village La Tablaza. A helicopter took them to Panama. The rupturing of the gas tank in the helicopter evacuating Gustavo's family forced an emergency landing. They ended up lost in the jungle for days until they found help in a village.

At midnight, the president declared a state of siege and a war without quarter against the traffickers, while promising to rescue the national dignity. His cabinet stayed up until 3 AM, debating their options. No cabinet minister had ever been assassinated in Colombia. Perhaps cocaine wasn't just an American problem. Trafficking was ruining Colombia's reputation in the eyes of the world. With the justice minister gone, it would appear that the president had lost control. Lara's death swung them in favour of extradition. In an emergency radio broadcast, Betancur declared war on the traffickers and said that drugs were "the most serious problem that Colombia has had in its history." Distressed by his friend's death, Colonel Ramírez vowed to capture the murderers, bring them to justice and remove them from the drug business.

Cocaine kingpins nationwide fled from Colombia. Immediately, Bogotá and Medellín were militarised and hundreds jailed, including the Ochoa brothers' father, Fabio Sr. Properties were raided and confiscated. Helicopters swooped on Hacienda Nápoles. With rifles and search dogs, troops in green battle fatigues stormed inside, provoking raucous cawing from Pablo's exotic birds. Seizing weapons and evidence, they trashed the property and handcuffed low-level workers, whom they lined up by a swimming pool. After the raid, they left the zoo animals to starve. Upon receiving complaints about the animals, the government was forced to reopen the zoo.

In the Rotunda of the Capitol Building, thousands visited

Lara's closed coffin, which military guards took to the National Cathedral. Outside, mourners from all sections of society were crying and chanting that they loved Lara. In the cathedral, emotions ran high. Amid the top brass from the military and the government, the president appeared tense.

A plane transported Lara to his hometown, Neiva, where he was buried in the presence of political leaders and ex-presidents. At the funeral, Betancur said, "We have reached a point where we must reflect on what is our nation. What does the word citizen mean? Stop, enemies of humanity! Colombia will hand over criminals wanted in other countries, so that they may be punished as an example." His eulogy received a standing ovation.

As the president had backtracked on his electoral promise to the traffickers, Pablo contemplated ruining his reputation by exposing his contributions to Betancur. But his lawyer, Guido Parra, advised him against it: "The remedy will be worse than the disease. The country is hurt and the president is strengthened. If he is attacked, the people will rally to him."

"[Lara] could have yielded," Galán said at the funeral, "to the various and intense pressures to which he was subject. He would be alive today had he given in and fled. But like a true man of honour he endured it all, and by accepting the entire challenge he became a victim, giving his life for his country and convictions. The struggle against drug trafficking cannot be considered as the quest of a handful of idealists who died like Lara, or as the responsibility of a specific political sector, while all the others remain silent out of cowardliness or complicity, convinced that this is mere Puritanism or a confrontation between naive and deluded moralists. Every political force and all social strata must interpret this reality as a common cause, essential for the survival of the state. In Colombia, we are all committed to persevere in this struggle until the foundations of a new era in the national life are laid. This is the duty his holocaust has imposed on us. It is the only possible consolation we can give his family, his people, his friends, his country. The government has lost a minister ... the

New Liberalism has lost one of its founders and his family has lost the core of their affection. But Colombian history has added to its registers, as of April 30, the heroic mission accomplished by Lara."

"A heroic and painful battle may have been lost, but not the war," wrote Guillermo Cano of *The Spectator*, determined to carry Lara's crusade forward by targeting not only the traffickers but everyone else in society profiting from them and tolerating their criminality. "The capos of the Mafia laugh at our judges, at our justice system, and none of them are in prison. In prison there are small drug traffickers, necessary accomplices, hired mules of no significance in this monstrous organisation. These godfathers only fear justice in the US and for this they mock our authorities, offering to hand themselves in on condition that they are not extradited."

The surviving hit man, Byron was hung by the feet at the hill of Monserrate, where he admitted that he had been hired due to the fame he had received for performing races and somersaults on the steep streets of his neighbourhood. He stayed alive in prison and was eventually sentenced to twenty-seven years, of which he served fourteen and was released. Although he never received the five million pesos, approximately $40,000, he had been promised for the job, he did receive just under $1,000 a month for the first six years of his incarceration.

General Maza was concerned by the rising power of the Medellín Cartel, which had supplanted the guerrilla groups in the field of high-profile assassinations. After investigating Byron's family history, he wrote an essay for the media about the origins of cartel hit men. He said that intermediaries tested young people with jobs of theft and extortion, and if they performed well, they moved up the ranks: driving and conditioning of cars and motorcycles, weapons handling, target practise, follow-up manoeuvres and finally assassinations.

Lara's sister blamed his death on a conspiracy between the traffickers and political elites: "The Mafia itself was used by people in government. [Lara] was killed because he knew too much and if he had escaped Colombia as planned he could have revealed all. Within four hours of his death, his office had been cleared of all but the most trivial of papers. It is very easy to blame everything on Pablo Escobar, but it is just too easy. His power depended on people in government."

At the hotel the hit men had used, a waitress told the police about their rude behaviour. In the call logs, they found a number to a house in La Estrella. The same address came up when a car-park owner reported the discovery of a getaway car, a green Renault, containing a grenade and a bulletproof vest. Tracing the car's origin brought the police to the seller, who had the same phone number of the house in La Estrella, which was raided. Inside were Big Guns' in-laws, who despised their son-in-law.

"Yes, he participated in the operation," his father-in-law said.

CHAPTER 26

PANAMA

Pablo and his family ended up in a house in Panama City's historic section, where they lived off deliveries from KFC and wore sandals in the mildewy shower because the water didn't drain properly. After a gynaecological examination at the house, Victoria was told that she was having a girl, which delighted Pablo. During a brainstorming session for a name, Juan Pablo came up with Manuela, his first girlfriend's name. The family approved, but Pablo warned his son that if his sister didn't like her name, she would hold him accountable after she had grown up.

In 1987, Pablo detailed the relationships he had established in Panama to a journalist:

"It happens that the day after the man [Lara] fell, all the mobsters of this country left for Panama, where there were already investments and connections and friendships and such. At that time, for example, it had already been achieved with General Noriega [the military dictator in charge of Panama] for us not to be disturbed.

"The story is simple: like a year prior or something like that, there was introduced a lieutenant colonel of the Panamanian National Guard saying that he offered us his services, and after meetings and to confirm that he was really supported by General Noriega – and yes he did come from him – he was given $4,600,000.

"This time it was planned that the sum would be $5 million for him to distribute, leaving two and a half million to General Noriega and the rest for him and other officers of the Guard in exchange for allowing us to be in the country without bothering us, and that, in addition, they'd let us set up a cocaine laboratory and distribute from Colón a German ether. We agreed that when the laboratory began to produce, General Noriega would participate and he said yes, go ahead with the operation.

"The full story is that a few months earlier, a man we had in Panama – we called him 'our man from Panama' – left a runway on the north coast of Colombia heading to the isthmus and above Cape Shark, which is where we border with them. He passed the coast, passed Puerto Obaldía and routed to El Bayano and, making his visual flight, discovered a large track that was built by the Germans during the Second World War.

"Such a track was hidden in the middle of the jungle and in the middle of the Darién reservoir, almost on the border with Colombia, and what most caught the attention of the man was that it was not entangled with high or low brush. There – right there – is a closed jungle, and from the edge of the jungle to the sea a forest of huge coconut palms covering it, but when you fly over with instructions, you can clearly see the hollow and the track – flat and green as a golf course. It happens that as the time passed, surely the breeze was throwing dirt at it which started covering it, and from the dirt was born a layer of fine grass which is what we found when we went in a helicopter to see it.

"So, we landed there and the pilot took out a tool to help us raise the grass and the layer of dirt and, man, we discovered that it was all asphalted. It was a track of one thousand six-hundred metres, at sea level which is how airplanes can get out while fully loaded, and with good safety zones, while at the same time quite camouflaged by the forest.

"We immediately went to work. The first thing that was done was to get natives from the region and put a crew to work to remove the grass, and then some foundations were placed in the ground to make it work. The idea was to assemble there a laboratory with the most modern instruments of the time. In the country, there was already a lot of experience in the processing of paste, and it was about making a bigger and more modern venture than Tranquilandia, which in itself was very large and very powerful.

"I was going to advance this: with the help of very important businessmen and economists from Medellín – that are my friends – I started to write down numbers about Tranquilandia and we have come to establish that this laboratory, in only eight months of production, gave more profits than Coltejer in its first twenty-two years. And what we planned in the Panamanian Darién was superior to Tranquilandia.

"Well, in more or less a month we started to set up the laboratory in that jungle that is very swampy. The first thing that was done was to buy wood, but in really large amounts. Sawn wood, wood in rolls of various dimensions, gallows, piles, flat wood for ramps, for enclosures. Look: I believe that the investment there was more than ten million dollars, but only in infrastructure. The wood was brought from far by rivers and by sea, because there on the site and in the surrounding places – I say nearby, about four or five kilometers – the trees were left untouched.

"What was done, as in Pascualandia or as in Tranquilandia or as in Horizontes or as in Villa Coca – which were big jungle kitchens in the south of Colombia – what was done there, I say, was to knock down the undergrowth and leave the trees with those gigantic crowns completely covering the set-up, so that no one could discover it, neither from above nor from below because we worked on top of an embankment, in the centre of the swamp.

"The kitchen area was large. Right now, I could not say how much, but only on roads and internal roads connecting all the units there could be [a span of] ten to twelve kilometres. To make the roads, or better, the pavement because they meant real footbridges, first we buried round poles of four metres on average and on the top lateral beams, and between the beams went through thin and strong logs, well nailed. There were other long and more consistent ramps to roll the barrels of ether, much better finished, with nails very well topped and hidden to the surface, and in a critical step they were tied with ropes and vines, so that when the barrel was pushed there, it did not produce a spark and thus avoided the danger of explosion that was frequent when handling these substances.

"Imagine how we had three Caterpillar generators that were bought in Panama and generated 600 kilowatts. We brought them in on a ship, and from there they went on some large rafts built by us, and from the rafts they were brought down to the ground and hoisted up on wooden rollers and we began to push them across the track. Further on began the swamp. When they were on the other side, they were transferred to a kind of raft, moved through the mud and, well into the jungle, they went up on a special ramp and we slid them onto wooden rollers. Once up there, you could count eighty men pushing, pushing, pushing a kilometre to the centre of the swamp. Do you know how much was spent on that effort? Ten days, working from sunrise to sunset. Ten days!

"The [cocaine] kitchens were as what most of the kitchens were like: massive ranches. These structures were mounted on wooden platforms about two metres above the swamp. And they were divided into weapons caches, dormitories, kitchen and dining rooms, warehouses for the refined merchandise, apartments for the administrator and foremen, a house for motor pumps to pump water out and motor-pumps for moving drinking water, a drinking water plant and water ozonation plant for human consumption, a section of power generators and fuel storage next to them, warehouses of liquid chemicals – different ones because they never put all the eggs in a single basket – a tool warehouse, oxidizer, drying ovens. Well. Everything a kitchen needs. All that is needed for a factory that produces over two tons of cocaine per day. Do you know how much that is? More than what Ford should produce daily. But all done by people here. That's why white people get annoyed. Because, look, look man: why do they have to mess with us so much?

"It's just that the issue is not that cocaine is the boogie man … All these stimulants and antidepressants, all those synthetic drugs from the big legal laboratories abroad – legal, they say and with that they think they fix everything – are more dangerous, deadlier, and more deceptive than cocaine. But they don't mention it because they are produced by them. The trouble is that, when it comes to money, cocaine leaves them behind and this is the first time in history that they do not have the money, nor the imagination, nor the power that we have. When I compared the numbers between Coltejer and those of Tranquilandia, what I wanted to tell is that this was the first time that white people didn't control an industry that could be called conventional. And that's what's hurting them, big deal.

"But speaking calmly, look: that kitchen was a whole city raised on thousands of wooden legs nailed with nails and tied with vines all under that swamp and humidity. It was so wet that clothes couldn't be dried. We brought there dozens of, I do not know how many dryers. And the mosquitoes, the mosquitoes, man: at the time we were there we did not know of a single case of malaria or infections or tetanus because we even had an infirmary with doctors and nurses and specialists in this most important [department]. We had a room for small surgeries and, if the condition was more serious, there was a plane there, ready to take off.

"From the beginning, we initiated that the ether would be taken by sea from Colón to the site. There it was thrown into the water and it was necessary to pollinate it, that is, rise it all on round wooden poles and push them to the beach. And already on the beach, they were rolled over the same poles to reach the track that was about four blocks away.

"The whole operation was manual because in those swamps tractors don't work, nothing works except the human being. In that way they crossed the track, they continued inwards through the mud and once in the middle of the jungle, they raised them on the liquid transport ramps and rolled them to their respective cellars.

"The first shipment of ether was 5,000 barrels, but another 11,000 were already sailing from Europe because the kitchen was planned by calculating the different stages to develop the project. Then the first ether arrived when the facilities were ready to receive it. There it was studied so much that, before starting to build, we had already bought a whole year's production of ether from a factory in Germany.

"That laboratory ate all the effort and all the money in the world, and all the experience, because, look at one thing: when you think about producing, you have to think about the market. And if you think about the market, then you have to think about things like transportation. I was telling you the story of the cloth planes [ultralight, made from tubes and cloth] and the sixty kilograms of cocaine, I'm going to tell you another one.

"Before developing that kitchen, we had thought about the need for large aircraft. Then I bought a company that was called Inair that was famous in Panama and Miami. I used those planes so much that they ended up getting annoyed, until they caught one in Miami with half a ton of cocaine. The other I had to leave at the Omar Torrijos airport in Panama …

"At Inair were two Boeing 707s that worked from before when the cocaine was taken from Colombia and we gathered it in a collection centre in Panama. There we would pack it up among supposedly nationally made refrigerators and so we sent it up north. That company worked well because the government, or rather, General Noriega, certified that the refrigerators were a Panamanian export product. And, in addition, Inair was run by Ricardo Bilonick Paredes in the United States who was at that time the ambassador of Panama to Washington.

"But on the other hand, let's say in the year 1983, there were already many links with Panama. The people of Medellín had enough business and projects to invest more. For example, a couple of my friends had bought Contadora Island from Noriega and they were ready to start building tourist developments, but the negotiation was not finished and Noriega was left with $2.5 million that he had been given as advance.

"That's when the death of Lara Bonilla comes and the next

day, thinking about that brave warrior that was going to come over, people said, 'Let's go to Panama because this run must be seen from the barrier.' That morning the hangars of the Olaya Herrera airport were almost empty because almost everyone left on their private planes and we arrived, some at the Paitilla airport and those with the largest planes at Omar Torrijos.

"To enter Panama was like going home because almost everyone had their houses or condos – the way they call apartments over there – cars and even yachts to go fishing in the middle of the morning or go to the Caribbean islands to play in the casinos. Perhaps the only one who had not wanted to buy was the late Pablo Correa who rented an entire floor at the Marriot Hotel.

"I remember that when the people were installed, we sent our man from Panama, in the company of his partner Michael Kalish – a gringo who was also a friend of the dictator – and César Rodríguez, supposedly the right arm of Noriega, an aviation pilot, and owner of a company called Aeroejecutivos or something like that, to talk to the general.

"Among other things, Cesar was later killed in Medellín for foul play: he stole 500 kilos of cocaine from someone and then they brought him here, but the man came with General Paredes' son – another of Noriega's relatives – and they shot them both. The two were killed: one for being a scammer and the other one for being nosy because nobody had requested for him.

"In the end the Colombian, the gringo and the Panamanian went to where the general was to ratify that everyone was there, that he remembered that he had a commitment with us, to not bother us. Our guy, Kalish and Rodríguez spoke with 'The Tiger' Noriega and he told us that we didn't have anything to worry about, as long as we behaved well."

On May 8, 1984, hoping to weaken the Medellín Cartel, the president signed an extradition order for Carlos Lehder. Betancur announced that traffickers would be tried in military courts and denied bail. Sentences would be increased, with limited possibility of parole. Suspected traffickers would have their gun permits cancelled. Thanks to the president's signature, Colonel Ramírez targeted Lehder. There would be no problem extraditing him, but if he arrested any of the other bosses, they would use their resources to manipulate the justice system.

At a press conference in Armenia, Lehder said that he would only be extradited over his dead body. Abandoning Armenia forever, he left behind his companies, properties, aircraft, newspaper, girlfriends, debts and bills. With him on the run, his property deteriorated. Lacking an expensive diet of fresh horsemeat, his tigers withered. The Humane Society stepped in. As the property crumbled from fire and rain damage, only one thing survived: his naked statue of John Lennon.

On his trail, Colonel Ramírez missed Lehder by four days, 100 miles south-east of Bogotá, but it raised his hopes. Moving around with twenty-three aliases and three passports, including a German one, Lehder was unfazed. He called radio stations to rant and penned open letters, criticising imperialism. Sources provided information about his whereabouts, but he remained elusive.

Raiding a Lehder property in Armenia, the police discovered a letter which revealed ties between the traffickers and the political class. In the letter dated December 1981, Lehder had written to the cousin of ex-president Alfonso López Michelsen about a banking arrangement. The cousin had presided over a banking conglomerate called Grupo Grancolombiano. Lehder had specified: "We also want to confirm our interest in Grupo Grancolombiano being the means for channelling our business abroad, amounting to about $20 million a year, which we will be ready to transfer to the country [Colombia] via your bank branches."

According to Pablo, the traffickers in Panama began to attract unwanted attention: "And we started enjoying ourselves so well that we'd spend time just doing what we liked: such as sports activities. For example, it became fashionable to go jogging every day at six in the morning on Balboa Avenue ... But take a look at where a dumb thing like this can actually lead you:

"Every morning we met before leaving and there was a line of Mercedes-Benzs and a large cloud of bodyguards: more bodyguards than mobsters, but all dressed in brightly coloured suits and headbands and even Lycra shorts that were the latest fad. For example, the Mexican [Gacha] had a green suit well lined to the body, with white sleeves and red legs like the flag of Mexico, and others were accompanied by their wives or [new] brides on tricycles with fat tyres for the beach, bringing their water bottles with iced tea or juice – and others, more liberal – brought one or two ladies from El Sombrero – a strip club that was famous in Panama – with their red hairs or their silvery wigs, dressed in the same uniforms as their respective men. The gangsters started with their women forward and the assassins and further back a caravan of pimped-out Mercedes-Benz cars driving along the avenue, with weapons almost in sight and accompanying cars with lights on. I mean c'mon!"

On May 22, his family moved into a luxurious house – owned by General Noriega – by a golf club. Protected by the general's bodyguards, his family enjoyed higher living standards. His associates entertained themselves by playing soccer on the golf course, working out at the gym and swimming. He gave his son a Honda motorbike, and flew in a man from Medellín to jog next to Juan Pablo as he rode his motorbike.

With a down payment, he had authorised the deal a few months before Noriega had come to power. Known as Pineapple Face due to his pockmarks, Noriega had ended up ruling Panama by having a bomb – provided by the CIA – planted in the plane of his predecessor. A master of playing every side, Noriega had profitable relationships with the CIA and the traffickers. He also collected fees on the billions that the drug cartels – and intelligence agencies such as the CIA – laundered through Panama. Noriega had agreed to provide sanctuary for the traffickers and their families in the wake of Lara's assassination. Despite the Panamanian leader's hospitality, Pablo didn't trust him.

Pablo summoned an American smuggler to visit him, Barry Seal, a burly ace pilot with flamboyant mutton-chop sideburns, who was addicted to living on the edge. The Colombians called him the Fat Man. El Patrón had recruited him to fly 600 kilos to America, but the DEA seized the drugs because Barry was a CIA pilot and DEA informant, operating under a fake name: Ellis MacKenzie.

To Panama, Barry delivered cash, daily reports from one of Pablo's business administrators in Florida and items from a shopping list of American goods. Asked to fly 1,500 kilos of cocaine, Barry said that he needed to inspect the airstrips. The job was urgent because chaos in Colombia had caused the cartel to dismantle its labs and move cocaine supplies to the mountains. If Barry could quickly transport 1,500 kilos, they would instruct him from their new headquarters in Panama.

In May, Barry met the cartel in the basement of a white stucco house. He later told his DEA handlers – whom he was trying to impress – that the cartel had introduced him to Federico Vaughan, a Nicaraguan government official. With slicked-back grey hair, Vaughan was sharply dressed in a silver business suit, tie, an expensive watch, sunglasses and cufflinks. He would accompany Barry to a Nicaraguan airfield, so he could inspect it. To avoid any harm in Nicaragua, Barry was to follow Vaughan's instructions. Vaughan introduced himself to Barry as the interior minister of the Nicaraguan Sandinista government, which was ready to process cocaine paste for the Medellín Cartel with ether from Germany.

With Pablo absent, his mother was in charge of assigning houses at the dump. She travelled to Moravia, where a pilgrimage of people had gathered, including some with wheelbarrows. "Pablo, to prevent the government from keeping the houses, asks that at all costs, with whatever sacrifices are needed, for you to move to the houses even though some are not finished." She asked for people to pray for no harm to come to her son.

Those living the highest on the dump received the first houses, which a priest blessed. Hermilda also designated a place to build a temple to the Holy Child of Atocha, honouring her pledge from decades earlier when she had prayed for the Holy Child to save her family from the mob attempting to break into her house during The Violence. "Child of Atocha, consolation of the afflicted, liberator of the prisoners and protection of the needy, I hope you will grant me what I am asking of you …"

After hearing the news of how joyfully the houses had been received, Pablo was glowing with pride during a meeting to discuss the traffickers surrendering to the government. He was congratulated by Gustavo, Gacha, Lehder, the Ochoa brothers, Kiko Moncada and Fernando Galeano. To determine who would be the ideal person to mediate with the president, they asked Diego Londoño White, the manager of the Medellín Metro, who had directed Betancur's presidential campaign. They considered the author Gabriel García Márquez, but settled on ex-president López. They asked Diego's brother, Santiago Londoño, who had directed the liberal campaign in Medellín, to ask López whether he would deliver their surrender proposal to Betancur.

The May elections in Panama brought high-profile independent observers from Colombia, including former president López. Approached by Santiago with the surrender proposal, López said, "Do you think it's a serious proposition?"

"As far as I managed to understand, it's a serious definitive proposal," Santiago said. "They know they are doing a great amount of damage and do not want to continue doing it."

After consulting the president, López agreed to meet Pablo and Jorge Ochoa at the Marriot Hotel. Before departing for the meeting, Pablo told Victoria that he was going to try to solve the problems they had in Colombia.

At the hotel, he told López and Santiago, "If the government will stop extradition and suspend prison sentences for convicted traffickers, we're willing to hand over our airstrips, labs and aircraft. We'll destroy the crops and close the routes to America." The traffickers asked whether the president would consider the possibility of their re-incorporation into Colombian society in the near future.

"I'll communicate your proposal to the president," López said. Convinced their surrender was in the best interests of Colombia, López detailed the proposal in a letter to Betancur. The president dispatched his attorney general, Carlos Jiménez, to meet the traffickers during an official trip to Panama to investigate the loss of $13.5 million from the Ministry of Defence, a famous robbery from the 1980s. Pablo told Victoria that he was optimistic about negotiating a deal, which would allow them to return to Colombia. His confidence was bolstered by the proposal of a second meeting in Panama with Colombian officials, including the attorney general.

On May 25, 1984, a call came from the hospital: Victoria was about to give birth. Pablo, Juan Pablo and Gustavo rushed over. In the waiting room, Gustavo reassured his nervous cousin. A doctor emerged. "Congratulations on your baby girl."

Pablo smiled. "Can we see them?"

"Yes. Come through." The doctor led them to an elevator, where a nurse was carrying a baby with a bracelet with the name, Manuela Escobar. Proudly, Pablo beamed at the sleepy newborn.

Near the end of May, Pablo and Jorge Ochoa met the attorney general at a hotel in Panama. "This is a serious thing," the attorney general said. "Therefore, we should send it to the president in writing. Not a letter, but a memorandum, so as not to put the president under any obligation to respond." After further contemplation, he said, "Mind you, if you want peace, you should also fix the situation with the DEA."

"By what way?" Pablo said.

"By sending another memorandum to the US Embassy."

The same night, lawyers from Medellín finalised a memorandum, which was divided into two parts: a proposal to end drug trafficking and a history of trafficking in Colombia up to the present. It claimed that their organisations "today control between 70 and 80 percent of Colombia's drug traffic," which generated "an annual income of around $2 billion ... of which a substantial proportion reached Colombia."

Pablo offered to dismantle his trafficking operation in Colombia, which would mean, in the short term, a spike in the prices of the final product abroad, the deterioration of quality, an increased difficulty of acquiring it and, as a consequence of all the above, the reduction in the number of consumers. A global dismantling of trafficking would require a one hundred per cent commitment by all of the participants. He offered to deliver his cocaine labs, definitively withdraw from political activity, put an end to the cocaine-paste market in the country and to repatriate billions in capital from abroad. The attorney general pledged to get a direct response from Betancur. The US Embassy received a similar memorandum.

The president was willing to negotiate with the traffickers, but during the inauguration of a bank building, he entrusted a journalist with details of the recent meetings, which *The Time* published on its front page:

"A group of drug traffickers, headed by Pablo Escobar Gaviria and who claim to represent eighty percent of the business, made a proposal to the government to reach an understanding on how to dismantle and eliminate drug trafficking in the country.

"The proposal was made a few weeks ago through former President Alfonso López Michelsen and the Attorney General of the Nation, Carlos Jiménez Gómez, who travelled to Panama to meet with Escobar Gaviria.

"The proposal is that the drug traffickers would collaborate with the US Embassy and the DEA to dismantle the laboratories and clandestine airstrips ... Escobar Gaviria's proposal took the government by surprise, whose answer is still unknown."

With the meeting exposed, the US announced that any proposals by the traffickers would be rejected and any rumours or allusions of discussions with the Mafia were false. "We do not negotiate with cartels but with people."

The attorney general offered to protect Betancur: "President, this is simply over, from now on, only one of us should speak because I think that if we start to make statements, [ex-president Alfonso] López Michelsen on the one hand, you on the other, and I on another, there will form a mess ... Let me face the consequences. I'll do that alone." Two years later, under fire from the press, the attorney general said that the president had taken far too seriously his last sentence about him taking the consequences alone.

Debates erupted in Congress. Photos emerged of a parliamentarian, William Jaramillo Gómez, using Pablo's planes. To deflect attention, he accused the attorney general and Santiago Londoño of conspiring with the traffickers.

In *The Spectator*, Cano stoked the fire: "How does a person who has received all the honours of the Republic, like former President López, sit down, with the still fresh corpse of Minister Lara, to negotiate with criminals?" With nobody wanting to be exposed for considering offers from the traffickers, the media reports scuppered any hope of a deal and revealed that Pablo was hiding in Panama.

By early June, Pablo feared that the US government was plotting to arrest him and was putting pressure on Noriega, whom he suspected was about to betray him. He told his family members that they needed to go on the run without the baby, whom he had arranged to be taken care of in Medellín. Sobbing, Victoria handed Manuela over to a trusted nurse for the journey to Colombia.

On June 15, 1984, the cartel lost 1.2 metric tons of cocaine packed in freezers and perfume cartons to US Customs agents in Miami. A Panamanian charter company owned the cargo jet transporting it. Pablo heard from a Panamanian colonel that Noriega was cutting a deal with the DEA. His military seized 16,000 barrels of ether destined for the new lab and arrested twenty-three Colombian workers. The angry traffickers demanded an explanation, but were told that Noriega was in Europe. They were granted a conference with the Panamanian government. Afterwards, Noriega released the Colombian prisoners and returned lab equipment and cash. Pablo advised his partners to leave Panama. Private planes and helicopters arrived. The Colombians fled. Some went to Medellín. Juan David Ochoa flew to Brazil.

According to Pablo, "In Panama, which is the base for the North Americans, the CIA, the FBI and the DEA, the gringos began to put pressure on Noriega. They wanted him to lay hands on us, to capture us, and Noriega, who was on our payroll but also on the payroll of the CIA and the payroll of the DEA, began to get nervous. He told César Rodríguez [a business associate] about his problems and César told us that the DEA was putting pressure on the General. For us to try to get away from Panama, we'd have to not fuck around anymore with the yachts or with the sports. Things started to get hot, and to wash his hands before the Americans, the bastard Noriega decided to hand them the ether first – 16,000 barrels – and then the laboratory that was about to start operating.

"So, when we saw that he gave everything to the DEA, we thought he was willing to sell his own mother and we started to flee. Some went to Brazil, others to Mexico, others to Spain and myself to Nicaragua where I already had connections with the government, thanks to the help of some M-19 leaders that I met when we made peace with them ..."

CHAPTER 27

NICARAGUA

Pablo's guerrilla contacts confirmed that he was welcome in Nicaragua, where a trade embargo enforced by America had created desperation for economic aid. Financial assistance donated by the traffickers enabled them to move to Managua, Nicaragua's capital.

Pablo, his family and a dozen bodyguards arrived at a massive old mansion with Gacha, his wife and four bodyguards, but they disliked being hemmed in by ten-foot security walls and towers with armed guards. They found a book describing the history of the house, which included several massacres. With a civil war in progress, gunfire erupted and surrounding buildings were damaged. Food was provided, but Pablo had nowhere to spend his money.

Clinging to a photo of her newborn, Victoria pined for Manuela. Her brother Mario took daily photos of the baby, but couldn't mail them as he didn't want the authorities to locate them. Without any toys, 7-year-old Juan Pablo cried and begged to leave Nicaragua.

"We'll all be killed if we go back right now," Pablo said.

Juan Pablo's respite from the gloomy house was to accompany Victoria to spa visits, where he sat with Pinina, listening to Colombian soccer games on a radio-telephone. Smothered by flies, they placed bets on how many they could kill within five minutes.

To assess transshipment routes, Pablo and Gacha flew over Nicaragua in a helicopter with Barry Seal, who was on a mission for George HW Bush, who wanted to trick Pablo into doing a cocaine deal with the Communist Nicaraguan government, which Bush hoped to use to justify providing arms to Nicaraguan rebels. Listed in Appendix C is the official version of what happened, according to Barry and the DEA, written in the interests of furthering American foreign policy. Barry returned with photos showing Pablo and Gacha loading twenty-five-kilo duffel bags of cocaine, which the American administration claimed had been facilitated by the Nicaraguan government.

While the US government planned its next move, Pablo relented to his son's demands to return home. "If it's so dangerous," Victoria said, "I promise he won't go out on the streets of Medellín."

Pablo told her that they would accompany Juan Pablo to the airport, and at the last minute, they would tell their son that he was travelling alone with a bodyguard. That way, he wouldn't get upset and refuse to go. At the airport, Juan Pablo wouldn't let go of his parents. Crying, he refused to leave without his mother. Pablo reassured him that they would join him in a few days.

Without her two children, stuck in a war-torn country, surrounded by armed bodyguards, Victoria grew depressed and cried constantly. Secretly plotting to return to Medellín, she insisted on travelling to Panama to meet her sister, who would bring photos of their children. Pablo approved of the visit provided that she promptly returned to Nicaragua. After she left, he called her daily to get updates on their children.

It took several days for her to muster the courage to tell him that she was joining their children in Medellín. Exploding on the phone, he warned she would be killed. Unwavering, she promised to stay inside of Nora's house and never leave. She had been absent from her baby for over three months, which she couldn't allow to continue because the newborn needed her.

Petrified of what might happen in Colombia, she landed at the Olaya Herrera airport, and headed straight to Nora, who had lost weight and was mired in depression. Unable to recognise

Victoria, Manuela cried in her mother's arms. Only Nora and the nurse could calm the baby. Juan Pablo clung to his mother.

Pablo later told a journalist, "Nicaragua will always be an important point in the transport of cocaine for the US, but we had lost the tracks [routes] and the freedom to go down from the time when Somoza fell. But now, with the problem of Noriega … I said, 'Let's try.' If I managed to open that route again, I was going to recover a series of routes that gave a lot of money previously. And so it was.

"Look: to not extend the story much, when we settled, my family and I were given the houses of those that had been seized by the rich from Somoza. And to keep the story even shorter: I'll tell you that not long after arriving there, I was travelling through parts of Nicaragua in a Russian helicopter, accompanied by Álvaro Fayad and a delegate of the President of the Republic. Do you know what we were doing? Choosing the place to install a kitchen, which, among other things, could never be assembled."

In July 1984, the Reagan-Bush administration leaked photos of the Barry Seal sting operation to the media. According to Pablo, "Now, there were some photos of me that were set up, supposedly to show that the Sandinistas were involved in drug trafficking. I don't know if you remember the photos: I appeared carrying a bag – according to them, full of cocaine – to a plane piloted by Barry Seal, on a track in Nicaragua, at night. In the first place, I have never been a freighter in my life. I have never been a pawn. I am a boss. And secondly, cocaine was never loaded in Nicaragua. Never.

"It happens that when I got back to where the Nicas were, we started to operate there with a Titan. A Titan aircraft is a ship with good space inside and will fly for about thirteen hours. A slow plane. Then when you get enough fuel to make a flight to the US, you can transport, maximum, 500 kilos of cocaine. But already with the help of that scale, we took off from tracks at sea level in Colombia with less gasoline and, loaded it with 1,200 kilos. So, in Nicaragua that was what the plane did: load fuel to go to another friendly country and do the same …

"But if you add to this the murder of Barry Seal, the pilot who betrayed us and went to work for the DEA and said he had taken those photos, then things get tangled up. We didn't kill that piece of shit nor did we ever load cocaine in Nicaragua.

"It seems to me that the photos were to try to cover up a scandal that was coming on top of us: that our cocaine was being handled by foreigners to finance the Sandinistas and our cocaine to finance the enemies of the Sandinistas. Rather said, Colombian cocaine was defining the wars of the continent.

"For this trade, it was a question of infiltrating our routes and they made it easy because at that time some Colombians who were assembling zoos and fine farms began to bring animals in a Howard 500 airplane that departed from Texas or Louisiana – depending on business – and went down to some tracks on the north coast of Colombia. That plane was from the government of the US and they did not know it was here. As always, the transport of cocaine is quite liked up there, so we negotiated with them and we started to load half a ton to the Howard on each trip. And they charged $500,000 per kilo transported or $2.5 million per flight. That's a lot of money. The Americans took the cocaine and gave it to our people up there and there they were paid that fortune.

"The truth is that much later we found that the Howard operated on tracks controlled by the CIA in Texas and Louisiana and that, once they got the transport money, they gave it to the Contras to acquire weapons, because the government of the United States had approved the sale, and that weaponry was transported to Costa Rica by a pilot on a Piper Cheyenne."

The kitchen in Nicaragua was never built because Pablo had to leave Managua in a hurry: "The story goes like this: President Ortega had returned from a trip to Europe – I think to Spain – and at night, listening to the radio, I found a station on which he was speaking. I do not remember what he was saying, but I heard someone ask him something and he answered in a way that I understood [the meaning of] very well. Immediately, I suspected that the Sandinista government could be in some negotiation with the North Americans and that they were going to deliver me. Then I called my pilot and ordered him to leave for the airport and get the plane ready. I picked up the three things that I needed to take with me and took off, mind you, at two in the morning. Later I learned that the Sandinista guards came for me at half past two."

With the international news showing his face, he was at risk of capture if he remained in unpredictable countries. Rather than battle the authorities overseas, he decided to return to his homeland to fight on familiar turf. Flying back with Gacha, calculating their next moves, Pablo could not have foreseen his next crisis. Having done everything possible to protect his family, he was devastated to learn from his sobbing mother that six heavily armed men in military uniforms had located his 72-year-old father at his farm in eastern Antioquia. After tying up Abel's colleagues, they took him and demanded $50 million. "You must do everything possible to rescue him safe and sound." The pain in his mother's voice upset El Patrón. To prevent a family kidnapping from ever happening again, he would use all of his resources to rescue his father and make an example out of the men.

CHAPTER 28

FATHER KIDNAPPED

On November 1, 1984, Abel rose at 5 AM at the farm he had named in his wife's honour: Villa Hermilda. After eating breakfast, he got in his Toyota truck and attended the 6 AM mass. He visited the market and returned home. Six men in uniforms claimed to be special agents seeking information about his son and asked him to accompany them. Complying, he was transported along the road that led to the town of Sonsón.

At his El Bizcocho estate, Pablo strategised with his men, some of whom blamed the guerrillas. "I don't think so," he said. "They cannot possibly have forgotten what happened with the kidnapping of Marta Nieves Ochoa."

"How about common criminals?"

"No one in the underworld would dare to challenge my dominance," he said.

He heard a rumour that the kidnapping had been orchestrated by an ultra-right-wing faction called Brigade Rodrigo Lara Bonilla who were seeking to avenge the assassination of the justice minister, but due to demands for money from the kidnappers, he discarded that possibility.

The kidnappers taunted him on a call. "You are only brave with ten assassins by your side." They demanded $10 million. Calmly, he responded that they had kidnapped the wrong person, a simple penniless farmer, they needed to come up with a realistic number and get back to him. He hung up.

He announced that if his father was so much as bruised the ransom money would be insufficient to pay for the kidnappers' burials. In the newspapers, he offered a $1 million reward for the culprits' whereabouts. The ad included descriptions of the two Toyota SUVs the men had used, including the licence plates. Enticed by the reward and wanting to ingratiate themselves with the boss, people from various backgrounds joined the hunt, including hit men from Medellín, Cali and the Colombian coast, young people from the barrios, members of the police, the Army, the political class, the industrial class, the Catholic Church, paramilitaries and guerrillas. But even with so many searching, the kidnappers remained elusive, which frustrated Pablo, whose family grew increasingly fearful.

Due to the lack of results, he adopted more cunning and creative strategies. He had the newspapers start a rumour that his father had a heart disease which required a pacemaker and medication. The story was reported in ads on the front page of *The Colombian* and *The World of Medellín*, authenticated by the signature of a doctor called Miguel Sepulveda. Many of the 200 drugstores in Medellín had security cameras. Cameras were installed in those that didn't. He offered a reward for photos of anyone buying the heart medicine.

As the kidnappers used payphones, he gave hundreds of radio transmitters to people with instructions to listen to a certain radio station. Whenever the kidnappers called Hermilda, the station announced a song dedicated to Luz Marina. After hearing this, the people with the transmitters rushed to the nearest payphones. Still lacking a result, he doubled the reward to $2 million and hired two ex-FBI agents with expertise in kidnapping cases.

Pablo went to a meeting at Montecasino, the headquarters of the United Self-Defense Forces, the paramilitary group run by the Castaño brothers. Amid 200 armed men guarding the headquarters, he was guided to a small office. Accompanied by Fidel Castaño, Don Berna arrived. Twelve years younger than Pablo, the hefty paramilitary leader was nervous because it was his first face-to-face talk with El Patrón. He believed that anyone willing to kidnap Pablo's father was suicidal and crazy.

"Here's a good man who works for our organisation," Fidel said, introducing Don Berna, who shook Pablo's hand. "You can count on us. As you know, our own father was killed in a kidnapping situation. Since then, I've had lots of experience and learned how to manage a crisis."

"Thank you," Pablo said. "The information coming in from people hoping to get the reward is fuzzy. I have nothing concrete. I'm eagerly awaiting a call from the kidnappers."

They waited until Pablo's phone rang. He told a kidnapper that he wanted to speak to Abel. After several seconds of silence, the kidnapper replied, "We have your father. He is in good health. For us to release him, we want $5 million, which is a small sum for a man of your great wealth."

"I will not pay you a single dime."

"If you don't pay, we'll kill your father, chop him up and send the pieces to you. Pablo, you think you are rich and tough, but if you don't pay, he dies."

With a rage swelling inside, he yelled, "If you lay so much as a finger on my father, I'll kill you all up to the third generation!"

"Get us the money. We'll talk later." The kidnapper hung up.

Red with fury, Pablo yelled, "I'll not rest until I kill the last of these bandits!" After an awkward silence, he said, "Fidel, I have worked hard in your fight against subversion and even though I don't agree with some of your methods, today more than ever, I need your help to find my father. I don't want my mother to suffer. For soon, I'll die of anguish. Mobilise your entire organisation to help get information that allows me to rescue him safe and sound."

"You can count on me," Fidel said.

Relaunching Death to Kidnappers, which had helped to rescue Marta Ochoa in 1981, Pablo hosted a meeting for 500 people at Hacienda Nápoles. Representatives from groups arrived, including senior army members and political advisers.

"I have a message for all of the kidnappers in Colombia," he said, "whether they are guerrillas or common criminals. If they choose to target family members or close friends of the cartels, many of their men are going to die in retaliation and there will be no considerations for sparing their lives." There was massive applause.

Supported by senior officers of the Fourth Army Brigade, Fidel Castaño was appointed the commander general of the organisation. Those present pledged millions of dollars and an assortment of weapons for the new Death to Kidnappers. Across Colombia, kidnapping organisations braced as their members were executed and hostages released. To generate publicity, their corpses were chained to the bars of buildings housing newspapers, with placards strapped to their bodies with messages such as, "For being a kidnapper: Sincerely, the MAS."

Pablo received a lucky break from Pachito, a paraplegic in Bello, a town in Antioquia. Abandoned by his band of kidnappers, he was resentful because he had no money to support his wife and child. He contacted the boss, who arranged to meet him in an office.

"I'm well acquainted with the men who kidnapped your father," Pachito said.

"I want to know every member of their band," El Patrón said. "What they look like. Where they live. Their real names and aliases. Everything about their family members." After hearing the details, Pablo thanked Pachito and gave him a down payment. "If I rescue my father safe and sound thanks to your information, you'll get a bigger sum. You'll never ever have to worry about taking care of your family."

In Medellín, Pablo met Fidel Castaño at an office called The Lake. Pachito's information was analysed and orders issued to abduct the family members of the kidnappers. In Pablo's helicopters, government forces assisted, including a retired lieutenant of the National Police. After the head of the band learned that his parents and sister had been snatched, even more of his relatives continued to vanish.

Pablo individually called the kidnappers. "I'm going to kill your entire families unless my father is released. There is nothing left to negotiate."

In a town south of Bogotá, Abel was released. Having been tied to a bed in a cold room, he emerged in surprisingly good health. Pablo announced: "The kidnappers, miserable and insensitive, did not take into account the conditions of the age and health of Mr Abel Escobar and, on the contrary, mistakenly believed they'd find a fearful and unprotected family. The demands of the kidnappers were not fulfilled in any way, because both Mr Abel Escobar and the other members of his family were willing to die before allowing the culprits of the most detestable of crimes to succeed."

After releasing the kidnappers' family members, he targeted the culprits. Located in a car heading for an airport hoping to escape to Miami, the head kidnapper fled several blocks only to be captured at a roundabout. Pablo removed from him a medallion he had given to Abel. To set an example, he shot him fifty times with a rifle, rendering him unrecognisable. The other culprits were tortured and killed. Having received his reward, Pachito was in his wheelchair outside of his home, relaxing in the sun, when he was executed.

CHAPTER 29

A LOVE RIVAL

In April 1984, Virginia went to Italy to film a stockings commercial, full of love for Pablo, who had given her $100,000 to spend. Twice weekly on the phone, they professed how much they were missing each other. She had been away for almost a month when Lara Bonilla was assassinated. The news shattered her happiness. She knew that Pablo would be a fugitive until he was captured or killed and she realised that the justice minister's assassination had been on his mind when he had given her the Beretta gun. She regretted going to Italy instead of remaining where she could have steered him away from such a big mistake, which the idiots he surrounded himself would have encouraged regardless of the consequences. She sobbed watching Lara's widow at the funeral.

On their next call, he asked not to be interrupted and for her to memorise his words. Due to the assassination, all communication had to stop because the authorities would target her. She needed to keep the gun ready and remember what he had taught her. She must distrust everybody, including her girlfriends. If anyone asked about him, she should say he had moved to Australia and she hadn't seen him in a year. Everything would calm down over time. He would return and send for her. He loved her and would miss her every day.

In Colombia, she received death threats from people angry at Pablo. Eventually, she stopped crying and toughened up. Perhaps the murderer was no good for her and he should stay in Australia.

On his visits to Bogotá, the Cali Cartel's Gilberto invited Virginia to his office at the radio station. "What's going on?" he asked, dressed in a navy-blue suit and Italian shoes. "As a simple man from the province, I don't get much news from Bogotá."

Aware that his political connections kept him informed, she suspected that he was bluffing. Sitting on the sofa, watching him take calls from important people, she thought that he was trying to impress her with his power. She had heard that the Medellín Cartel had lost a few billion dollars due to the raid of the jungle labs, and Gilberto was becoming one of Colombia's wealthiest at Pablo's expense.

After she had listened to the majority of the callers requesting money, Gilberto hung up. "My friends get 100 percent of what I've promised. Those I dislike get 10 percent, and when I know their price, I promise that they'll get the rest later. Ex-president Alfonso López Michelsen gets first-class tickets to Europe. He and his wife are frequent visitors to London, Paris and Bucharest, where they get procaine injections from a famous gerontologist, whose patients stay healthy and alert for up to 100 years."

While their topics of conversation varied, Pablo was never mentioned by name. Describing her as a goddess and a beautiful queen, Gilberto pointed out that she was marriage material, but unfortunately, he had already wedded a beast. Between the bitterness of his wife and the contempt from the bankers, he was treated like an outcast. He appreciated that Virginia understood his predicament.

She was noticing differences between the bosses. Pablo never insulted her intelligence with flattery, deprecated his associates, lowered his guard around anybody or accepted defeat. He refrained from small talk and nothing was ever big enough. Gilberto was more elegant, refined and less confrontational. Pablo prioritised sex, the talk came later, but Gilberto did it in reverse. Pablo preferred jeans, sneakers and a shirt whereas Gilberto dressed like a banker and lacked the close-set shark eyes of a killer. Pablo did business on a handshake and never asked for receipts, whereas the Orejuela brothers hired accountants to document everything.

Gilberto was charming and relaxed, whereas Pablo was full of surprises that pushed her to the limits of feeling.

Gilberto invited her to a soccer event, where she met his brother Miguel, who came across as serious and lacking Gilberto's charm and intellectual curiosity. After posing for photos with them, she met Gilberto's children from his first wife, who were all friendly and polite. When she was ready to go, Gilberto insisted on walking her to her car even though she said it was unnecessary. Spotting her Mitsubishi, he remarked how lovely his queen's car was. After telling him to stop his nonsense, she said it wasn't exactly Cinderella's chariot, it was the tiny vehicle of a journalist exploited by his radio company. Besides, her heart wasn't in cars, it was in the fleet of planes she had at her disposal. Asked whose hangars they were in, she said a man in Australia who would soon return. Didn't she know that he'd been back for a while, Gilberto said, and invited her to dinner in Cali.

Pablo was back and hadn't told her! The thought pierced her heart, but she tried to hide the explosion of pain. "Since colonialism, Bogotá has had restaurants, but I'm going to Cali on Saturday to buy antiques from my friend, so I accept your invitation."

On Saturday, she cried for most of the day after learning that Pablo had been partying with models and beauty queens in jacuzzis while high on cannabis. She appreciated that Gilberto wasn't obsessed with cannabis or lesbian shows, nor was he on the run. The king of the Valle del Cauca had spent hundreds of hours wooing her, during which they had discussed everything under the sun from art to philosophy, whereas Pablo just wanted to get her naked.

Over dinner, she asked Gilberto for his cocaine formula. After smiling, he stated that she must have become a Mafiosa or at least done some intensive classes on the subject. What had she been talking about with the Australian other than counting sheep? She said that she had explained to him step-by-step the theory of relativity until he had a eureka moment and saw stars. Gilberto needed to stop asking her about that psycho because she never talked about her ex-lovers with another. She demanded his cocaine recipe, which she promised not to sell for less than $100 million.

He said that in business sometimes you win, sometimes you lose, someone steals 200 kilos here, 300 kilos there. What else can you do other than resign yourself? However, if someone stole five kilos from his competitor, at least five people would be killed. At that rate, he would eventually murder all of humankind. He detailed his formula for cocaine. After finishing, he said he had a business proposal that would make her a multimillionaire and asked how well she got along with Gacha.

"I'm respected by all the bosses," she said. "At the forums against extradition, I'm the only TV star. I realised my involvement would eventually end my career. That's why I took the job at your radio company. It was my parachute."

He said a queen like her shouldn't worry about such silly things. As he must spend more time in Bogotá, he'd like her to help convince Gacha what was in his best interest. After the raid on the jungle labs, Gacha would benefit from them being Colombia's largest importers of chemicals. In LA, there are a million honourable Mexicans desperate for work and those involved with Gacha's merchandise don't steal any of it; whereas in Florida, you have to work with the murderers, rapists and criminals Castro sent on boats from Cuba. Dealing with them would send you crazy. He wasn't so ambitious that he needed to win every battle. The Wall Street and Studio 54 crowds provided enough for him and his children to live peacefully forever.

With the bosses of the Medellín Cartel being so tight-knit, even more so now they were fugitives, Virginia didn't expect Gacha to welcome Gilberto's proposal. But as her passion was collecting information, she requested a meeting, aware that in the emerald-dealing underworld, Gacha had committed more horrific crimes than Pablo. She arrived in the countryside where Gacha's soccer team, Millonarios Fútbol Club, trained. After walking by beautiful gardens and duck ponds, she waited until he appeared smiling, dark-skinned and thin, about 5 foot 7 and a couple of years older than Virginia and Pablo. After exchanging greetings, she said, "I like Pablo's friends much better than Pablo himself."

He laughed. "It's hard for me to speak freely. Even in my offices they can hide microphones." After she conveyed the message from the Cali godfather, he said that Gilberto was Pablo's sneakiest enemy and a scoundrel to send a princess like her to do his dirty work. If he wanted to be his partner, he needed to stop acting like a great lord and get blood on his hands by joining the MAS and slaughtering kidnappers and Communists. Like all of them, Gilberto was nothing but an Indian-made-good and a drugstore messenger with a bicycle. Gacha knew his territory and partners, but apparently Gilberto didn't. His chemicals would last until the year 3000, so he didn't need Gilberto's. The business was not for angels like her, but for a son of a bitch like him, but with balls like Pablo's. Although he wouldn't tell anybody about the meeting, he wanted Gilberto reminded that there was nothing more deadly anyone could do in life than to provoke El Patrón.

Gacha said that whatever was going on between her and Pablo, he couldn't intervene because Pablo was his friend. He believed that Pablo had been crazy about her ever since they had met. Due to Lara's assassination, Pablo hadn't dared to show his face to her because the government had hit back hard. He updated her on what had happened in Panama and said that ex-president López was helping them get everything back on track. Thanks to the civil aviation director, their planes had been safely moved to Central America.

"Since Lara's death," she said, "I've been receiving daily threats and living in terror."

"If you want, I can have my men trace the calls and eliminate the callers."

"That's OK. I've got enough on my conscience with all the people Pablo has killed. I prefer to be a victim than a victimiser, but I understand why in our country people take justice into their own hands."

"You can always count on me even if Pablo isn't around. I'm eternally grateful for the TV programme you made about Medellín Without Slums and for you attending the forums on extradition."

"Pablo has never thanked me for anything."

He said that Pablo was too proud to say anything. After he had won her heart, he believed he was the king of the world. But he had told Gacha about her courage and loyalty. He really needed her. In his life, he never had an educated adult woman who could put him in his place. Nor would anyone from her class have made such sacrifices and not asked for anything in return. She left with a deeper understanding of the divisions among the traffickers and how the toughest always supported Pablo. Their fierce loyalty and admiration was perplexing. Despite Gacha's monstrous reputation, he had the character of a real man, which was rare in Colombia, and a solid friendship with Pablo.

Gilberto insisted on meeting Virginia in Cali to discuss the meeting because her phone was tapped and she was under surveillance. In Cali, she said that Gacha had thanked him for the offer, but had declined because he had supplies until the year 3000. The Cali godfather responded that Gacha must have told him to go to hell and that he was Pablo's partner, not his, because he wasn't a member of the MAS. She said that due to his busy schedule they had only spoken for fifteen minutes. He said not to lie, not only did nobody talk to her for only fifteen minutes but because she was such a good interviewer and obtainer of information, he probably spoke to her for three enjoyable hours. What had been said during the rest of the time?

She said Gacha considered him and his brother too liberal to kill Communists, but he did respect their ideological differences, and as a brilliant man you would know what that means. He frowned on you having a princess like me convey your message. The good news was that she had convinced one of her wealthy friends to provide banking for his drugstores. She had assured her friend that Gilberto paid all of his taxes, which her friend appreciated because he was the largest taxpayer in the country. Her friend was ready to meet whenever he liked. Gilberto praised her for being a dream girlfriend, but then corrected himself, saying she was born for more important things such as being a guardian angel, who would selflessly do favours. She said she understood the problems stemming from having $2 billion in only one bank. He needed to stay on the correct path, and never to join the MAS.

To celebrate the banking arrangement, they danced at his brother's nightclub, where alcohol reduced his self-control. At the Intercontinental Hotel, he said, "I'm walking you back to your room." Going through the lobby, all eyes turned towards the high-profile couple. Upon reaching her door, he insisted upon opening it. He pushed her inside and onto the bed.

In Bogotá days later, Gilberto apologised and claimed that he had memory loss. "I don't remember anything either, thank God," Virginia lied.

"To prove how important you are to me, I want to take you to Panama to meet ex-president Alfonso López. Do you know him?"

Of course she did. She used to sit at the main table during the presidential campaign with the ex-presidents: López and Turbay. At the forums against extradition, Pablo had also sat at the main table. With news, she was the perfect person to cover it.

In Panama, Virginia met Gilberto's partners and company directors, mostly middle-aged men who were experts in accountancy and finance. They only talked business, whereas Pablo's associates mostly talked about politics. She concluded that they had all been summoned so that Gilberto could display them to her.

In Bogotá, *Show of the Stars* started to receive phone calls from someone impersonating Virginia claiming that she could not attend any more recordings because her face had been mutilated with a razor blade on the orders of Pablo's wife, who wanted the big black SUV that Virginia had supposedly received as a gift from El Patrón. Entering the studio, she heard her co-workers whisper that her face had been reconstructed by plastic surgery in Rio de Janeiro the previous weekend, financed by Pablo. The scandal spread throughout the country. She suspected Gilberto's wife.

After participating in a product launch, Virginia returned home to find her living room lights on. Inside, Pablo was holding one of her photo albums. As if they had never spent months apart, they smiled and embraced. His adoring gaze suggested that he was unaware of her fling with Gilberto, but he quickly detected something was amiss and for the first time resorted to the flattery that she despised. "You're the most beautiful woman I've ever laid eyes on. In that long gown with your hair pulled up you resemble a goddess from Olympus."

She prepared a large drink. "My whole life I've made a living from looking like this."

"In your dozens of magazine covers, I don't understand why they don't show how you look in real life."

"They have insufficient budgets and they are too busy plastering serial killers on the covers to turn them into modern legends." She asked about Panama and whether he'd struck a deal with the government to abolish extradition in return for repatriating his wealth. He asked how she knew that and who had been calling her every fifteen minutes. "Let's wait for the next call for you to find out and you can listen to the description of torture."

"Don't worry. The threats can only be from Galán's harmless supporters. Now where are my gifts from Rome? Your girlfriends said you didn't leave anything with them." Shocked that her friends had lied, she protested that she had spent over $10,000. Her girlfriends must have assumed that he had fled permanently, stolen the gifts and resold them. "For our safety, don't tell anybody that I'm back or that we have seen each other. Who knows what your girlfriends are capable of if they will steal $10,000. It's time to accept that you shouldn't be having girlfriends." He opened a suitcase and threw cassettes onto the floor. "These are your phone calls recorded by the F2 Unit of the police, who work for me. They are scrambled, so you wouldn't understand them if you listened to them."

Refusing to believe him, she was too tired to engage. He demanded to know whose wife had contacted the media with the story about his wife and Virginia's face getting slashed. She said the culprits were probably supporters of Galán, and that her lover is always Colombia's richest man. Perhaps the F2 could provide his name. For five hours, she had listened to him insult her in a disguised way, so exhausted, she said goodnight.

"For the rest of your life, you'll never ever see me again!" he stormed off and took the elevator down.

Hoping to relax, she turned on music, rested in a bath and closed her eyes. She rejoiced that she had looked superb for Pablo's last impression of her. She had no need for a Mafia serial killer in her life, so why was she crying? Perhaps because she couldn't relate to or trust anyone like she had with him. Journalism was a nest of vipers. She was tired of society women, jilted men and her gift-thieving girlfriends. An object splashing into the bath jolted her eyes open. Floating on the water was her favourite toy boat.

Pablo yelled that was her first yacht and if she didn't tell him the name of the Mafia boss she had been speaking to on the phone, he would confiscate the boat and drown her. He imagined lifting her feet up slowly and her lovely hair getting soaked, which would be revealed to the world when they photographed her corpse. If she didn't want there to be a headline 'Goodbye Goddess,' then she needed to name the son of a bitch, so that he could cut him into pieces, so he'd learn not to mess with his woman and his wife.

Sarcastically, she said bravo and suggested that they search together for the woman who had started the rumour in the media, so that they could both dismember her. Laughing, she pumped her fist in the air and tried to snatch the boat. He grabbed it. On his knees next to the bathtub, he said he wasn't joking anymore, he'd returned to electrocute her even if he regretted it eternally. The desperation and jealousy in his eyes seemed funny and pathetic to Virginia. It was as if their roles had reversed since he had saved her from the whirlpool. Suddenly, she felt that the only thing that fulfilled her in the present moment was him, so she reached out, grabbed his shirt and put her arms around his neck. She suggested that they electrocute themselves together, so that they could be united in heaven for eternity.

Pretending to fall into the tub, he swayed. He crouched and scooped her from the water. "The only place I'll be accepted is hell." He wrapped her in a towel and dried her frantically, while she sang to a song on the radio called 'Fever.'

With Lara's replacement, Enrique Parejo, stepping up extradition, Jorge Ochoa and Gilberto fled to Spain. The Cali godfather claimed that he was retiring from the business to concentrate on European investments. He told Virginia that he would miss her, and he hoped to see her soon because she was the only person he could confide in. She said she would miss their intellectual conversations. When Gilberto left Colombia, she felt the loss of someone she was fond of but not in love with.

She entered a second honeymoon period with Pablo. So much organisation went into their clandestine meetings, they appreciated every second, while aware that due to the danger every time they met could be their last. Rented planes flew her to airports, and two armed bodyguards – different each time – transported her to him. Not wanting to become a liability for knowing too much, she never asked his men where they were going or where he was hiding. Usually, she traversed dangerous roads slippery with mud and full of potholes, while clutching her Beretta handgun. Sentry booths indicated the proximity of Pablo's safe house, which was often small, still under construction and usually within the Hacienda Nápoles estate. She would arrive before Pablo, wait in silence and listen for his jeeps. The noise of engines would prompt her to turn off the lights, so she could gaze out of the window in case the authorities arrived, in which case she was supposed to kill herself to avoid getting interrogated. To prevent his extradition, she had decided to shoot him if he were arrested at a safe house.

Pablo would arrive with his bodyguards, and they would quickly disperse. Watching through the window some of their faces became familiar, and years later she would recognise them in the media as famous hit men. Some had evil faces, whereas others such as Pinina appeared angelic. Although he loved his men, Pablo told Virginia that all mercenaries had their price and would succumb to the highest bidder. With so much money in cocaine, betrayal was an ever-present threat. He was convinced that his men would switch sides to whomever orchestrated his death. Hoping to prevent the leaking of information, he said he never discussed his cocaine labs with his accountants or politics with the pilots or smuggling routes with Santo. To hide their money, his brother used corporations and banks in the Bahamas, Luxembourg, Panama and the Grand Cayman Islands. Travelling back, the driver always quickly found the highway, while Virginia wondered what would happen to her if Pablo were killed. She prayed that he would strike a deal with the government and retire.

The second honeymoon period ended when he announced that he had to leave the country to take care of business. She warned him about bribing Communists because that was putting money into the hands of America's main enemy, which would provoke a US response against him. He promised that they would meet soon, perhaps in Central America. "Be careful with what you say on the phone, with your friends and take care of your gun." She promised to sleep with the gun under her pillow. Watching him leave, she was concerned about the relationships he had cultivated with the extreme left and right and his increased use of anti-imperialist language directed at America.

Her fears were realised when the US published the photos taken by Barry Seal of Pablo and Gacha trafficking cocaine in Nicaragua, which transformed the bosses into two of the most wanted men in the world. She believed that his mistake was irreparable and the consequences would be enormous.

For two months, she assumed that he was too busy with beauty queens to see her, so she accepted an invitation from Gilberto to travel to Spain. In a restaurant, she met Gilberto and Jorge Ochoa, who reiterated that they had retired from the business and were investing their fortunes in construction and Spanish fighting bulls instead of financing wars in Colombia. Although El Patrón's name wasn't mentioned, she felt his presence at the table.

On Saturday, Gilberto took Virginia to lunch by the Segovia Fortress, an impressive castle built upon a large rock promontory. Pointing at a turret, he said, "Centuries ago, a girl enslaved by the Moors dropped a baby prince from there and then threw herself over." On Sunday, his executives took her to an art gallery. Although she enjoyed the sights, she felt inexplicably sad. In the evening, she met Gilberto for dinner.

"How is your career going?" he asked.

"My fame and beauty create envy, which the media stirs up and people call with death threats."

"I've missed you a lot. I really need a woman I can talk to in Colombian about everything." Holding her hand, he said, "I'd like to have you nearby, in Paris not Spain. It's my favourite city. I never imagined that someone from my humble background would ever see it." He offered to fall in love with her over time, and for them to have a more serious relationship. If she were to start her own business, they could see each other on the weekends.

Taken aback, she contemplated the beauty of Paris, which she esteemed above Bogotá and was far removed from the turmoil in Medellín. The prospect of becoming the spoiled Parisian lover of one of the world's wealthiest men had its appeal. She specified her terms. If they fell in love, she would make him feel like a king. He would always be proud to be with her, in public and private. Her contacts would open doors for him. If they separated, she would take only her jewels unless she were marrying another man, in which case she would need her designer clothes.

He smiled. "We should meet again as soon as everything is settled in Spain and I've made all of my investment decisions. Moving our money over here is complicated. I can't call you because your phone is tapped. You need to withdraw all your money from the First Interamericas Bank in Panama because the US is putting pressure on General Noriega. The bank could be closed and its assets frozen at any time." The bank's biggest share-holders were Gilberto, his brother, Miguel, and Edgar Alberto Garcia Montilla, who laundered money for the Cali Cartel. Gilberto knew what was about to happen because he had bribed General Rogelio Cruz Rios, one of the most powerful people in Panamanian law enforcement, who served as secretary of the board of directors of First Interamericas Bank, and protected the cartel's interests. Virginia managed to withdraw her money before the trouble erupted.

In Zürich, she sought advice from a high-society friend, who said to decline Gilberto's offer and to find work at a Spanish TV channel in America. She objected on the grounds that her chemistry with Gilberto was excellent, they laughed continuously, and with his billions, her hotel room would be decorated as if she were British royalty, with art from Sotheby's and Christie's, and she would have a driver in a Bentley, a chef, the prettiest flowers, the most coveted tables in the fanciest restaurants, tickets to the opera and concerts, vacations anywhere in the world ... He responded that any human would kill for that. Regarding Gilberto's offer of helping her set up a business, she could use his labs to create her own line of cosmetics. Her friend said that it was great that she knew how to use Gilberto's billions, but the Mafia boss would never know what to do with a woman like her. The next morning at breakfast, her friend handed her the newspapers and said that she was lucky to have dodged the incident in Spain: Colombians were all over the news: Gilberto, Jorge Ochoa and their wives had been arrested and were facing extradition to America.

An informant had betrayed the bosses by notifying Spain's Special Prosecutor for the Prevention and Repression of Drug Trafficking that Ochoa was in Madrid and using the alias Moisés Moreno Miranda. The authorities had set up surveillance on Ochoa, who had occupied an 8,000-square-foot mansion, complete with a swimming pool, tennis courts, a disco and four Mercedes-Benz. They had watched him live a luxurious life, including frequenting expensive restaurants and concerts. They saw his wife deposit hundreds of thousands of dollars in local banks, which they believed was drug money.

They had notified the DEA, and the agency had told Washington: "Intelligence ... has indicated that suspected Colombian trafficking group intends to create an investment company with unlimited funding and is in the process of purchasing several extremely expensive residences, indicating intent to remain in Spain."

Both bosses were monitored for three months. After Ochoa asked about buying 10,000 acres in southern Spain, the police feared that he was about to set up a global cocaine hub. On November 15, 1984, the two bosses and their wives were arrested. The Americans hoped to parlay their misfortune into obtaining their extradition, which set the stage for a legal battle.

Virginia flew to Madrid and attempted to enter Carabanchel prison. "What's the nature of your relationship with Gilberto Rodriguez and Jorge Ochoa?" a guard asked.

"I'm a Colombian journalist."

"We can't allow you into the prison."

At her hotel, Gilberto's associates advised her to leave Spain immediately because she was at risk of arrest and interrogation. She packed and rushed to the airport, where the police followed her. In first class, she drank champagne and cried so much that the passenger next to her offered a handkerchief. At home, her answering machine played endless death threats. She decided to sleep with the phones left on in case news came about Gilberto.

The phone ringing roused her from slumber. A familiar voice asked where she had been. She responded that on Friday, she had dinner with a Sicilian prince in Rome. On Saturday, she had consulted with an English lord about moving to Europe. On Monday, she was in Madrid contemplating her move. On Tuesday, she was sobbing outside of a prison which she was barred from entering. On Wednesday, she was drinking champagne to rehydrate from shedding so many tears. Yearning to sleep, she said goodbye.

"Change," Pablo responded to indicate that he was switching

phones to prevent any call lasting from over three minutes. He said she had been living the fairy-tale life of a princess, and asked whether she was going to replace the two richest men she had lost with another who was noble or handsome. She blamed his loss on his affinity for beauty queens and hiding overseas. She was sad, busy and just wanted to sleep. He said if she didn't come to him nicely, his men would drag her out in her négligée. He still had her keys. She threatened to use his gun on them in self-defence.

Using another phone and a secret code based on numbers and the names of his zoo animals, he said he wanted to introduce her to the leader of the FARC and the heads of other guerrilla groups. After saying that people from every section of society dreamed of meeting the people headlining the news, she hung up.

Calling back, he grabbed her attention with news about her lover [Gilberto] and his best friend [Jorge Ochoa]. He and his partners would ensure that the prisoners went down [to Colombia] and not up [to America]. He would have to tell her the details in person. She protested that Gilberto had not been her lover, but he was going to be. She enjoyed Pablo simmering angrily in silence. He told her to bring rubber boots and a poncho for her trip to the jungle. She wanted to rest for a day to recover from jetlag and she didn't want to get wet. He insisted on seeing her that night as he had already seen her wet in the river, from jugs of water in the Rolligon, in the bath, in the shower, in the swamp, in the ocean and wet from her own tears. A little clean water wouldn't hurt her.

Rather than wear a poncho, she went in a parka, Wellington boots and with a Louis Vuitton bag in the hope of provoking a reaction from the guerrillas. With two bodyguards, she arrived at night in a deserted encampment with the only sign of life a radio playing. The bodyguards left her outside of a tiny house under construction. To ensure the house was empty, she circled it, while holding her gun in her pocket. She entered through a white door into a room with a huge white mattress on the floor with a pillow and a blanket.

Spotting a radio, flashlight, shirt, machine gun and kerosene lamp, she reached to light the lamp when a figure jumped behind her, slid his right arm under her neck and applied pressure. Pablo told her to observe how he slept in the open around people fighting for causes, while his princess cavorted around Europe with his enemy. After releasing her and lighting the lamp, he said that the camp was the last thing she was ever going to see, not the Ritz Hotel in Paris. She admonished him for living like Che Guevara in the Bolivian jungle, who never had $3 billion. It didn't matter what she had done because they had separated a while ago. What did he want from her? Why wasn't he wearing a shirt in the cold? She wasn't going to spend the night with him on a flea-bitten mattress.

He said she would soon find out why she was there. The woman of the boss of bosses should never have cheated on him with his enemy in front of his friends. She said no one should ever cheat on the boss of all divas, especially with models. She was not his woman as that term only applied to his nanny. He threatened to have his men come in and cut off her expensive clothes with razors if she didn't remove them herself. She challenged him to do it on the grounds that it was the only dishonourable thing he hadn't done to her yet. If he killed her, he would do her a favour because she had never much liked life and wouldn't miss it. If he mutilated her, no women would come near him. She yelled for him to order in a 200-man army. What was he waiting for?

He tore off her clothes and threw her around. While choking her and howling like an animal, he forced his penis inside her. Why had she chosen Gilberto as the rich pig she had once told him he would be traded for? Did she know what Gilberto had told his friends about her? The pathetic jailbird would soon know that she had returned to Pablo the day after sobbing over losing him. Incarcerated, he would hurt deeply.

By listening to the F2 tapes, Pablo had learned that she had called Gacha, who had revealed everything to El Patrón. He was flabbergasted that Gilberto had used his princess to do his dirty work. He knew the Cali godfather's witch of a wife had started the rumour about Victoria having Virginia's face slashed and had contacted the media. Gilberto had attempted to steal his girlfriend, his best friend, his business partner, his territory and even his president. If Jorge Ochoa wasn't in jail as well, he would have paid the Spaniards to extradite Gilberto to America.

He hated Virginia now and constantly dreamed about killing her. She had destroyed his adoration for her. He should have let her drown in the whirlpool. By choking her, she would know what drowning feels like as she died in his arms. He wanted to see all signs of life leave her face as she drew her last breath. They were going to hell together with him on top of and inside her.

Repeatedly, he brought her close to suffocation by putting a pillow over her face, covering her mouth with his hands, pinching her nose and choking her neck. She resolved to reduce his satisfaction by suffering in silence and affirming to herself to stay alive. After experiencing every type of suffocation, she imagined a tunnel with a light at the end. She felt her life slipping away until he released his grip and she gulped air. He yelled at her to beg for her life and to scream. Remaining silent, she gazed as he exploded upon her and she lost track of whether she was alive or dead. She contemplated the nature of the slippery liquid gluing their bodies together. Drifting into unconsciousness, she heard him say how horrible she looked. He thanked God that he would never see her again. He much preferred little girls and whores. In one hour, he would return and if she wasn't ready, she would be abandoned naked in the jungle.

After he left, her body slowly revived. In the mirror, she saw her face had altered like on the day she had lost her virginity. His beard had sandpapered her face, while she had cried. By the time he returned, she had decided to get the last word in a way that he would never forget.

Sitting on the mattress with his elbows on his knees, he rested his head in his hands. Knowing that she would never forgive him or forget what he had done, she gazed down while sat in a director's chair, her left boot over her right thigh. He got up, leaned against a wall and stared blankly. She found it odd that the gazes of her former lovers always formed a 45° angle at the end of the relationship instead of looking at each other.

In a sweet voice, she asked about his baby daughter. He said she was the most beautiful thing in the world, whom she had no right to talk about. As he had previously used the name Manuelita as a nickname for Virginia, she asked why he had named his baby after her. He said her name was Manuela not Manuelita. She asked if he were working to have Gilberto and Jorge Ochoa extradited to Colombia. Yes, he said, but journalists were excluded from such business, which was private except for the families in his trade.

She decided to launch her attack by stating that she was taught that an honest woman owns only one fur coat. She had bought hers five years ago with her own money. Scowling, he said his wife had dozens in a cold-storage room and she was more honest than Virginia. If she wanted a new one from him, she had lost her mind.

Anticipating his reply, she said a girl should be taught that honest men don't own more than one plane. She would never fall in love with a man who owned his own fleet because he would be cruel. He responded that not many men had their own fleet. How many did she think existed? She said three and asked whether he thought he were the first. She knew that moguls were terrified of being traded for rivals and tortured themselves by imagining their ex-lovers in bed with another, mocking their inadequacies and shortcomings. With a victorious expression, he said that was exactly why he preferred innocent girls who didn't make comparisons with moguls or anyone.

Sighing, she picked up her travel bag and stood. She had repeatedly practised what she was about to say and the tone of voice. She wanted to deliver the blow precisely. After admitting that women who could make comparisons like her were scarce, she said that she had something to say that she had always been sure of. The real reason he preferred young girls wasn't because of their inability to draw comparisons with other moguls, but because they couldn't compare him to any sex symbols. After saying goodbye, she hurried away in the rain, leaving him to stew, while enjoying the sense of liberation that replaced her rage. Behind her, he whistled at his men to escort her home. When she reached her house, she finally took her hand off her gun.

CHAPTER 30

GABRIEL GARCÍA MÁRQUEZ'S PEACE NEGOTIATION

The success of his book, *One Hundred Years of Solitude*, launched Gabriel García Márquez to international fame. Writing about injustice and corruption earned him the respect of the guerrillas and the traffickers, not to mention his views on American imperialism, which had caused the US to deny him travel visas and some people to classify him as subversive. With doors open to him at the highest levels of society, he became a mediator between the Colombian government and the guerrillas, including the M-19.

Based in Mexico, García Márquez received a visit from Germán Castro Caycedo, a writer who had cultivated a relationship with Pablo. In the study of García Márquez's colonial house, Castro Caycedo said, "I'm sorry for the situation in Colombia."

"I'm willing to do whatever is necessary," García Márquez said, "and within the law to help seek peace in the country."

"Upon my return, I'll seek contact with Escobar and tell him what you said."

With President Betancur scheduled to visit Mexico, García Márquez planned to talk to him, but first he needed Pablo to relay the traffickers' demands and what they were willing to do to appease Betancur. "In the Presidency of the Republic of Mexico, they have let me know the draft agenda of Betancur's visit, which is tight, but there is a free afternoon in Cancun during which we are going to stay alone and I think there may be an opportunity to talk to him about the traffickers, so that it is definitive that based on this contact, and the previous contacts, that things should go well."

Back in Colombia, Pablo's increased security made it more difficult for Castro Caycedo to establish contact. After nine days, they talked briefly. Pablo said, "I propose to the Teacher [García Márquez] that he come to Colombia because things are made better here. Let him decide in what type of plane he is more confident to fly and in which of these twenty tracks he wants to land … and what security he demands. We will supply all of that, but the ideal is to talk here with all the people."

Back in Mexico, Castro Caycedo relayed Pablo's message to the author, who responded, "I'm not going to the White Mountain to meet with them no matter what. Handle them, so that they say what they want or else to hell with everything."

Castro Caycedo arrived in Medellín on a Friday, scheduled to meet Dr Carlos Echevarría –Pablo's alias for the occasion – at 10:30 AM at Zazcandyl's Workshop. While waiting for El Patrón, the journalist watched cars owned by the traffickers driving around: Alfa Romeos, Maseratis, Jaguars, Ferraris and Mercedes-Benz.

At noon, a bus arrived and the journalist recognised some of the passengers as men who worked for Pablo. A recreational vehicle came and a taxi with two passengers in the back seat. Wearing a black baseball cap with a Padres logo, Pablo was driving the taxi. Noticing the passengers' weapons, the journalist got in the taxi, which left Medellín. At a country house, they were greeted by Gacha, who was sporting a beard and responding to the name Andrés.

After drinks were distributed to the group of traffickers, El Patrón explained that García Márquez was going to try to broker peace with President Betancur. Pablo removed his baseball cap and lowered his forehead. "Man, Andrés, stop saying bullshit because García Márquez has more power than you, than me and more than all of the mobsters in this room."

"What the fuck!" Gacha said in an accent that was a blend

of peasant and countryman. "Who is that piece of shit who has more money than me?"

"No, it isn't like that, brother," Pablo said, "but that man can call the one in charge in Russia or the President of France right away and they will immediately call him on the phone. They will listen to him and, in addition, if Gabito [García Márquez] wants, they send him a plane so he can talk to them. But for us, they will not take our calls, not even by those who are the major [players] of Medellín. If you don't believe me, call him and see for yourself."

The traffickers wanted the journalist to take a letter to García Márquez, but he responded, "What you need to do is send your own emissary and inform me who and I will let the Teacher know because I'm retiring from the negotiation."

The journalist told García Márquez the day the emissary was due to arrive, but he failed to show up for another two days. Later, the author would describe the emissary as young, tall, blond, strong, friendly, extremely well educated and respectful. He came with a briefcase that recorded the conversation, which unsettled García Márquez as they discussed the conflict with the government. Reluctant to tell the emissary to stop recording, he measured his words in the hope of preventing them from being used against him.

"Look, Escobar proposes the following things," the emissary said, "including maintaining all the points proposed in Panama, and resigns, in this first negotiation, to the problem of extradition, so that it is discussed later on."

The author believed that leaving extradition for later was a new development that created a path to peace. "Marvellous, do not worry that President Betancur is coming that day. I will talk to him and then I will let you know the results of my meeting through German [the journalist], but this bloodbath has to end because Colombia is suffering in a way that it does not have to."

In Mexico, the president was on a tight schedule because he had decided to go to Guatemala. Unable to get him alone as planned in Cancun, García Márquez invited him to his home. There, the president was received by a group of the author's friends. While they chatted, the author waited for the precise moment to talk, but none arose. With his calculations astray, he formulated a plan and said to the president, "Come and I'll show you something." After leading Betancur to his studio at the other end of the patio, he presented him Hemingway's book, *Across the River and into the Trees*, with corrections made in pencil by Hemingway.

Holding it, the president fell silent and after a pause excitedly said, "What a wonder!"

"I give it to you as a gift!" They gazed at each and the author said, "Take it, but first, I want to give you a message."

"From whom?"

"From Escobar."

"No. No. Nooooo!"

Betancur hastened for the door, so the author yelled, "Hey, President, you are President of the Republic and you cannot say no to a message without knowing what it is because the country's faith is involved."

"In regard to any message coming from Escobar, I will tell you in advance that they are going to kill me anyway." The president went through the patio to return to the meeting.

At night, the author contemplated his options and decided not to tell Pablo out of fear that men would be dispatched to kill Betancur.

Hoping to save the life of a government minister whom the M-19 had sentenced to death for betraying them during the peace process, García Márquez called the journalist. Contact with the M-19 led the author to believe that the death penalty had been called off by the guerrillas, but there was still an outstanding death penalty from the traffickers. The journalist asked what had happened with Pablo's emissary, and the author detailed Betancur's visit.

Five days later in Medellín, the journalist met Pablo, who guaranteed that the traffickers were not going to assassinate the minister, so everybody must remain calm. "Look, I'm so serious when I say that we don't have anything against him that I am going to send an emissary to the Teacher [García Márquez] in Mexico to confirm it and tell him that the opposite is true: that if Dr Castro wants to be President of the Republic one day, we'll finance the campaign." Pablo asked about the negotiations with Betancur.

"García Márquez was never able to speak to Betancur," the journalist lied.

Pablo's face reddened as if he were about to explode. "Then this motherfucking president will have to die."

APPENDIX A

HISTORY OF COCAINE

For thousands of years, the indigenous people of South America have chewed coca leaves, just like the British enjoy drinking tea. A coca leaf in the mouth combined with a small amount of an alkaline substance is sucked for up to forty-five minutes. The stimulant effect is similar to a boost of energy from coffee. Ancient Andean tribes cherished the coca leaf as a gift from the gods, reserving its use for royalty and high priests. Over time, the masses discovered that it helped them to suppress appetite, increase stamina and overcome altitude fatigue in the Andes Mountains. It was thought to cure everything from stomach complaints to snow blindness. The Incas used it as an anaesthetic for primitive brain surgery on injured warriors.

In the nineteenth century, European chemists focussed on coca leaves in the hope of developing new drugs. Using leaves imported to Germany, Albert Niemann extracted the primary alkaloid in 1859 and named the crystalline substance cocaine. Having stripped the leaf of its moderating substances, he'd unwittingly unleashed an addictive drug.

In 1863, cocaine made its way to America as an anonymous ingredient in Vin Mariani, a tonic wine named after the Corsican chemist who created the concoction. It consisted of ground-up coca leaves with red Bordeaux wine, at the rate of six milligrams of coca per ounce of wine. The label claimed it, "Fortifies Strengthens Stimulates & Refreshes the Body & Brain. Hastens Convalescence especially after Influenza." The recommended dose was two to three glassfuls per day, taken before or after meals, and half of that for children.

Helped along by Vin Mariani's advertising genius, the wine became a worldwide sensation. He had 3,000 physicians endorse it, and countless monarchs, politicians, actors, writers and religious leaders, including Queen Victoria, Thomas Edison, Alexandre Dumas, Émile Zola and President William McKinley. It was said that Pope Leo XIII never left the Vatican without a flask of Vin Mariani under his robes, and that he'd awarded Vin Mariani a gold medal. When Ulysses S. Grant was dying from throat cancer, struggling to write his memoirs, Mark Twain sent him Vin Mariani, which revived him sufficiently to pick up his fountain pen.

An American pharmacist, John Pemberton, made a non-alcoholic health drink, a mineral-water beverage laced with cocaine, which softened his morphine addiction. It became so popular that Pemberton received an offer of $2,300 from Asa Candler for the rights and recipe. Thirty-eight years later, Candler's $2,300 investment was worth $50 million. The name of the health drink was Coca-Cola. It was advertised as a tonic that gave you energy and cured headaches. People would enter a drugstore, sit on a high stool, hand over a couple of pennies and receive a glass of Coca-Cola. Popular amongst members of the temperance movement, it pepped them up to protest against alcohol.

Viewed as a miracle cure, cocaine was widely adopted in self-administered medicines. The Hay Fever Association latched onto cocaine because it constricted blood vessels. Many asthma preparations contained coca or cocaine. By 1890, it was everywhere, with quacks claiming it cured everything from impotence to baldness and dandruff. As it boosted work performance, it was used by all sections of society, ranging from baseball players to dock workers. White business owners doled it out to black employees, to squeeze more work out of them. An anti-opium crusader, Dr Hamilton Wright, advocated its distribution to black dock workers and labourers to increase their productivity. In literature, it was heralded by Sherlock Holmes, who eagerly injected it every day, as described in *The Sign of the Four* by Arthur Conan Doyle:

> Sherlock Holmes took his bottle from the corner of the mantelpiece, and his hypodermic syringe from its neat morocco case. With his long white fingers he adjusted the delicate needle and rolled back his shirt cuff. For some little time his eyes rested thoughtfully upon the sinewy forearm and wrist all dotted and scarred with innumerable puncture marks. Finally he thrust the sharp point home, pressed down the tiny piston, and sank back into the velvet-lined armchair with a long sigh of satisfaction.

> "Which is it today," I asked, "morphine or cocaine?"

> He raised his eyes languidly from the old black-letter volume which he had opened.

> "It is cocaine," he said, "a seven-per-cent solution. Would you care to try it?"

Cocaine was used to treat Civil War veterans addicted to morphine and alcohol. This was noticed by an Austrian neurologist called Sigmund Freud. Born in 1856 in the Moravian town of Freiberg, now Příbor – a historic town in the Czech Republic – Freud developed an unnatural interest in reading at an early age. He stacked his bedroom with books, where he remained cloistered even during mealtimes. In 1873, he joined the medical faculty at the University of Vienna, where his studies included physiology, philosophy and zoology. He dissected hundreds of male eels in a quest to find their genitals. In 1882, he started work at the Vienna General Hospital, where his research included cerebral anatomy. He also fell in love with Martha, a petite and intelligent friend of his sisters. Two months later they were engaged. Her family responded by sending her away to live near Hamburg. On April 21, 1884, Freud wrote to Martha:

"I have been reading about cocaine, the essential constituent of coca leaves which some Indian tribes chew to enable them to resist privations and hardships. A German has been employing it with soldiers and has reported that it increases their energy and capacity to endure. I am procuring some myself and will try it with cases of heart disease and also of nervous exhaustion, particularly in the miserable condition after the withdrawal of morphium ... Perhaps others are working at it; perhaps nothing will come of it. But I shall certainly try it, and you know that when one perseveres, sooner or later one succeeds. We do not need more than one such lucky hit to be able to think of setting up house. But don't be too sure that it must succeed this time. You know, the temperament of an investigator needs two fundamental qualities: he must be sanguine in the attempt, and critical in the work."

Hoping to make a breakthrough in medicine to generate the resources to marry Martha, Freud purchased a gram of cocaine from a pharmacy, supplied by Merck of Germany. He tried one twentieth himself. With his mood elevated and appetite suppressed, he wondered about its application for depression and stomach problems. His enthusiasm for cocaine increased after it provided relief for a patient suffering from gastritis. He ordered more, which he shared with his friends, associates and Martha, "to make her strong and give her cheeks a red colour." Using it throughout the day, he documented its effects, including his shifts in emotion, body temperature and muscular strength. Pining for Martha, whom he hadn't seen in over a year, Freud experienced a depression, which he increasingly self-medicated with cocaine. High on the substance, he wrote to Martha in the summer of 1884:

"Woe to you, my princess, when I come. I will kiss you quite red and feed you till you are plump. And if you are forward you shall see who is the stronger, a little girl who doesn't eat enough or a big strong man with cocaine in his body. In my last serious depression I took cocaine again and a small dose lifted me to the heights in a wonderful fashion. I am just now collecting the literature for a song of praise to this magical substance."

His first published medical article was "Über Coca" in 1885, which lauded the use of cocaine in depression and morphine addiction, while also commenting on its anaesthetic qualities. Pleased with his progress, he took time off to visit Martha. When he returned in September, cocaine was causing a stir, but not because of his paper. Karl Koller, a colleague he had conducted experiments with, had made a breakthrough with cocaine and become an instant celebrity. He'd developed it as a local anaesthetic for eye surgery. Although Freud had touched on cocaine's anaesthetic properties, Koller had identified its tissue-numbing capabilities. As it would have enabled him to marry Martha, he envied Koller's success. In later life, he claimed that it was Martha's fault that he was not famous earlier.

While Koller was at his house, Freud received a visit from his father, who had an eye complaint. After diagnosing glaucoma, they operated on him the next day, using cocaine as an anaesthetic. His father's eyesight was saved. The medical community scrambled to use it as an anaesthetic in a variety of procedures ranging from tooth extraction to haemorrhoid surgery. It was soon heralded as a cure for hay fever, asthma, opium and morphine addiction and for every complaint imaginable ranging from ingrowing toenails to nymphomania. It was sold in lozenges, cigarettes, cough medicines and cold cures. Bars offered shots of whiskey with cocaine. In America, its price jumped from $2.50 to $13 a gram. The lead producer, Merck, ramped up production from fifty grams in 1879 to thirty kilos in 1885.

Even though medical professionals had certified cocaine as being safe, by 1885, its side-effects were apparent, especially among those who'd used it first: physicians, chemists, pharmacists, doctors, dentists and their wives, some of whom ended up in the madhouse.

To a friend, Freud had recommended cocaine for morphine addiction. The friend ended up hooked on cocaine and morphine. Freud spent "the most frightful night" of his life babysitting his friend, who, suffering from cocaine psychosis, kept picking at imaginary insects and snakes crawling beneath his skin.

It was determined that cocaine did not cure morphine addiction. It just substituted one addiction for another, and sometimes left people addicted to both. One doctor predicted it would be the third great scourge of the human race after alcohol and opium. A Russian doctor gave twenty-three grains of cocaine to a girl he was about to operate on. She died and he committed suicide. Perhaps the last straw for Freud occurred when he fatally overdosed a patient.

Dr Albrecht Hirschmüller of the University of Tübingen traced the error back to work Freud had originally read concerning cocaine's use for morphine addiction in a journal called the *Therapeutic Gazette*, which Freud had discovered in the index catalogue of the Surgeon General's Office. Seven papers he had quoted in "Über Coca" were from the *Therapeutic Gazette*, which, unknown to Freud, was owned by the Parke-Davis pharmaceutical company of Detroit, the American manufacturer of cocaine. Freud had accepted $24 from Parke-Davis to vouch for their cocaine, which he had claimed was as good as Merck's.

Flak rained on the claims in "Über Coca." Even though he'd finally managed to marry Martha in 1886, Freud described 1887 as "the least successful and darkest year" of his life. He never published any more papers on cocaine. He buried the theories and went on to found psychoanalysis. With the zeal of enemy combatants, researchers still argue over whether cocaine gave him the inspiration and vivid dreams that contributed to his later theories.

Although most of its supposed medical benefits were debunked, cocaine use in America climbed as people became addicted to patent medicines. But that was all about to stop, at least for black people. At the turn of the nineteenth century, agricultural depression and labour struggles increased tension among the whites, some of whom channelled their discontent into the despicable act of lynching blacks. Gangs of vigilantes grabbed innocent blacks and hung them from the nearest tree. When they dared to fight back, the whites got it into their heads that the cause of retaliation was cocaine.

For decades, the whites had felt threatened by the customs of the blacks. After the Civil War, the blacks in southern states were banned from drinking alcohol on the grounds that when intoxicated they became dangerous to whites. The majority of politicians believed that the whites were able to behave themselves while drunk, whereas blacks lacked that ability.

In 1901, Henry Cabot Lodge spearheaded a law that banned the sale of liquor and opiates to "uncivilised races," including blacks, aborigines, Eskimos, Hawaiians and immigrant railroad workers. Cocaine dodged inclusion, until a decade later when headlines courtesy of William Randolph Hearst reported on the new southern menace: cocaine. The same reasoning that had outlawed alcohol and opium to blacks now spread to cocaine.

Thus was born the myth of the cocaine-crazed Negro with superhuman strength who you could shoot, but wouldn't die. One newspaper stated, "In attempting to arrest a hitherto peaceful negro who had become crazed by cocaine, a police officer in self-defence drew his revolver, placed the muzzle over the negro's heart, and fired. And yet, this bullet did not even stagger the crazed negro, and neither did a second."

The police were so spooked that they demanded higher-calibre bullets to shoot blacks under the influence of cocaine because anything less would be repelled by their superhuman strength. Calibres .25 and .32 were replaced by .38, which decades later were replaced by Glocks when the Reagan-Bush administration propagandised black crack use to terrify the nation into tightening drug laws, and to spend hundreds of millions of taxpayers' dollars on the War on Drugs and to hunt down Escobar.

In the early 1900s, according to politicians and the tabloids, cocaine not only made blacks bulletproof, but it turned them into something much worse: deviants out to rape every white woman in sight. As with opium smoking in San Francisco fifty years earlier, the idea that a drug was being used to seduce white women was the final straw. Southern states banned cocaine, but illegality did not stymie its availability. The first cocaine dealers were newspaper boys and shoe-shiners offering a sniff of powder for ten cents or a day's supply in a pillbox for twenty-five cents. Cocaine prohibition created a black market that would grow exponentially around the time of Escobar.

These first drug laws were enacted at the local level. There were no federal laws. While local laws prohibited cocaine from the uncivilised races, the whites still devoured cocaine-based medicines. It was considered legitimate to take a drug if you were sick, but a no-no if you were feeling good. With cocaine tonics having been around for four decades, most addiction was medicine-based. By 1900, it was estimated that five per cent of the American public was addicted to cocaine-based drugs. Hardest hit were middle-class white women in rural areas.

While making grandiose advertising claims, patent-medicine manufacturers refused to label their ingredients, so men, women and children were unknowingly dosing themselves on cocaine. An article in *Collier's* magazine by Samuel Hopkins Adams caught the attention of Congress. It commenced with:

"GULLIBLE America will spend this year some seventy-five millions of dollars in the purchase of patent medicines. In consideration of this sum it will swallow huge quantities of alcohol, an appalling amount of opiates and narcotics, a wide assortment of varied drugs ranging from powerful and dangerous heart depressants to insidious liver stimulants; and, in excess of all other ingredients, undiluted fraud. For fraud, exploited by the skilfulest of advertising bunco men, is the basis of the trade. Should the newspapers, the magazines and the medical journals refuse their pages to this class of advertisement, the patent medicine business in five years would be as scandalously historic as the South Sea Bubble, and the nation would be the richer not only in lives and money, but in drunkards and drug-fiends saved."

Adams' exposé included false advertising claims and stories of addiction, abuse and death caused by patent medicines. It motivated Congress to pass the 1906 Food and Drug Act, which required habit-forming medications to be labelled with the contents. It didn't ban drugs. Cocaine, heroin, morphine, opium and marijuana were legal and readily available. But it put most patent medicines out of business. Even Coca-Cola dropped the hard stuff, though it retained the name.

Research by Professor Paul Gootenberg revealed the more sinister role of corporate interests. Making cocaine illegal eliminated the competition for the two producers in America: Merck and Maywood. Before shipping to Coca-Cola, Maywood removed the cocaine from its coca to minimise the risk of Coca-Cola staining its wholesome image. Coca-Cola and Maywood kept the drug czar, Harry Anslinger – a racist who believed that marijuana and jazz music were the work of the devil – informed about events in Peru, where their plantations grew, and in return, he protected Coca-Cola by putting loopholes in international legislation that allowed Coca-Cola the right to import leaves. The wrath of Anslinger would come down on any potential competitors to Coca-Cola, who wanted to import leaves, guaranteeing Coca-Cola's monopoly. If the Peruvian government didn't keep its prices down, Anslinger threatened that Coca-Cola would take their business to Bolivia. Anslinger and Coca-Cola were always on the lookout for the results of any new studies on the coca plant. If it were declared safe, Anslinger would have difficulty maintaining his ban on importation, and the Coca-Cola monopoly would be eliminated by copycats. At the same time, Coca-Cola didn't want coca to be deemed too dangerous because minus its cocaine, it was still a main ingredient, which carried a constant risk of a scandal erupting. Outside of helping Coca-Cola, Peru was discouraged from producing coca, which, according to Gootenberg, boosted the black market, which fed the rise in demand for cocaine from the 1960s onwards. With no legal outlet for coca due to United Nations laws put forward by Anslinger, the Peruvian farmers exported coca paste to traffickers – Escobar's progenitors – or as Gootenberg put it, "There was a continual rise in cocaine production throughout Peru in the 1950s and 60s. The United States created the cocaine problem itself."

When the Harrison Narcotics Tax Act was proposed, southern legislators seized upon the opportunity to include cocaine. They backed up their demand with stories about black men murdering and raping entire families. Now not only did cocaine give black men superhuman strength, but it also improved their pistol aim. The federal law passed in 1914 included cocaine, opium, morphine and heroin. It required anyone handling those drugs – doctors, druggists, pharmacists, distributors, importers – to pay an annual tax, to keep strict records, and to only prescribe it "in the due course of medical treatment." Except for licensed handlers, possession of cocaine was illegal. Over-the-counter medicines were not allowed a scintilla of cocaine, bankrupting the producers of patent medicines who had survived the 1906 Food and Drug Act.

In 1919, the Supreme Court ruled that addiction was not a disease, preventing doctors from prescribing drugs for addicts, criminalising addicts and causing the closure of drug-maintenance clinics. By 1928, one-third of the federal prison population was made up of violators of the Harrison Act, including numerous doctors. To avoid prison, addicts switched from cocaine to drugs outside of the Harrison Act such as amphetamines, which, just like cocaine decades earlier, were being touted as completely safe wonder drugs.

Methamphetamines were sold in patent medicines and nasal decongestants, recommended for heroin addiction, and mass disseminated to troops to improve their performance. The police and prohibitionists hailed the drop in cocaine use as a success, demanded even more severe punishments and cited the large number of addicts in prison as proof that drugs made people commit crimes; after all, only criminals ended up in jail. With cocaine users scarce in the face of an expanding anti-drugs bureaucracy, the authorities moved onto potheads, where their focus remained for decades, which allowed Escobar to get cocaine into America unnoticed.

In the following decades, the most famous cocaine abuser was Adolf Hitler. After a failed assassination attempt, he was treated by Dr Erwin Giesing, who prescribed cocaine in ten per cent solutions for Hitler's sore throat. After his throat was cured, he demanded more cocaine from his reluctant doctor. Towards the end of the war, he was receiving multiple injections a day of drug cocktails and popping pep tablets such as Pervitin, an early version of crystal meth. Unable to sleep on Pervitin, he took sedatives. As Hitler intensified his evil treatment of the Jews, Freud escaped to London in 1938, but four of his elder sisters were killed in concentration camps. In September 1939, in agony with mouth cancer from smoking, Freud was given enough morphine to end his life. With his decision-making processes scrambled by drugs, Hitler shot himself in the head in 1945 to avoid capture by the Russians.

Making cocaine illegal created a black market that would remain small at first and wither during the Great Depression and World Wars, only to accelerate in the latter half of the century to generate enough mayhem to make the authors of the early drug laws squirm in their graves, including hundreds of thousands of murders in Colombia and Mexico as rival cartels fought for control. It was a market that would rain dollars down on exporters of coca paste in Peru and Bolivia, and generate even bigger profits for their customers in Colombia such as Escobar.

Prior to 1973, Chile was a centre of cocaine production. Using Peruvian coca leaves and paste, refiners made cocaine in Chilean labs, which was shipped to wealthy US customers. The refiners often hired Colombian smugglers, which is how the Colombians learned the early routes. The good times for the Chilean producers ended abruptly due to regime change. As General Pinochet was a sworn enemy of Communism, the CIA backed his coup in 1973. Once in power, he had the Army execute thousands of his own citizens, including traffickers. He shut down dozens of cocaine labs, and arrested hundreds of people associated with trafficking. With the competition eliminated, Pinochet and his son organised a cocaine production and distribution network, which supplied Europe and America. Pinochet had the Army build a lab in Talagante, a rural town twenty-four miles from Santiago. Chemists mixed cocaine with other chemicals to make black cocaine, which could be smuggled much easier than the obvious white stuff – a trick that Escobar would employ. Pinochet earned millions from cocaine.

In Colombia, three cities set about competing for cocaine business: Bogotá, Medellín and Cali. On November 22, 1975, a plane was busted in Cali with 600 kilos on board. This sparked a cocaine war. In one weekend, over forty people were murdered. But not in Cali. They had died in the city dominating the cocaine business: Medellín. The authorities started to watch the slum neighbourhoods, where young people armed to the teeth hustled to stay alive, and dreamt of raising themselves out of the barrio through fast cash from cocaine.

Escobar had started in the cocaine business a hundred years after the previous boom in American use, when it had been touted as a cure-all by pharmacists and was an original ingredient in Coca-Cola. The scourge of what followed – addiction, insanity, deaths – had long been forgotten. Americans were receptive to this cool new drug that they were told they couldn't get addicted to and there was talk of decriminalising it.

APPENDIX B

NORMAN'S CAY

Born in Boston in 1942, George Jung was a high-school football star and a natural leader. At the University of Southern Mississippi, he studied advertising, but dropped out to lead a life of smoking and dealing cannabis. Mesmerised by West Coast culture, he became a hippy, embracing LSD and free love. Noticing a discrepancy in the price of weed in South Los Angeles – $60 a kilo – versus on the East Coast – $300 a kilo – Jung started to bulk buy it from the owner of a hairdressing salon. Demand far exceeded the amounts smuggled by the airline stewardesses he'd hired as mules – including his girlfriend – so he invested in motorhomes.

Soon he had hundreds of thousands of dollars. He bought a plane to fly weed from Mexico that cost $8–$10 per kilo. Only 26, he hired a team of pilots. In 1974, he was busted smuggling 660 pounds of cannabis to Chicago. He bonded out and went on the run. When he visited his parents, they called the police. His sentence was reduced after he argued with the judge.

In 1974, serving a four-year sentence, Jung was bracing to receive a new cellmate in his seven-by-nine-foot room with a view of the countryside. When Carlos Lehder walked in, Jung was relieved by the presence of such a polite young man. After exchanging pleasantries, Lehder said, "What are you in for?"

"Flying pot out of Mexico," Jung said. For an hour, they discussed their experiences in the cannabis trade.

Standing in the line for the chow hall, Carlos said, "You must know a lot about airplanes and have a lot of people in the US who buy drugs. Do you know anything about cocaine?"

"No," Jung said. "Tell me about it."

"It sells in the US for $40–$50,000 a kilo."

"How much do you get it for, Carlos?"

"Like $2–$5,000."

"Tell me everything you know about cocaine, Carlos. Everything."

For sixteen months, the cellmates ironed out the logistics for distributing cocaine across America. Lehder told Jung that he could obtain unlimited amounts of it from two cousins: Gustavo Gaviria and Pablo Escobar. Aiming to make millions from air transportation, they obtained maps from the prison library and plotted trafficking routes. Banker inmates taught them about money laundering and offshore accounts. After a doctor incarcerated for Medicare fraud mentioned Belize, which lacked an extradition treaty, Lehder contemplated setting up a regional haven for traffickers.

Jung wanted to transport cocaine to America in light aircraft, just like he'd done with weed. A pilot advised them that a small plane couldn't carry enough fuel for such a long trip. The plane would have to stop somewhere to refuel. If a plane were to fly from Miami to the Bahamas, as if taking its occupants on a vacation, it could continue to Colombia, get the cocaine and return to the Bahamas. If the plane returned with the end-of-the-week traffic, it would be invisible to the authorities.

Lehder affectionately referred to incarceration as his college days because he learned so much. He obtained a high-school diploma. Due to his excellent grades, he ended up teaching Hispanic inmates. He never stopped reading. Jung introduced him to Machiavelli, Plato, Nietzsche, Carl Jung, Hermann Hesse and Hemingway.

In 1975, Jung was released to his parents. In 1976, he received a telex from Colombia: "Weather beautiful. Please come down. Your friend, Carlos." Unwilling to violate parole, Jung sent a friend to Lehder in Medellín on a fact-finding mission. They arranged a fifteen-kilo transaction.

In April 1976, Lehder called Jung with instructions to send two female mules to Antigua with baggage. "Don't tell them anything. We'll explain everything when they get there."

Jung approached his girlfriend and her friend at a schoolyard where they were watching a softball game. "Would you be interested in a free Caribbean vacation?"

"When?"

"Now."

The women took hard-shell Samsonite cases and spending money. They had a blast with the charming Lehder and returned home with different cases. Jung took the new cases home and removed the aluminium lips protecting the fibreglass false bottoms. Snorting the product, he thought it was wonderful. Carlos paid Jung five kilos to distribute the cocaine. He sold four kilos for $180,000. He paid his female smugglers in cocaine. More trips were organised.

A setback occurred on October 19, 1976, when Lehder was arrested for smuggling Chevrolet wagons into Colombia. Through bribery, he arranged to serve his time in a special terrace in the Bellavista prison in Medellín. While most of the prisoners occupied the filthy floor, he had his own bed and ordered food from restaurants to avoid the rotten-meat soup.

Buddying-up with an American incarcerated for smuggling weed, he said that he wanted to form, "a conglomerate of small-time cocaine producers, and to put all their merchandise together into one shipment, so it would pay for the equipment necessary to get into the United States." After two months inside, he was released in time for Christmas. Jung sent him $30,000 and business resumed.

In February 1977, Jung received fifty kilos in Miami, which he transported to Boston, but Lehder was a no-show. Unbeknown to Jung, Lehder had run into difficulty crossing the Canadian border and was on the run. Jung gave the cocaine to his former weed dealer, the Hollywood hairdresser. Two weeks later, it had been sold for over $2 million.

Lehder showed up at Jung's parents, concerned about the fate of the cocaine and that Jung may have ripped him off. Many Colombians had lost cocaine by trusting Americans. When he saw his share of the cash – $1.8 million – he was so delighted that he bought a new BMW. Soon, Jung was making $500,000 a week. Hidden in cars, millions were smuggled back to Medellín by Lehder. By 1977, a plane was needed to move the cocaine, so Jung hired a Learjet. But constantly smuggling and using cocaine were debilitating Jung.

Lehder was such a strict disciplinarian that he put everybody he knew to work. An exhausted Jung asked Lehder to find someone to bring cocaine to California. "I'll call you as soon as I have that person in transit," Lehder said. The next day he called Jung. "I have someone. They're on the plane now."

"Who is it?"

"It'll be a surprise."

The next day, Jung heard knocking on the door of his Holiday Inn room. Opening it revealed a little grey-haired lady: Lehder's mother. When Jung objected, Lehder said that everybody had to work, and she had wanted a free trip to Disneyland.

As the business grew, the former cellmates fell out. Lehder viewed Jung's cocaine habit as detrimental to performance. Jung was snorting a gram at a time, earning him the nickname I-95 because his long lines of white powder reminded the Colombians of that Interstate Highway. Attempting to squeeze Jung out of the picture, Lehder demanded to know the name of the Hollywood hairdresser.

In August 1977, a pilot tested the Bahamas route – the plan hatched in prison – with 250 kilos picked up from one of Pablo's farms outside Medellín. The plane refuelled in Nassau, the capital city of the Bahamas, on its eleventh largest island. It landed in the Carolinas, and the cocaine was transported to Florida. The cocaine sold within days. The profit was $1 million, which Jung and Lehder split. Lehder wanted to move the base of their operations to the Bahamas, but Jung argued against it.

"Look, Carlos, the only way to do this business is to hit-and-run. Keep changing our smuggling routes. Never stay in one place. Then we don't have to be under anybody's thumbs. We make ourselves a hundred million apiece, or whatever. You go your way. I go mine."

To achieve his revolutionary goals, Lehder wanted rapid expansion, whereas Jung favoured slow and steady progress. For cocaine supply, Jung had stepped on Lehder's toes by marrying a Colombian whose brother was a supplier. Lehder obtained the contact details for the Hollywood hairdresser, so he didn't need Jung as an intermediary. Jung accused Lehder of going behind his back.

Lehder obtained a boat, and searched for an island in the Bahamas. He settled on Norman's Cay, a fishhook-shaped landmass twenty miles south-east of Miami surrounded by some of the clearest blue water on earth, teeming with marine life. The central curvature harboured yachts. At the top of the island, a dozen beach cottages sat on a rocky coast. At the tip of the fishhook was a 3,000-foot airstrip adjacent to four miles of sparkling white sand, forming a beach that curved around water known as Smugglers Cove. On a hill by the airstrip was a yacht club with a four-stool bar, a restaurant and the only telephone on Norman's Cay. Amid hundreds of islands, it was paradise. Lehder paid $190,000 cash for Beckwith House on the north-eastern bend. He deposited millions in a trust company, which he used to buy property on the island.

With Jung out of the way – or so Lehder thought – Lehder got down to running all of the wealthy inhabitants off the island, so that he could turn it into a smuggling hub. He started by showing up at cottages with a suitcase full of cash and telling the owners to name their price. Flashing money and introducing himself as Joe Lehder, he came off as polite and intriguing.

"Joe, how much money are you worth?" a neighbour asked on Lehder's 30th birthday.

"Oh, about $25 million."

He bought the rights to the guesthouse, the bar and the airstrip. He closed the airstrip down for general use by painting a giant yellow X on it, which prevented the other residents from flying in and out. He closed the yacht club, the diving school and stopped the hotel from taking reservations. The remaining residents were starting to wonder what was going on, but Lehder was only just getting started. He decided that the homeowners who'd refused his cash had to go. To pressure them into moving, he filled the island with intimidating characters, including bodyguards and traffickers.

"In case I didn't make myself clear," he told a resident, "if you're not off this island today, your wife and children will die."

A college professor who ran a diving business was told that it must stop. When he returned for his gear, his plane was surrounded and he was prevented from leaving. After shooting the plane's radio, Lehder's bodyguards instructed him to fly away and never return. In the air, he noticed that the plane lacked fuel. It had been siphoned. The plane had to emergency land on a nearby island's beach. The police did nothing about the complaints from the residents. Lehder had paid off everybody. A Bahamian immigration officer initiated deportation proceedings against a remaining resident. On the beach, Lehder pulled a gun on a former Bahamian politician.

Emulating his hero, Adolf Hitler, in a way that would have made his father proud, Lehder hired forty German bodyguards, who arrived in the Aryan tradition with Doberman pinchers, automatic weapons and blonde hair. Toting black satchels, they patrolled in Toyota jeeps and Volkswagen vans. Any yachts that approached with tourists, sightseers, or remaining residents were shadowed along the perimeter of the island by vehicles full of armed neo-Nazis and canines capable of tearing off limbs. If they got too close to the shore, a helicopter would hover over them.

The famous TV anchorman for *CBS Evening News*, Walter Cronkite, travelled by yacht to Norman's Cay on a Christmas vacation. Finding the harbour empty, he dropped his anchor. "You can't dock here and you can't anchor out there!" yelled a man on the pier. Cronkite continued to the next island, where he was told that it was common knowledge that the people who had taken over Norman's Cay didn't want any visitors.

The last resident to leave was Floyd, a handyman who had built his own house on the island. Lehder had hired him to assemble a couple of prefabricated hangars to store planes and cocaine. While working on a hangar, Floyd watched a plane land, men with rifles jump out, and a truck arrive, from which suitcases were loaded onto the plane. When his work was done, Floyd was ordered to leave the island, but he refused. He told the superintendent that he wasn't interested in selling the house he had built.

"He [Lehder] doesn't have to buy it. He's just going to take it."

A foreman warned Floyd, "Look, he's [Lehder's] coming by and he has some pretty rough men there, and they probably won't kill you, but they could certainly knife you up pretty bad." After that, Floyd fled.

Planes landed every day. Lehder's associates lived in several of the houses. Out of his twenty-two cars, he preferred driving a 1932 Ford Replica, a classic car with a rectangular elongated body with two round lights at the front.

Even though he had warned Jung about the detrimental effects of cocaine on business judgement, Lehder started to use it heavily. His associates joined in, and they became paranoid. To calm them down, planes full of women arrived. Wild orgies ensued to the music of the Beatles and the Rolling Stones. Naked women picked up new arrivals from the runway. Cocaine-crazed neo-Nazis hauled a houseboat onto the top of the island's only hill, and left it there as a lookout. Luxury properties were destroyed and vandalised. Laden with cocaine, a DC-3 crashed in the lagoon and was left to rot. Like one of his other heroes, Che Guevara,

Lehder started dressing in army fatigues and brandishing guns. His alter ego continued to assert itself.

Meanwhile, Jung had been reduced to the man who had launched Lehder. In a confrontational mood, he flew to Norman's Cay. Making only $500,000 a year, he coveted Lehder's tens of millions. "It's over," Lehder said, flanked by two armed Germans. "You have your brother-in-law … You can do your own operation, but this is my island. I own it."

Interviewed for PBS's *Frontline* TV programme, Lehder's personal pilot said, "Carlos played a very special role in establishing the business in the US because he had Norman's Cay. He was the key person who readily expanded the Medellín Cartel's view of the business. He was the only one who really had the idea of being able to move the thousands and thousands of kilos to the States."

Jorge Ochoa disclosed to *Frontline* that, "Norman's Cay was a bridge used by everybody in the business. At the time, it was something that helped me and it helped many people … It was almost as if law enforcement hardly existed at that point in time. It was easy to buy an island in the Bahamas. Everybody used the routes that Carlos had."

APPENDIX C

BARRY SEAL

According to the DEA's official account, the cartel bosses' contact in the Nicaraguan government, Federico Vaughan, took Barry Seal and his Honduran co-pilot to an airfield and told them not to worry about the guards and checkpoints, which were a mere formality. Five miles outside of Managua in a rural setting, they stopped at a large oil refinery.

"This is the country's only refinery. Never fly near or over it." Vaughan pointed at anti-aircraft batteries on the perimeter. "Any aircraft that flies over the refinery, friend or foe, will be shot down immediately." He took them to a massive sunken lake, a volcanic crater full of clear blue water. "This is the purest water in the country. The only unpolluted drinking water for Managua. In its own way, it's as vital as the oil refinery. If you fly near it, you will be shot down."

They travelled around a mountain, across a railroad track and onto a military airfield called Los Brasiles, with a lone paved runway. At roadblocks and checkpoints, Vaughan was waved through by guards wielding AK-47s. He took them to a hangar designated for their mission. Inside was a Piper Cheyenne owned by Pablo. Barry asked about the length of the airstrip and its foundation and texture. Vaughan escorted them along the 3,500-foot runway.

When Barry and his co-pilot walked onto the grass to examine a drainage ditch, Vaughan yelled, "Stop! It's mined with landmines. If you have any problem landing your aircraft, don't veer to the western side, or you'll be killed."

Afterwards, they ate at a steakhouse. Vaughan produced a map of Nicaragua and drew arrows to indicate the smuggling mission's entry and exit routes. "You need a code for entering Nicaraguan airspace. You are to call the Sandino tower on a certain VHF frequency and identify yourselves as Yankee November Whiskey X-ray Yankee. Then the tower will reroute you to Los Brasiles. All approaches to the city of Managua are covered by anti-aircraft guns to protect against night attacks by the Contra rebels." On the map, Barry drew circles around the gun emplacements, the oil refinery, Vaughan's house and the Sandinista People's Army headquarters.

Barry told Pablo that the runway was ideal, but the hangar was too small for the plane he had in mind. Pablo said that Barry's mission had changed: he needed to go to Bolivia for 6,000 kilos of cocaine base. To his DEA handlers, Barry claimed that the paste was for the cartel's new labs in Nicaragua, but this was unlikely because no labs had yet been established. The claim did however promote the link with the Nicaraguan government that George HW Bush was attempting to establish.

In America, Barry showed up for a routine court appearance and ended up in jail. The DEA got him out, eager for him to set up a sting operation on the traffickers. He immediately called his Honduran co-pilot, who asked where Barry had been. He said he had been busy. With a shipment scheduled to be transported from Colombia the next day, they had no time to waste. Paranoid after free-basing cocaine, the co-pilot dropped out of the mission, so Barry brought in his trusted friend, Emile Camp. They flew a Learstar from Arkansas to over the Colombian jungle.

"That strip looks mighty wet!" Barry yelled.

"So," Emile said. "You gonna try it?"

"I didn't fly all this way to turn around."

"That mountain's awful close, and that river's pretty high. Do not enter that banana grove. It'll take the wings off. That grass is too wet. You're gonna pay hell getting out of there, I'll tell you that."

"Anything else?" Barry asked.

"It's a piece of cake."

With its propellers roaring, the plane swerved to land. Water and mud splashed off the wheels as it skidded on the landing strip. Barry was talking to the ground crew when a long-haired man galloped towards the plane on a white Arabian stallion, brandishing a machine gun and barking orders.

"Who the hell are you?" Barry asked.

"Carlos Lehder!" he yelled. Barry had heard stories about Lehder. "Now you will do what I say! Immediately! Before someone sees your plane from the air!"

A tractor appeared, pulling over a ton of cocaine. "Holy shit!" Emile said. "They expect us to fly out of this swamp with all of that shit."

"No, of course not," Barry said.

"We can't get up with that much weight."

"Don't you worry. I'm gonna reason with the man." Barry laughed. "Hey, lifting off this muddy strip with all of that weight is impossible."

He ended up pinned against the tractor with Lehder shoving a gun under his chin. "I don't care what you say. You'll fly every last gram of it out of here, just like you contracted to do. And if you refuse, I'll kill you right now, and your co-pilot will do it. We're going to load this plane and you're going to get out of here. You start loading fuel."

With a defeated expression, Barry complied. In fifteen minutes, 1,500 kilos of cocaine in duffel bags and burlap sacks were loaded. Barry manned the plane. "You ready?"

"No," Emile said.

"I knew I could count on you."

As it picked up speed on the muddy runway, the plane rumbled and bounced, but failed to gain height. "C'mon, baby," Emile said.

Lehder galloped alongside, shooting into the earth, his workers lined up at the periphery of the jungle, yelling for the plane to rise. It lifted to cheering, but fell and skidded. The right wheel sank into the mud and was ripped from its undercarriage. The plane crashed with a mechanical groan.

"Get out, man! The fuel's gonna blow!" Barry said, scrambling to exit.

Lehder appeared, bursting off more gunfire. "Gringos! Maricones!" Anticipating an explosion, Barry and Emile dived into the jungle. Lehder ordered his workers to rescue the cocaine from the burning plane.

"That crazy bastard's making them go to the plane," Emile said, clutching a tree. "They'll be barbecued." Barry and Emile leapt from the jungle and tried to stop the two-dozen workers charging towards the plane.

"Help them now!" Lehder yelled, shooting his gun at the dirt around their feet.

Barry and Emile joined the men grabbing packages of cocaine from the plane. As they charged away, the plane exploded, knocking men over. Flames shot dozens of feet in all directions. Two workers were burnt. The tractor transported the cocaine back to its storage facility, where it was inventoried.

"Cabrones, we have another plane!" Lehder yelled.

"I don't give a damn what kind of plane you've got," Barry said, his face muddy. "We can't take off with that load. We've gotta wait for this field to dry."

A replacement plane was found: a Titan 404. "Certainly you're not going to be able to carry the full 1,500 kilos that you tried to carry with the larger plane. Can you carry half of it?" a cartel worker asked.

"No, sir," Barry said, worried about the plane going down in the Gulf of Mexico. "Because then I wouldn't be able to add any fuel."

"And with a stop in Nicaragua? How much can you take?"

"Well, with a stop in Nicaragua, we can probably take 700, 750 kilos." The crash had played into Barry's hands because the sooner he could get to Nicaragua, the more predisposed the Reagan-Bush administration would be to remedying his legal trouble.

At the Intercontinental Hotel in Medellín, Barry called the DEA to appraise them about the new flight schedule. In Gulfport, DEA agents were in a recreational vehicle waiting for the cocaine. The seizure would make their careers.

The next day, Barry and Emile returned to the jungle airstrip. They spent three days with Lehder, who was guarding the cocaine. Lehder showed them 3,000 kilos and claimed that 6,000 kilos of cocaine base were waiting to be shipped from Bolivia.

At the next meeting with Pablo, Barry advised using a large plane. "You should buy a military cargo plane like those I've seen advertised in the aviation-trade magazines." Pablo authorised it for the first 700 kilos.

In Escobar's Piper Cheyenne, which required maintenance in America, Barry and Emile flew home with Pablo's latest shopping list, which included night-vision goggles and a dozen high-frequency radios that cost $12,000 each.

The CIA provided Barry with a Fairchild C-123K Provider, a massive camouflage-green twin-engine military cargo plane from the Vietnam War. He nicknamed it the Fat Lady. On June 18, 1984, Barry flew it to Rickenbacker Air National Guard Base near Columbus, Ohio. Repairing and retrofitting the plane, Air Force employees worked around the clock.

Barry was instructed to take pictures of Nicaraguan officials associated with cocaine. He told the CIA, "Let me explain something to you, mister. There's gonna be a lot of men with guns down there. Nervous men, who aren't gonna exactly say cheese to some gringo pilot with a camera."

Five days later, the plane was at Homestead Air Force Base near Miami. A transponder was installed to allow the DEA to track its flight. The CIA added a hidden 35-mm camera in the nose cone and another was put inside of a fake electronics box in the rear cargo hold, facing the doors. A pinhole lens in the box allowed the camera to film the cocaine coming into the back of the plane. The radio-controlled trigger for the cameras had a long wire antenna.

"What! Where in the hell do you expect me to hide that? Stick it up my ass?" Barry said, referring to the antenna.

"You can put it in your pocket."

"All five feet of it?"

"Put it in your pocket and let the antenna slide down your leg."

Barry did so and pressed the remote control. Enraged by the loud noise the camera made, he cursed the CIA men in suits. "I'm tired of wasting my time with you assholes. I'll get your fucking photographs. Autographed! But what are you gonna do for me?"

"We have a deal, Mr Seal."

"The judge. Say it, dammit!"

"We'll speak to the judge on your behalf."

In a Miami hotel room, Barry called Vaughan, recording the call for the DEA. "I was going to see my grandmother at noon on Saturday," Barry said, using code for the cocaine shipment. Referring to the Fat Lady, Barry said, "It's a big Cadillac ... Very big, big car ... I just wanted to make sure that my grandmother was going to tell the landlord that the car was very big, so that the landlord wouldn't be excited when they saw it." Worried about getting shot down again, Barry wanted the Nicaraguan government to stay calm when they saw the Fat Lady.

"No, no, no," Vaughan said. "Everything is OK about that."

On June 24, 1984, Barry told Vaughan about a party tomorrow at his grandmother's, meaning the cocaine was coming the next day. "I mean, everybody is coming to the party, and you've notified those boys in green." Barry was still concerned about getting shot down.

"Right," Vaughan said.

"Everybody is notified?" Barry said.

"Yes," Vaughan said.

"Excellent. OK. I just want to make sure. I don't want any problems."

"Yes, everybody is going to be there."

"OK, good. And is Pedro coming? Because I have that liquor

for him," Barry said, referring to Pablo and the items on his shopping list.

"Yes, yes, he's coming," Vaughan said.

"I'm leaving for the party at midnight. Has it been raining on the yard where we park the cars at the party?" Barry said.

"It's dry and hard and only a little bit muddy in one small area."

"I can't stay at the party long. I have to try to leave as soon as possible," Barry said, hoping for a fast refuelling.

"Yeah, we're going to be ready for that."

"OK. Now remember this motorhome is very big, and it's a funny, funny colour, so don't let anybody get excited."

Vaughan laughed. "No, that's perfect."

At 1 PM on June 25, 1984, Barry landed at Los Brasiles near Managua and dropped open the back of the plane. He'd brought $454,000 for Pablo. He later claimed that on the ground were Vaughan, Pablo, Gacha and a group of soldiers. "How do you like the plane?" Barry yelled over the engine noise. "I call her the Fat Lady."

Soldiers started loading duffel bags of cocaine into the cargo hold. Every time Barry pressed the remote control to take a picture, the camera clicked so loudly that it could be heard outside the Fat Lady. To drown out the noise, Barry switched on the plane's generators. An American spy plane above took pictures.

"Shut down your engines!" Pablo yelled.

"I can't. We gotta keep them hot," Barry said, maintaining the sound to disguise the camera noise.

An overweight bodyguard with a gun entered the plane and started looking around as if he could hear the camera noise. Emile revved the propellers to camouflage the sound. The bodyguard checked around and finally left. After being loaded with 700 kilos of cocaine and 2,000 gallons of fuel – which took about an hour – the plane took off. The following morning, the Fat Lady landed at Homestead Air Force Base near Miami. The DEA seized the cocaine and the CIA took the camera film.

REFERENCES

Bowden, Mark. *Killing Pablo*. Atlantic Books, 2001.

Bowen, Russell. *The Immaculate Deception*. America West Publishers, 1991.

Castaño, Carlos. *My Confession*. Oveja Negra, 2001.

Caycedo, Germán Castro. *In Secret*. Planeta, 1996.

Chepesiuk, Ron. *Crazy Charlie*. Strategic Media Books, 2016.

Chepesiuk, Ron. *Drug Lords: The Rise and Fall of the Cali Cartel*. Milo Books, 2003.

Chepesiuk, Ron. *Escobar vs Cali: The War of the Cartels*. Strategic Media, 2013.

Cockburn, Leslie. *Out of Control*. Bloomsbury, 1988.

Cockburn and Clair. *Whiteout*. Verso, 1998.

Don Berna. *Killing the Boss*. ICONO, 2013.

Escobar, Juan Pablo. *Pablo Escobar: My Father*. Ebury Press, 2014.

Escobar, Roberto. *Escobar*. Hodder & Stoughton, 2009.

Grillo, Joan. *El Narco*. Bloomsbury, 2012.

Gugliotta and Leen. *Kings of Cocaine*. Harper and Row, 1989.

Hari, Johann. *Chasing the Scream*. Bloomsbury, 2015.

Hopsicker, Daniel. *Barry and the Boys*. MadCow Press, 2001.

Leveritt, Mara. *The Boys on the Tracks*. Bird Call Press, 2007.

Levine, Michael. *The Big White Lie*. Thunder's Mouth Press, 1993.

MacQuarrie, Kim. *Life and Death in the Andes*. Simon & Schuster, 2016.

Márquez, Gabriel García. *News of a Kidnapping*. Penguin, 1996.

Martínez, Astrid María Legarda. *The True Life of Pablo Escobar*. Ediciones y Distribuciones Dipon Ltda, 2017.

Massing, Michael. *The Fix*. Simon & Schuster, 1998.

McAleese, Peter. *No Mean Soldier*. Cassell Military Paperbacks, 2000.

McCoy, Alfred. *The Politics of Heroin in Southeast Asia*. Harper and Row, 1972.

Mollison, James. *The Memory of Pablo Escobar*. Chris Boot, 2009.

Morris, Roger. *Partners in Power*. Henry Holt, 1996.

Noriega, Manuel. *The Memoirs of Manuel Noriega*. Random House, 1997.

North, Oliver. *Under Fire*. Harper Collins, 1991.

Paley, Dawn. *Drug War Capitalism*. AK Press, 2014.

Porter, Bruce. *Blow*. St Martin's Press, 1993.

Reed, Terry. *Compromised*. Clandestine Publishing, 1995.

Rempel, William. *At the Devil's Table: Inside the Fall of the Cali Cartel, the World's Biggest Crime Syndicate*. Random House, 2011.

Ross, Rick. *Freeway Rick Ross*. Freeway Studios, 2014.

Ruppert, Michael. *Crossing the Rubicon*. New Society Publishers, 2004.

Salazar, Alonso. *The Words of Pablo*. Planeta, 2001.

Salazar, Alonso. *Born to Die in Medellín*. Latin America Bureau, 1992.

Saviano, Roberto. *Zero Zero Zero*. Penguin Random House UK, 2013.

Schou, Nick. *Kill the Messenger*. Nation Books, 2006.

Shannon, Elaine. *Desperados*. Penguin, 1988.

Stich, Rodney. *Defrauding America* 3rd Ed.
Diablo Western Press, 1998.

Stich, Rodney. *Drugging America* 2nd Ed. Silverpeak, 2006.

Stokes, Doug. *America's Other War: Terrorizing Colombia*.
Zed Books, 2005.

Stone, Roger. *The Clintons' War on Women*. Skyhorse, 2015.

Stone, Roger. *Jeb and the Bush Crime Family*. Skyhorse, 2016.

Streatfield, Dominic. *Cocaine*. Virgin Publishing, 2001.

Tarpley and Chaitkin. *George Bush*. Progressive Press, 2004.

Tomkins, David. *Dirty Combat*. Mainstream Publishing, 2008.

Valentine, Douglas. *The Strength of the Pack*.
Trine Day LLC, 2009.

Vallejo, Virginia. *Loving Pablo, Hating Escobar*. Vintage, 2018.

Velásquez Vásquez, Jhon Jairo. *Surviving Pablo Escobar*.
Ediciones y Distribuciones Dipon Ltda, 2017.

Woods, Neil. *Good Cop Bad War*. Ebury Press, 2016.

Get A Free Book:

Join Shaun's Newsletter

www.shaunattwood.com/
newsletter-subscribe/

SHAUN'S BOOKS

English Shaun Trilogy
Party Time
Hard Time
Prison Time

War on Drugs Series
Pablo Escobar: Beyond Narcos
American Made: Who Killed Barry Seal?
Pablo Escobar or George HW Bush
The Cali Cartel: Beyond Narcos
We Are Being Lied To: The War on Drugs (Expected 2019)
The War Against Weed (Expected 2019)

Un-Making a Murderer:
The Framing of Steven Avery and Brendan Dassey
The Mafia Philosopher: Two Tonys
Life Lessons

Pablo Escobar's Story (Expected 2019)
T-Bone (Expected 2022)

SOCIAL-MEDIA LINKS

Email: attwood.shaun@hotmail.co.uk
YouTube: Shaun Attwood
Blog: Jon's Jail Journal
Website: shaunattwood.com
Instagram: @shaunattwood
Twitter: @shaunattwood
LinkedIn: Shaun Attwood
Goodreads: Shaun Attwood
Facebook: Shaun Attwood, Jon's Jail Journal,
T-Bone Appreciation Society

Shaun welcomes feedback on any of his books.
Thank you for the Amazon and Goodreads reviews!

SHAUN'S JAIL JOURNEY STARTS IN HARD TIME NEW EDITION

Chapter 1

Sleep deprived and scanning for danger, I enter a dark cell on the second floor of the maximum-security Madison Street jail in Phoenix, Arizona, where guards and gang members are murdering prisoners. Behind me, the metal door slams heavily. Light slants into the cell through oblong gaps in the door, illuminating a prisoner cocooned in a white sheet, snoring lightly on the top bunk about two thirds of the way up the back wall. Relieved there is no immediate threat, I place my mattress on the grimy floor. Desperate to rest, I notice movement on the cement-block walls. *Am I hallucinating?* I blink several times. The walls appear to ripple. Stepping closer, I see the walls are alive with insects. I flinch. So many are swarming, I wonder if they're a colony of ants on the move. To get a better look, I put my eyes right up to them. They are mostly the size of almonds and have antennae. American cockroaches. I've seen them in the holding cells downstairs in smaller numbers, but nothing like this. A chill spread over my body. I back away.

Something alive falls from the ceiling and bounces off the base of my neck. I jump. With my night vision improving, I spot cockroaches weaving in and out of the base of the fluorescent strip light. Every so often one drops onto the concrete and resumes crawling. Examining the bottom bunk, I realise why my cellmate is sleeping at a higher elevation: cockroaches are pouring from gaps in the decrepit wall at the level of my bunk. The area is thick with them. Placing my mattress on the bottom bunk scatters them. I walk towards the toilet, crunching a few under my shower sandals. I urinate and grab the toilet roll. A cockroach darts from the centre of the roll onto my hand, tickling my fingers. My arm jerks as if it has a mind of its own, losing the cockroach and the toilet roll. Using a towel, I wipe the bulk of them off the bottom bunk, stopping only to shake the odd one off my hand. I unroll my mattress. They begin to regroup and inhabit my mattress. My adrenaline is pumping so much, I lose my fatigue.

Nauseated, I sit on a tiny metal stool bolted to the wall. *How will I sleep? How's my cellmate sleeping through the infestation and my arrival?* Copying his technique, I cocoon myself in a sheet and lie down, crushing more cockroaches. The only way they can access me now is through the breathing hole I've left in the sheet by the lower half of my face. Inhaling their strange musty odour, I close my eyes. I can't sleep. I feel them crawling on the sheet around my feet. *Am I imagining things?* Frightened of them infiltrating my breathing hole, I keep opening my eyes. Cramps cause me to rotate onto my other side. Facing the wall, I'm repulsed by so many of them just inches away. I return to my original side.

The sheet traps the heat of the Sonoran Desert to my body, soaking me in sweat. Sweat tickles my body, tricking my mind into thinking the cockroaches are infiltrating and crawling on me. The trapped heat aggravates my bleeding skin infections and bedsores. I want to scratch myself, but I know better. The outer layers of my skin have turned soggy from sweating constantly in this concrete oven. Squirming on the bunk fails to stop the relentless itchiness of my skin. Eventually, I scratch myself. Clumps of moist skin detach under my nails. Every now and then I become so uncomfortable, I must open my cocoon to waft the heat out, which allows the cockroaches in. It takes hours to drift to sleep. I only manage a few hours. I awake stuck to the soaked sheet, disgusted by the cockroach carcasses compressed against the mattress.

The cockroaches plague my new home until dawn appears at the dots in the metal grid over a begrimed strip of four-inch-thick bullet-proof glass at the top of the back wall – the cell's only source of outdoor light. They disappear into the cracks in the walls, like vampire mist retreating from sunlight. But not all of them. There were so many on the night shift that even their vastly reduced number is too many to dispose of. And they act like they know it. They roam around my feet with attitude, as if to make it clear that I'm trespassing on their turf.

My next set of challenges will arise not from the insect world, but from my neighbours. I'm the new arrival, subject to scrutiny about my charges just like when I'd run into the Aryan Brother-hood prison gang on my first day at the medium-security Towers jail a year ago. I wish my cellmate would wake up, brief me on the mood of the locals and introduce me to the head of the white gang. No such luck. Chow is announced over a speaker system in a crackly robotic voice, but he doesn't stir.

I emerge into the day room for breakfast. Prisoners in black-and-white bee-striped uniforms gather under the metal-grid stairs and tip dead cockroaches into a trash bin from plastic peanut-butter containers they'd set as traps during the night. All eyes are on me in the chow line. Watching who sits where, I hold my head up, put on a solid stare and pretend to be as at home in this environment as the cockroaches. It's all an act. I'm lonely and afraid. I loathe having to explain myself to the head of the white race, who I assume is the toughest murderer. I've been in jail long enough to know that taking my breakfast to my cell will imply that I have something to hide.

The gang punishes criminals with certain charges. The most serious are sex offenders, who are KOS: Kill On Sight. Other charges are punishable by SOS – Smash On Sight – such as drive-by shootings because women and kids sometimes get killed. It's called convict justice. Gang members are constantly looking for people to beat up because that's how they earn their reputations and tattoos. The most serious acts of violence earn the highest-ranking tattoos. To be a full gang member requires murder. I've observed the body language and techniques inmates trying to integrate employ. An inmate with a spring in his step and an air of confidence is likely to be accepted. A person who avoids eye contact and fails to introduce himself to the gang is likely to be preyed on. Some of the failed attempts I saw ended up with heads getting cracked against toilets, a sound I've grown familiar with. I've seen prisoners being extracted on stretchers who looked dead – one had yellow fluid leaking from his head. The constant violence gives me nightmares, but the reality is that I put myself in here, so I force myself to accept it as a part of my punishment.

It's time to apply my knowledge. With a self-assured stride, I take my breakfast bag to the table of white inmates covered in neo-Nazi tattoos, allowing them to question me.

"Mind if I sit with you guys?" I ask, glad exhaustion has deepened my voice.

"These seats are taken. But you can stand at the corner of the table."

The man who answered is probably the head of the gang. I size him up. Cropped brown hair. A dangerous glint in Nordic-blue eyes. Tiny pupils that suggest he's on heroin. Weightlifter-type veins bulging from a sturdy neck. Political ink on arms crisscrossed with scars. About the same age as me, thirty-three.

"Thanks. I'm Shaun from England." I volunteer my origin to show I'm different from them but not in a way that might get me smashed.

"I'm Bullet, the head of the whites." He offers me his fist to bump. "Where you roll in from, wood?"

Addressing me as wood is a good sign. It's what white gang members on a friendly basis call each other.

"Towers jail. They increased my bond and re-classified me to maximum security."

"What's your bond at?"

"I've got two $750,000 bonds," I say in a monotone. This is no place to brag about bonds.

"How many people you kill, brother?" His eyes drill into mine, checking whether my body language supports my story. My body language so far is spot on.

"None. I threw rave parties. They got us talking about drugs on wiretaps." Discussing drugs on the phone does not warrant a $1.5 million bond. I know and beat him to his next question. "Here's my charges." I show him my charge sheet, which includes conspiracy and leading a crime syndicate – both from running an Ecstasy ring.

Bullet snatches the paper and scrutinises it. Attempting to pre-empt his verdict, the other whites study his face. On edge, I wait for him to respond. Whatever he says next will determine whether I'll be accepted or victimised.

"Are you some kind of jailhouse attorney?" Bullet asks. "I want someone to read through my case paperwork." During our few minutes of conversation, Bullet has seen through my act and concluded that I'm educated – a possible resource to him.

I appreciate that he'll accept me if I take the time to read his case. "I'm no jailhouse attorney, but I'll look through it and help you however I can."

"Good. I'll stop by your cell later on, wood."

After breakfast, I seal as many of the cracks in the walls as I can with toothpaste. The cell smells minty, but the cockroaches still find their way in. Their day shift appears to be collecting information on the brown paper bags under my bunk, containing a few items of food that I purchased from the commissary; bags that I tied off with rubber bands in the hope of keeping the cockroaches out. Relentlessly, the cockroaches explore the bags for entry points, pausing over and probing the most worn and vulnerable regions. *Will the nightly swarm eat right through the paper?* I read all morning, wondering whether my cellmate has died in his cocoon, his occasional breathing sounds reassuring me.

Bullet stops by late afternoon and drops his case paperwork

off. He's been charged with Class 3 felonies and less, not serious crimes, but is facing a double-digit sentence because of his prior convictions and Security Threat Group status in the prison system. The proposed sentencing range seems disproportionate. I'll advise him to reject the plea bargain – on the assumption he already knows to do so, but is just seeking the comfort of a second opinion, like many un-sentenced inmates. When he returns for his paperwork, our conversation disturbs my cellmate – the cocoon shuffles – so we go upstairs to his cell. I tell Bullet what I think. He is excitable, a different man from earlier, his pupils almost non-existent.

"This case ain't shit. But my prosecutor knows I done other shit, all kinds of heavy shit, but can't prove it. I'd do anything to get that sorry bitch off my fucking ass. She's asking for something bad to happen to her. Man, if I ever get bonded out, I'm gonna chop that bitch into pieces. Kill her slowly though. Like to work her over with a blowtorch."

Such talk can get us both charged with conspiring to murder a prosecutor, so I try to steer him elsewhere. "It's crazy how they can catch you doing one thing, yet try to sentence you for all of the things they think you've ever done."

"Done plenty. Shot some dude in the stomach once. Rolled him up in a blanket and threw him in a dumpster."

Discussing past murders is as unsettling as future ones. "So, what's all your tattoos mean, Bullet? Like that eagle on your chest?"

"Why you wanna know?" Bullet's eyes probe mine.

My eyes hold their ground. "Just curious."

"It's a war bird. The AB patch."

"AB patch?"

"What the Aryan Brotherhood gives you when you've put enough work in."

"How long does it take to earn a patch?"

"Depends how quickly you put your work in. You have to earn your lightning bolts first."

"Why you got red and black lightning bolts?"

"You get SS bolts for beating someone down or for being an enforcer for the family. Red lightning bolts for killing someone. I was sent down as a youngster. They gave me steel and told me who to handle and I handled it. You don't ask questions. You just get blood on your steel. Dudes who get these tats without putting work in are told to cover them up or leave the yard."

"What if they refuse?"

"They're held down and we carve the ink off them."

Imagining them carving a chunk of flesh to remove a tattoo, I cringe. He's really enjoying telling me this now. His volatile nature is clear and frightening. *He's accepted me too much. He's trying to impress me before making demands.*

At night, I'm unable to sleep. Cocooned in heat, surrounded by cockroaches, I hear the swamp-cooler vent – a metal grid at the top of a wall – hissing out tepid air. Giving up on sleep, I put my earphones on and tune into National Public Radio. Listening to a Vivaldi violin concerto, I close my eyes and press my tailbone down to straighten my back as if I'm doing a yogic relaxation. The playful allegro thrills me, lifting my spirits, but the wistful adagio provokes sad emotions and tears. I open my eyes and gaze into the gloom. Due to lack of sleep, I start hallucinating and hearing voices over the music whispering threats. I'm at breaking point. Although I have accepted that I committed crimes and deserve to be punished, no one should have to live like this. I'm furious at myself for making the series of reckless decisions that put me in here and for losing absolutely everything. As violins crescendo in my ears, I remember what my life used to be like.

SHAUN'S INCARCERATION CONCLUDES IN PRISON TIME

Chapter 1

"I've got a padlock in a sock. I can smash your brains in while you're asleep. I can kill you whenever I want." My new cellmate sizes me up with no trace of human feeling in his eyes. Muscular and pot-bellied, he's caked in prison ink, including six snakes on his skull, slithering side by side. The top of his right ear is missing in a semi-circle.

The waves of fear are overwhelming. After being in transportation all day, I can feel my bladder hurting. "I'm not looking to cause any trouble. I'm the quietest cellmate you'll ever have. All I do is read and write."

Scowling, he shakes his head. "Why've they put a fish in with me?" He swaggers close enough for me to smell his cigarette breath. "Us convicts don't get along with fresh fish."

"Should I ask to move then?" I say, hoping he'll agree if he hates new prisoners so much.

"No! They'll think I threatened you!"

In the eight by twelve feet slab of space, I swerve around him and place my property box on the top bunk.

He pushes me aside and grabs the box. "You just put that on my artwork! I ought to fucking smash you, fish!"

"Sorry, I didn't see it."

"You need to be more aware of your fucking surroundings! What you in for anyway, fish?"

I explain my charges, Ecstasy dealing and how I spent twenty-six months fighting my case.

"How come the cops were so hard-core after you?" he asks, squinting.

"It was a big case, a multi-million dollar investigation. They raided over a hundred people and didn't find any drugs. They were pretty pissed off. I'd stopped dealing by the time they caught up with me, but I'd done plenty over the years, so I accept my punishment."

"Throwing raves," he says, staring at the ceiling as if remembering something. "Were you partying with underage girls?" he asks, his voice slow, coaxing.

Being called a sex offender is the worst insult in prison. Into my third year of incarceration, I'm conditioned to react. "What you trying to say?" I yell angrily, brow clenched.

"Were you fucking underage girls?" Flexing his body, he shakes both fists as if about to punch me.

"Hey, I'm no child molester, and I'd prefer you didn't say shit like that!"

"My buddy next door is doing twenty-five to life for murdering a child molester. How do I know Ecstasy dealing ain't your cover story?" He inhales loudly, nostrils flaring.

"You want to see my fucking paperwork?"

A stocky prisoner walks in. Short hair. Dark eyes. Powerful neck. On one arm: a tattoo of a man in handcuffs above the word OMERTA – the Mafia code of silence towards law enforcement. "What the fuck's going on in here, Bud?" asks Junior Bull – the son of "Sammy the Bull" Gravano, the Mafia mass murderer who was my biggest competitor in the Ecstasy market.

Relieved to see a familiar face, I say, "How're you doing?"

Shaking my hand, he says in a New York Italian accent, "I'm doing alright. I read that shit in the newspaper about you starting a blog in Sheriff Joe Arpaio's jail."

"The blog's been bringing media heat on the conditions."

"You know him?" Bud asks.

"Yeah, from Towers jail. He's a good dude. He's in for dealing Ecstasy like me."

"It's a good job you said that 'cause I was about to smash his ass," Bud says.

"It's a good job Wild Man ain't here 'cause you'd a got your ass thrown off the balcony," Junior Bull says.

I laugh. The presence of my best friend, Wild Man, was partly the reason I never took a beating at the county jail, but with Wild Man in a different prison, I feel vulnerable. When Bud casts a death stare on me, my smile fades.

"What the fuck you guys on about?" Bud asks.

"Let's go talk downstairs." Junior Bull leads Bud out.

I rush to a stainless steel sink/toilet bolted to a cement-block wall by the front of the cell, unbutton my orange jumpsuit and crane my neck to watch the upper-tier walkway in case Bud returns. I bask in relief as my bladder deflates. After flushing, I take stock of my new home, grateful for the slight improvement in the conditions versus what I'd grown accustomed to in Sheriff Joe Arpaio's jail. No cockroaches. No blood stains. A working swamp cooler. Something I've never seen in a cell before: shelves. The steel table bolted to the wall is slightly larger, too. *But how will I concentrate on writing with Bud around?* There's a mixture of smells in the room. Cleaning chemicals. Aftershave. Tobacco. A vinegar-like odour. The slit of a window at the back overlooks gravel in a no-man's-land before the next building with gleaming curls of razor wire around its roof.

From the doorway upstairs, I'm facing two storeys of cells overlooking a day room with shower cubicles at the end of both tiers. At two white plastic circular tables, prisoners are playing dominoes, cards, chess and Scrabble, some concentrating, others yelling obscenities, contributing to a brain-scraping din that I hope to block out by purchasing a Walkman. In a raised box-shaped Plexiglas control tower, two guards are monitoring the prisoners.

Bud returns. My pulse jumps. Not wanting to feel like I'm

stuck in a kennel with a rabid dog, I grab a notepad and pen and head for the day room.

Focussed on my body language, not wanting to signal any weakness, I'm striding along the upper tier, head and chest elevated, when two hands appear from a doorway and grab me. I drop the pad. The pen clinks against grid-metal and tumbles to the day room as I'm pulled into a cell reeking of backside sweat and masturbation, a cheese-tinted funk.

"I'm Booga. Let's fuck," says a squat man in urine-stained boxers, with WHITE TRASH tattooed on his torso below a mobile home, and an arm sleeved with the Virgin Mary.

Shocked, I brace to flee or fight to preserve my anal virginity. I can't believe my eyes when he drops his boxers and waggles his penis.

Dancing to music playing through a speaker he has rigged up, Booga smiles in a sexy way. "Come on," he says in a husky voice. "Drop your pants. Let's fuck." He pulls pornography faces. I question his sanity. He moves closer. "If I let you fart in my mouth, can I fart in yours?"

"You can fuck off," I say, springing towards the doorway.

He grabs me. We scuffle. Every time I make progress towards the doorway, he clings to my clothes, dragging me back in. When I feel his penis rub against my leg, my adrenalin kicks in so forcefully I experience a burst of strength and wriggle free. I bolt out as fast as my shower sandals will allow, and snatch my pad. Looking over my shoulder, I see him stood calmly in the doorway, smiling. He points at me. "You have to walk past my door every day. We're gonna get together. I'll lick your ass and you can fart in my mouth." Booga blows a kiss and disappears.

I rush downstairs. With my back to a wall, I pause to steady my thoughts and breathing. In survival mode, I think, *What's going to come at me next?* In the hope of reducing my tension, I borrow a pen to do what helps me stay sane: writing. With the details fresh in my mind, I document my journey to the prison for my blog readers, keeping an eye out in case anyone else wants to test the new prisoner. The more I write, the more I fill with a sense of purpose. Jon's Jail Journal is a connection to the outside world that I cherish.

Someone yells, "One time!" The din lowers. A door rumbles open. A guard does a security walk, his every move scrutinised by dozens of scornful eyes staring from cells. When he exits, the din resumes, and the prisoners return to injecting drugs to escape from reality, including the length of their sentences. This continues all day with "Two times!" signifying two approaching guards, and "Three times!" three and so on. Every now and then an announcement by a guard over the speakers briefly lowers the din.

Before lockdown, I join the line for a shower, holding bars of soap in a towel that I aim to swing at the head of the next person to try me. With boisterous inmates a few feet away, yelling at the men in the showers to "Stop jerking off," and "Hurry the fuck up," I get in a cubicle that reeks of bleach and mildew. With every nerve strained, I undress and rinse fast.

At night, despite the desert heat, I cocoon myself in a blanket from head to toe and turn towards the wall, making my face more difficult to strike. I leave a hole for air, but the warm cement block inches from my mouth returns each exhalation to my face as if it's breathing on me, creating a feeling of suffocation. For hours, my heart drums so hard against the thin mattress I feel as if I'm moving even though I'm still. I try to sleep, but my eyes keep springing open and my head turning towards the cell as I try to penetrate the darkness, searching for Bud swinging a padlock in a sock at my head.

OTHER BOOKS BY SHAUN ATTWOOD

Pablo Escobar: Beyond Narcos

War on Drugs Series Book 1

The mind-blowing true story of Pablo Escobar and the Medellín Cartel beyond their portrayal on Netflix.

Colombian drug lord Pablo Escobar was a devoted family man and a psychopathic killer; a terrible enemy, yet a wonderful friend. While donating millions to the poor, he bombed and tortured his enemies – some had their eyeballs removed with hot spoons. Through ruthless cunning and America's insatiable appetite for cocaine, he became a multi-billionaire, who lived in a $100-million house with its own zoo.

Pablo Escobar: Beyond Narcos demolishes the standard good versus evil telling of his story. The authorities were not hunting Pablo down to stop his cocaine business. They were taking over it.

American Made: Who Killed Barry Seal?
Pablo Escobar or George HW Bush

War on Drugs Series Book 2

Set in a world where crime and government coexist, *American Made* is the jaw-dropping true story of CIA pilot Barry Seal that the Hollywood movie starring Tom Cruise is afraid to tell.

Barry Seal flew cocaine and weapons worth billions of dollars into and out of America in the 1980s. After he became a government informant, Pablo Escobar's Medellin Cartel offered a million for him alive and half a million dead. But his real trouble began after he threatened to expose the dirty dealings of George HW Bush.

American Made rips the roof off Bush and Clinton's complicity in cocaine trafficking in Mena, Arkansas.

"A conspiracy of the grandest magnitude." Congressman Bill Alexander on the Mena affair.

We Are Being Lied To: The War on Drugs

War on Drugs Series Book 3

A collection of harrowing, action-packed and interlinked true stories that demonstrate the devastating consequences of drug prohibition.

The Cali Cartel: Beyond Narcos

War on Drugs Series Book 4

An electrifying account of the Cali Cartel beyond its portrayal on Netflix.

From the ashes of Pablo Escobar's empire rose an even bigger and more malevolent cartel. A new breed of sophisticated mobsters became the kings of cocaine. Their leader was Gilberto Rodríguez Orejuela – known as the Chess Player due to his foresight and calculated cunning.

Gilberto and his terrifying brother, Miguel, ran a multi-billion-dollar drug empire like a corporation. They employed a politically astute brand of thuggery and spent $10 million to put a president in power. Although the godfathers from Cali preferred bribery over violence, their many loyal torturers and hit men were never idle.

The Mafia Philosopher

"A fast-paced true-crime memoir with all of the action of Goodfellas" – UNILAD

"Sopranos v Sons of Anarchy with an Alaskan-snow backdrop" – True Geordie Podcast

Breaking bones, burying bodies and planting bombs became second nature to Two Tonys while working for the Bonanno Crime Family, whose exploits inspired The Godfather.

After a dispute with an outlaw motorcycle club, Two Tonys left a trail of corpses from Arizona to Alaska. On the run, he was pursued by bikers and a neo-Nazi gang blood-thirsty for revenge, while a homicide detective launched a nationwide manhunt.

As the mist from his smoking gun fades, readers are left with an unexpected portrait of a stoic philosopher with a wealth of charm, a glorious turn of phrase and a fanatical devotion to his daughter.

Hard Time New Edition

"Makes the Shawshank Redemption look like a holiday camp" – NOTW

After a SWAT team smashed down stock-market millionaire Shaun Attwood's door, he found himself inside of Arizona's deadliest jail and locked into a brutal struggle for survival.

Shaun's hope of living the American Dream turned into a nightmare of violence and chaos, when he had a run-in with Sammy the Bull Gravano, an Italian Mafia mass murderer.

In jail, Shaun was forced to endure cockroaches crawling in his ears at night, dead rats in the food and the sound of skulls getting cracked against toilets. He meticulously documented the conditions and smuggled out his message.

Join Shaun on a harrowing voyage into the darkest recesses of human existence.

Hard Time provides a revealing glimpse into the tragedy, brutality, dark comedy and eccentricity of prison life.

Featured worldwide on Nat Geo Channel's Locked-Up/ Banged-Up Abroad Raving Arizona.

Prison Time

Sentenced to 9½ years in Arizona's state prison for distributing Ecstasy, Shaun finds himself living among gang members, sexual predators and drug-crazed psychopaths. After being attacked by a Californian biker in for stabbing a girlfriend, Shaun writes about the prisoners who befriend, protect and inspire him. They include T-Bone, a massive African American ex-Marine who risks his life saving vulnerable inmates from rape, and Two Tonys, an old-school Mafia murderer who left the corpses of his rivals from Arizona to Alaska. They teach Shaun how to turn incarceration to his advantage, and to learn from his mistakes.

Shaun is no stranger to love and lust in the heterosexual world, but the tables are turned on him inside. Sexual advances come at him from all directions, some cleverly disguised, others more sinister – making Shaun question his sexual identity.

Resigned to living alongside violent, mentally-ill and drug-addicted inmates, Shaun immerses himself in psychology and philosophy to try to make sense of his past behaviour, and begins applying what he learns as he adapts to prison life. Encouraged by Two Tonys to explore fiction as well, Shaun reads over 1000 books which, with support from a brilliant psychotherapist, Dr Owen, speed along his personal development. As his ability to deflect daily threats improves, Shaun begins to look forward to his release with optimism and a new love waiting for him. Yet the words of Aristotle from one of Shaun's books will prove prophetic: "We cannot learn without pain."

Un-Making a Murderer:
The Framing of Steven Avery and Brendan Dassey

Innocent people do go to jail. Sometimes mistakes are made. But even more terrifying is when the authorities conspire to frame them. That's what happened to Steven Avery and Brendan Dassey, who were convicted of murder and are serving life sentences.

Un-Making a Murderer is an explosive book which uncovers the illegal, devious and covert tactics used by Wisconsin officials, including:
- **Concealing Other Suspects**
- **Paying Expert Witnesses to Lie**
- **Planting Evidence**
- **Jury Tampering**

The art of framing innocent people has been in practice for centuries and will continue until the perpetrators are held accountable. Turning conventional assumptions and beliefs in the justice system upside down, *Un-Making a Murderer* takes you on that journey.

The profits from this book are going to Steven and Brendan and to donate free books to schools and prisons. In the last three years, Shaun Attwood has donated 20,000 books.

ABOUT SHAUN ATTWOOD

Shaun Attwood is a former stock-market millionaire and Ecstasy supplier turned public speaker, author and activist, who is banned from America for life. His story was featured worldwide on National Geographic Channel as an episode of Locked Up/ Banged Up Abroad called Raving Arizona.

Shaun's writing – smuggled out of the jail with the highest death rate in America run by Sheriff Joe Arpaio – attracted international media attention to the human rights violations: murders by guards and gang members, dead rats in the food, cockroach infestations…

While incarcerated, Shaun was forced to reappraise his life. He read over 1,000 books in just under six years. By studying original texts in psychology and philosophy, he sought to better understand himself and his past behaviour. He credits books as being the lifeblood of his rehabilitation.

Shaun tells his story to schools to dissuade young people from drugs and crime. He campaigns against injustice via his books and blog, Jon's Jail Journal. He has appeared on the BBC, Sky News and TV worldwide to talk about issues affecting prisoners' rights.

As a best-selling true-crime author, Shaun is presently writing a series of action-packed books exposing the War on Drugs, which feature Pablo Escobar and the cocaine Mafia.

Lightning Source UK Ltd.
Milton Keynes UK
UKHW021012201120
373762UK00015B/1590

9 781912 885039